Edward North Buxton

Short Stalks

Or, hunting camps, north, south, east, and west

Edward North Buxton

Short Stalks
Or, hunting camps, north, south, east, and west

ISBN/EAN: 9783337426279

Printed in Europe, USA, Canada, Australia, Japan

Cover: Foto ©Lupo / pixelio.de

More available books at **www.hansebooks.com**

SHORT STALKS:

OR

HUNTING CAMPS

NORTH, SOUTH, EAST, AND WEST

BY

EDWARD NORTH BUXTON

WITH NUMEROUS ILLUSTRATIONS

NEW YORK: G. P. PUTNAM'S SONS
LONDON: EDWARD STANFORD
1892

Copyright, 1892, by
G. P. PUTNAM'S SONS

Entered at Stationers' Hall, London, 1892, by
EDWARD STANFORD

PREFACE

Most of the papers which I have collected in this volume have appeared before in various magazines and journals. My thanks are especially due to the Editors of *The Nineteenth Century*, *The New Review*, *The Field* newspaper, and *The Alpine Journal*, for their permission to reprint them.

All but one of them describe the chase and death of some wild animal. Perhaps the criticism will be made that it is sad that a man cannot enjoy himself in foreign countries without killing something. I freely admit that it is a pity, but I cannot deny that, to most of us, the pursuit of creatures which are hard to catch, whether butterflies or buffaloes, is very pleasant. If the predatory instincts which we have inherited—one of my ancestors was sarcastically described as "worshipping, leaning on his gun"—cannot be altogether eradicated, I may at least urge, in mitigation, that in all these journeys, spreading over more than a quarter of a century, I am personally responsible for the death of less than eighty four-footed animals.

I do not profess to be a distinguished sportsman, such as those who have devoted years to the pursuit of great game; nor am I competent to instruct aspirants to that title. If I remember rightly, only one of my trips has exceeded the limit of six weeks. My only excuse for writing a book on such subjects, is the keen enjoyment which I take in reviving the memory of the scenes described in it.

Mr. J. E. Harting has most kindly corrected my imperfect observations from the point of view of a trained naturalist.

I must acknowledge the assistance which I have derived from the art of the wood-engraver, to which my book will owe any charm which it may possess. First and foremost to Mr. Edward Whymper, whose work is almost good enough to convert a bad book into an attractive one, and in the next place to Mr. Lodge, whose birds are a triumph, I am grateful for the pains they have taken to carry out my ideas. To Mr. W. Biscombe Gardner I am indebted for two or three admirable pictures, which make me desire more from the same workshop. Mr. G. H. Putnam has procured for me some beautiful examples of the skill of American artists. These have been reproduced by the "half-tone" process, and it must be admitted, that for certain subjects it treads hard upon the heels of the older and more laborious method.

Characteristic drawings of unfamiliar wild animals are hard to get. Several of mine are from the veteran pencil of Joseph Wolf, which is a guarantee of faithful study.

In expeditions such as these, everything depends upon the choice of a partner. In this respect I have always been singularly fortunate. I have taken liberties with the features of some of them—both my own companions, and others, racy of the soil. I like to recall these my friends in association with the incidents in which they shared. To their congenial society I owe the chief part of the brightness of those holiday hours, and if there is such a thing nowadays as a dedication, to them I hereby address it.

The final revision of these pages has been made under the shadow of a personal calamity, which has darkened my house, and with which a light-hearted volume like this may seem out of keeping. But, apart from the circumstance that the son whom I have lost took a keen interest in its preparation, I have found it a relief from the heart-ache to recur in memory to joyous labours, in some of which he was a happy and strenuous participator.

E. N. BUXTON.

KNIGHTON, *September* 1892.

CONTENTS

CHAPTER I
Sardinia and its Wild Sheep — 1

CHAPTER II
Recollections of Chamois Hunting — 36

CHAPTER III
The Rocky Mountains — 73

CHAPTER IV
On the Rim of the Desert — 122

CHAPTER V
The Elk — 159

CHAPTER VI
The Father of all the Goats — 193

CHAPTER VII
The Pyrenean Ibex — 229

CHAPTER VIII
BEAR HUNTING — PAGE 257

CHAPTER IX
A TANTALISING QUEST — 279

CHAPTER X
REINDEER STALKING — 323

CHAPTER XI
THE IZZARD — 349

CHAPTER XII
PEAKS AND PASSES — 370

LIST OF ILLUSTRATIONS

FULL PAGE

	PAGE
The Sardinian Mouflon	19
Two to one against the Horse	57
He takes us for a Rival	70
A Flat Crawl	84
The Challenge	89
The Tetons from Buffalo Fork	97
They must be hereabouts	119
The Desert from Jebel Metlili	129
The Barbary Sheep	135
The Mountain Gazelle	156
Skraemt	175
A Race for Life	189
The Salt Lake from Maimun Dagh	196
A Turkoman Shepherd	207
The Capra Ægagrus	209
A Likely Spot	214
Cyril engineers the Water-supply	221
In the Cane Brake	227
Our Camp	232
He moved straight towards us	269
Love and War	304
The Reindeer	329
The Herd clattered down the Cliff	358
The Aiguille de Bionnassay	380
Jakob invites us to leap	392

IN THE TEXT

	PAGE
Celestin	3
A Nuragho	5
Gigi	13
An Old Chamois Hunter	45
The Lämmergeier	48
Andreas	69
Indian Dick	78
The Tetons over the Divide	87
An Indian Arrow-head	105
Cris	106
Sunday Dinner	121
An Arab Geitoun	124
Willie	131
Abdullah	139
The Algerian Buzzard	158
The Capercailzie	162
Watering the *Forra*	165
Tump	168
John Wallan with Peyas and Luft	178
Ernest is stalked	184
Hazel-Grouse	192
The Griffon Vulture	199
Bouba	201
Junk takes well-earned Repose	228
The Wall Creeper	239
Cyril	244
Falling Ibex	246
Narcissus Moschatus	251
Geof	275
The Big Head	280
Jani	285
"Smoke"	287
Alfred's Mount	315

LIST OF ILLUSTRATIONS   xiii

	PAGE
The Great Bustard	316
One Touch of Nature	317
The Caravan Barber	319
Arabas	322
Kenny	337
The Brèche	354
Mac	384
Jakob	386
The Author	399

SARDINIA AND ITS WILD SHEEP

NOTWITHSTANDING the perpetual struggle to make life more comfortable, it is a master passion with some of us to emancipate ourselves from Babylon, and from time to time to escape from this complex civilisation to some barbarous land, there to become for a few weeks happy savages like our ancestors. If, in addition, one can so far imitate those noble creatures as to spend the time in killing something, the deception is more perfect. One's happiness is complete if the animal to be hunted lives in a mountainous country, and is difficult to obtain, but may be fairly stalked in the open. At least, that is my case.

A fit of this unquenchable longing had seized me at the beginning of 1889, and the particular excuse which served was the County Council Elections. I was personally responsible for the conduct of fifty-six of them, and I ask any candid person whether that did not justify the Buck-fever from which I was suffering. On 18th January I learned that the contests had all passed off without a hitch, and the anxieties of the previous weeks were forgotten. People congratulated the victors and condoled with the victims, but nobody pitied the High Sheriff, so he consoled himself in his own way. On the following morning I packed up my camping outfit, and, accompanied by two kindred spirits, fled to the land of the free. To a busy man the scope for this sort of thing is limited. If six weeks be the outside of his tether, dreams of Arctic bears or *Ovis Poli* are unattainable and unreal. Time and distance have to be considered: but Scandinavia, the Alps, the Pyrenees, the Mediterranean Islands, can be reached within six days even in their remoter parts, and open out possibilities of elk, reindeer, chamois, bear, ibex, and deer of several kinds. Of all these I possessed memories and trophies, and besides, the season for them was over. But there is another land of forests which I had for long marked down in my agenda, and gathered stray scraps of information about, as a squirrel hoards his acorns—no doubt, with all the pleasures of anticipation. This was the island of Sardinia, where dwell many wild animals—red deer, fallow deer, boar, ducks, and longbills innumerable; but, chief of all, in the wildest parts, the curly-horned mouflon, desired by many sportsmen, seriously hunted by few, and obtained by very few.

The old numbers of the *Field* had been ransacked, travel books searched, H.B.M.'s consuls resident on the island written to, still the information about these particular animals was meagre and contradictory. The authorities all differed as to what was the close season for the mouflon, but they all concurred in saying that it didn't much matter. They were also unanimous in declaring that the method of hunting them was by driving, whereas

I was convinced that, being sheep, they must feed in the open, and therefore might be honestly spied and stalked. Possessed by this idea, I had engaged Celestin, keenest of chamois hunters, cheeriest of companions — though he knew no world wider than his own mountain valley. His friend Benjamin had begged to be allowed to come too,

CELESTIN.

content to be a hewer of wood and drawer of water without pay if only he might see some new thing. These two joined us at Genoa, and were eyed suspiciously by the swallow-tailed waiters when their iron-clad boots clinked along the marble halls.

My immediate companions were G——, one of those overworked country bankers who are expected to shoot with their customers four days a week, and F——, of the numerous army of Anglo-American cowboys who return to Bond Street and Leicestershire when the autumn "round-up" is over. After being clothed and in his right mind for two months, his soul hungered for scalps and the war-path. I was due back within six weeks to receive one of Her Majesty's judges at Assizes. So there should be no avoidable delays—and of course delays occurred, perverse and irritating.

Instead of following my own instincts as to route, I took advice—always a mistaken thing to do—and thereby lost, for hunting purposes, three whole days. But, as every expedition has its share of bad luck, perhaps it was as well to take ours in this way. Our intention was to be landed at a small harbour within easy reach of the range where we desired to hunt; but when, the morning after leaving Leghorn, we got among the islands in the Straits of Bonifacio, the Tramontana wind blew so furiously that it became certain that no landing could be effected between the sheltered harbour of Terranova, at the northern end of the island, and that of Cagliari at the other extremity. Our plan of campaign had to be changed at an hour's notice, and a landing effected at Terranova, many weary leagues from our hunting ground. Not liking the look of the *trattoria*, where we supped, we got the stationmaster to lend us an empty room in his station. Here we spread our mattresses and waited for the morning train. Heavens! how the wind hissed all night! It was some consolation that no landing would have been possible on the open coast.

The early train took us through a broken rocky country, the little ravines covered with cork and arbutus. It would be picturesque if it were not marred by numerous straight stone walls, under which the little smoke-coloured cattle cowered from the storm. In some parts the landscape was dotted with *nuraghi*, the ancient fortified dwellings of primeval Sards—conical stone towers, yellow with

A NURAGHO.

the moss of three or four millenniums—into which they retired with their families on the approach of Phoenicians, Moors, or other predatory navigators. But this hypothesis is quite unauthorised, and very likely wrong.

As we rose to a higher level the snow fell heavily, driven before a raging gale, and the Highland Railway in mid-winter could not have presented a more desolate picture. I blessed my fur coat and reindeer-lined boots, if I blessed nothing else. It was merely a foretaste of the weather which we were to endure with few respites for a month.

Foiled in our first attempt to reach our destination by water, we now proposed to enter the hill country from a certain point on the railway, whence the map indicated a road of some sort in the direction we desired. Fortune, for the moment, seemed to favour us, as we found a fellow-traveller who knew the country we proposed to traverse. He warned us of *malviventi*, but my companions were a sufficient bodyguard, so we telegraphed inquiries for a vehicle. When we reached the station from which we hoped to start, a message met us that this road was blocked with snow-drifts, and that there were no means of entering the mountains that way. We could only bow to the perversity of fate, which doomed us to spend our precious days in wandering round the charmed circle of our land of promise, while we gazed wistfully at the leaden clouds which covered the Paradise. There was nothing for it but to re-enter the train and continue the journey to Cagliari at the southern extremity of the island. We now descended to the great plain of Oristano—chocolate-coloured and dank—and traversed it from end to end. It is a pestilential hotbed which has helped to give the island a bad name for two thousand years. Miles away the mountains rose with sudden steepness from the plain, as they do on the Italian littoral. We passed several *stagni*, or brackish lagoons, covered with wild fowl, which would have stirred our sporting instincts if we had not been thinking of higher game, and cursing the fate which kept us at arm's length. The natives pop at them all day and sometimes kill them, for they brought ducks for sale to the carriage windows, along with fresh-gathered oranges.

The next morning saw us again on board the train—

this time on a narrow-gauge railway which winds for fifty miles into the mountains. At the terminus we found the "post" waiting—a small edition of a Rocky Mountain mud-waggon, already occupied by three passengers, and into which we were invited to stow our five selves. At first the conductor volubly refused all luggage, but by dint of heavy bribery we got our rifles allowed and such a minimum of equipment as would serve at a pinch. The rest was left forlorn on the platform, and did not rejoin us for a week.

Somehow we all squeezed in—six inside, two in the *coupé*, driver and conductor in front of that—and started for a twenty hours' continuous drive. We saved our lives by walking nearly all the way; and this was not difficult, as we were always either diving into a ravine or climbing out of one. The road continually returns upon itself, and short cuts were numerous. As we rose, the cultivation became scantier, and the *macquia* or scrub more frequent, till it covered the whole hillside. The population is exceedingly thin, and the houses are all huddled together for mutual protection in little towns, separated by long intervals. In the evening we stopped at such a one, and the conductor wired an inquiry as to the state of the road. Somewhat to our relief, the answer came back that there was too much snow to traverse it in the night, and six feet two inches was able to stretch itself on the flat. The *padrone* of the telegraph office was hospitably inclined—as indeed we found all the Sards—and put bread and wine before us, and a room to lie in. We had rescued from our stores two bottles of that traveller's friend, British jam, and with the *padrone*, and his brother the priest, enjoyed a jovial meal. The jam took the priest's fancy immensely, and his conversation was confined to blessings on that condiment and curses on Garibaldi, whom he seemed to think still a militant enemy of the Church. One of the bottles was broken and the glass scattered among the contents, and we told the priest it was "molto pericoloso" for him to eat it, but I fancy he elected to chance it after we had left. In the room where we slept were the first signs which we had seen of the *caccia grossa* for which we were enduring so much—skins of boar, moufflon, red and fallow deer. It is not correct in Sardinia to offer any payment for such casual hospitality, but a little keepsake to the *signorina*, who waits in the background with curious eyes, is taken in good part.

In the morning we resumed our journey on the frozen road, and passed through some grand ilex woods—alas! rapidly disappearing before the charcoal-burner. Once in the snow we found tracks of moufflon, or were they tame pigs? I am not sure, but they served the purpose of raising our spirits. The horses, which are small, but well-bred and wiry, did their work well, and in due course we reached the little town which was to be the base of our operations. It is piled on the steep side of the mountain, facing a lovely view of purple plain and distant sea. We were greeted by the kind-hearted sportsman who is familiarly known in these parts as Signor Carlo. Blessings on his head for the good things he showered on us, not only then and there, but during the whole time we were in the mountains! What bread, short in the grain, white and tender! what succulent kids, what honey, more divinely flavoured than that of Hymettus; and above all, what

Ogliastra wine, of which the tally *said* that we and our followers had drunk six hundred bottles! But it was only twopence a bottle, so a fig for the expense!

The next morning, being Sunday, the whole male population were on the little Piazza. The women seem to be kept in almost Oriental seclusion. The national costume is peculiar. It has the appearance of being too hot above the waist and too chilly below it. A heavy Phrygian cap, fur waistcoat, and the universal hooded capote, constitute the upper part, while below there is nothing but a short linen petticoat and gaiters. Nearly all wore a heavy knife, fully two feet long, across the stomach; this is used indifferently to chop wood, slice a sausage, or avenge a quarrel. Varied and strongly-marked features seem to denote that every conquering nation of the Mediterranean has set its seal on the physiognomies of the island. Spaniards, Greeks, Moors, Arabs, and Jews reproduce, after many generations, their respective types, distinct, and apparently unmixed. Notwithstanding the very predatory appearance of some of these gentry, we found them universally civil, though we were advised not to carry a large sum of money with us, and it would probably be rash to go into the wilder parts unarmed. The island is well patrolled by police, and these carabinieri were, as we thought, needlessly solicitous about our safety. The only approach to marauding habits which we experienced was on one occasion when one of our party was walking, alone and unarmed, on the hill, when three sportsmen whistled to him to halt, and approaching with their guns pointed at him from the hip, demanded cigars, and then money. He turned out his purse, which contained an English shilling, with which booty they retired, apparently well pleased with the result of their little game of brag. When he wanted to examine their guns, they sprang back, spurred by guilty conscience. This very mild case of highway robbery came round to the ears of the carabinieri, though we had carefully concealed the incident from them. They professed great indignation that we had not reported it, and the row waxed so hot that at one time we thought we were to be locked up for having been robbed. Ultimately they offered to intern the whole countryside in their villages as long as we remained! The only recent crime of which we heard in the neighbourhood was recorded by a little cross on the road, a mile from the cantoniera where we stayed. Here, a merchant, returning with the proceeds of a sale of wine, had been murdered for his money the previous summer. There was a hue and cry, and a demand for justice, and *somebody* was shot "at sight" by one of the carabinieri a month afterwards. As far as I could learn, there was only the barest suspicion against this man, but if he hadn't murdered the merchant, perhaps he had "booed the police." The carabiniero was decorated! The custom of the *vendetta* has been almost stamped out, and what remains is merely a residue of commonplace sordid crime, and very little of that. As impulsive as children, the Sards are also as susceptible to praise or blame. If the least thing went wrong I have seen them blubber like overgrown babies, with heaving shoulders and streaming eyes. Our coachman, on one occasion having to get an extra load up a rather steep hill, was so overcome by such a paroxysm that he actually rolled off the box from sheer inability to hold himself upright. I am afraid it cannot be said that they are as simple as doves. Many of them are, it must be confessed, sad rogues and snappers up of unconsidered trifles; but their *bonhomie* covers a multitude of sins, and I confess I liked them.

The language bears traces of the same mixed origin as the people, and many Arabic words are used; but three hundred years of Spanish occupation has left the most marked impression. Some of our party who knew Spanish and no Italian had no difficulty in making themselves understood.

We had intended to establish a camp in some valley high up in the best mouflon ranges, but our camp equipage had had to be left behind with the bulk of our heavy luggage, so that until it arrived this scheme was out of the question; and though we began with two or three brilliant days, for the rest of our stay the weather was such as to make four walls and a roof a necessity of existence. I have said that there were no houses outside of the villages and towns. The exceptions to the rule are the *cantoniere*. These houses are placed about ten miles apart on the Government roads, which now traverse the mountains in various directions. They are used primarily for the accommodation of the cantonieri, who keep the roads in order; but they also contain, as a rule, a large empty barrack-room for the shelter of travellers, and a similar one for their horses. In one of these houses, at a height of nearly four thousand feet, and close under some of the highest peaks on the island, we took up our quarters, afterwards moving to the guard-house of a mine, a few miles farther on. The nearest habitation, a small village of five or six houses, was six miles off. This *cantoniera* contained a fairly comfortable room, reserved for the use of the engineer of the road on his periodical visits, and this, by leave of the head official at Cagliari, we used. It was furnished with a rough table and two camp bedsteads, and we soon felt quite at home. The two cantonieri quartered here had each his separate tenement under the same roof, and as their abodes contained the only fireplaces, we had to mix a great deal in the family circle. I daresay we were as great a nuisance to them as they were to us, but we made very free with the family hearth, and were always greeted with a friendly invitation to take the warmest place. Here every evening we had a jovial hunting symposium, as we dried ourselves and our telescopes. The man himself, with his wife and progeny, retired at night to an inner room; but the hospitality of the kitchen was extended indifferently to carabinieri—several of whom slept there every night—goats, dogs, and casual wayfarers. I used to get up early, and it was always a difficulty to pick my way to the fireplace across the floor, which was literally covered with the sleeping figures. As soon as we saw these surroundings, we of course expected to be devoured : but during our stay of four weeks I only once caught a flea, and that was a very little one—in fact, a mere kid, not worth hunting. Perhaps they were hibernating, and in warmer weather this kind of *caccia* might be more lively.

We had added to our party two Sards—Gigi and Enricetto—reputed to be knowing hunters. They were cheery companions and willing workers, and never lost their tempers, but their ideas of the art of venerie differed

GIGI.

partridges, seldom failing to score; but his favourite occupation was to draw a stocking on to his stump and darn it—I mean the stocking; the stump was sound enough. Enricetto had a mercurial temperament, which occasionally vented itself in irrepressible shouts when he saw any wild animal—an inconvenient practice during a stalk. The worst thing he did was to break up one of my mouflon heads and take it out for his luncheon. After this we chiefly used him to fetch supplies from the nearest town, at a distance of seventeen miles; and he and his horse seldom failed to perform the double journey in the day, and to return laden with huge demijohns of wine and sacks of bread.

On the first evening our anticipations were raised to the highest pitch by the accounts which the carabinieri gave of the moufloni, or "mufli" as they familiarly styled them, which they saw daily from the road—an account which we thought too good to be true, but which our own experience afterwards confirmed. And now arose a tremendous controversy as to how they ought to be hunted. One writer says, "These animals are almost impossible to get except by driving them, and this is a very uncertain proceeding." With the last part of this statement I agree. As to the first I believed there was a better way. I had come to stalk them, and stalk I would. The Sards on the other hand vehemently maintained that their method had always been pursued; that it was to fly in the face of Providence to try any other, and that none but a pestilent radical would suggest such a thing. Willing to humour them I stooped to conquer. On the first day we would go all together, and the Sards were to show us how to hunt mouflon, but I secretly determined not to let pass a fair chance of a stalk.

We started before daylight. Indeed, if I may make a harmless boast, I saw every sunrise during the five weeks I remained in the island—that is to say, when there was one. Nor will any one be successful at this sport who does not do likewise. But I am bound to confess there were so many mornings when the sky shook out the feather beds, instead of producing any sun at all, that the conceit does not amount to much. We ascended a ridge immediately behind the house, and followed its crest. The snow, in spite of the three previous fine days, still lay everywhere except on some southern slopes. Alternate sun and frost had produced a crust upon its surface, in plunging through which our feet made a terrible noise, which did not promise well for "still hunting." However, whatever its disadvantages, one learns more of the habits of an animal in one day on the snow, than in three without it. And, oh! the exhilaration of that moment! Here was fresh "sign." In the neighbourhood of one of these clear slopes there were unmistakable mouflon tracks. Telescopes were immediately busy, notwithstanding the impatience of the natives, who thought this a needless waste of time. A few minutes later those blessed words, "I have them," from Celestin, brought us all, eager worshippers, to his side. There they were sure enough—four brown spots on one of the southern slopes a mile or more distant. We had never seen mouflon before, but there was no mistaking the identity of the animal. The Sards were sceptical and said it was impossible to see mouflon at that distance, but that they might be pigs. It was worth the delay of a few minutes to give these gentlemen a lesson, so we carefully posed a telescope on the rocks, and presided over the peepshow. As each man came up to look, it was amusing to watch his face. He would apply his eye with an expression of supercilious pity for our credulity. After a long gaze this would suddenly give place to an eager look, while the glass was convulsively clutched; then a broad grin and a volley of smothered oaths followed. Ross's 30-inch stalker was a new revelation to them, and visibly altered their attitude towards us. From that moment they recognised that we did know a thing or two which they had not dreamed of in their philosophy.

These mouflon were close above the high road, and as they would obviously be put away by the first person that passed along it that morning, we did not attempt to stalk them, especially as they were all females or kids, and were separated from us by a deep valley. We went on along the ridge till we came to another favourable spying-place, and again called a halt. Again the telescope, or rather the practised eye behind it, was successful. This time the mouflon were in a shallow hollow in the ridge upon which we stood, and by dropping down to our left and keeping along parallel to the ridge, we could reach them in twenty minutes. The Sards assumed an air of profound wisdom, and showed how they were to be driven. I pointed out how they might be approached with certainty if they remained where they were. We compromised. They were to place themselves and the other guns as though for a drive, and I was to make the stalk. A long tramp through drifted snow took us to the rock which we had marked as overlooking the *macquia* where they were. Lying flat on the top of it, we scanned the slope below us with infinite precautions. There was nothing to be seen but the *macquia*, which was here so high and dense that it might have concealed a hundred. I sent Celestin to a point on the ridge three hundred yards farther back, which commanded the slope from a different angle, and whence I hoped he might see them. But while he was gone I continued to watch the waving covert below me, and at last saw a little brown patch in the dark green. This presently developed into the head and shoulders of a mouflon. It was a long shot, but I had had plenty of time to get my hand steady. She fell stone dead in her tracks. At the sound another, darker and more conspicuous, jumped up and stood for a moment; I rammed in a second cartridge, and as he moved off I felt sure I had hit him. As a matter of fact, he had received as deadly a wound as the other, and had fallen within ten yards, but the covert was so dense that I was some time finding him. This was a handsome young male. The other, I regret to say, was a female, but it was the first one I saw, and though this chance came thus early, I could not tell that I should have another. After this we always let the ewes alone. The natives make no such distinction, but fire a charge of slugs into the brown at short range, as they are driven by the *poste*. Two of those subsequently killed by us had old wounds thus given.

So triumphant a beginning was beyond the dreams of avarice. Incidentally it raised us several pegs in the estimation of the natives, and proved to them the efficacy of our method. The great difficulty was to teach the importance of finding the game before the game found them. But from this time Celestin's superior skill was recognised, and brute force bowed to science. While at luncheon under a clump of fine ilex, F—— made a clever spy of a small herd of mouflon containing some good males, on the farther side of the valley. They were lying in some thin covert, and the master ram lay on the top of a rock, only his dark brown shoulder and fine head being visible. In accordance with our plan for the day, while two of us were "posted," the third took the stalk, but this was a very different business from the first trial. For the first time we discovered the exceeding shiftiness of the wind among these hills. A back current carried a warning message to the herd, and F—— got only a long running shot. The Sards said it was all the fault of this beastly stalking.

I came home by myself, following the stream, where the *macquia* was tallest and the snow was most drifted. When these long flexible shoots are bowed down by masses of snow, and interlaced, they constitute a temper-trying obstacle comparable only with the *leg-föhren* of the Eastern Alps. On the way I saw another lot of mouflon which I had unwittingly disturbed in my struggle through the covert. Now it is not to be supposed from this grand day's sport that it is easy to put salt on the tails of these wily beasts. To some extent, as often happens, we exhausted our luck on the first day, and we did not get another chance for many days.

To enable sportsmen to appreciate the difficulties of the sport, let me endeavour to describe this little wild sheep, and his ways and surroundings. The mouflon is a small edition of the big-horn sheep of the Rocky Mountains. Though only about a fifth of the size, he carries the same sturdy body on short legs. Like that animal, his horns spring well back, and then curve downwards and forwards, parallel with his cheeks; and like him, instead of the wool of a sheep, he has the close hair of a deer. The colour of the ewes is also the same

THE SARDINIAN MOUFLON.

gray dun as the *Ovis montana*, but the rams are distinguished by the rich dark brown of the shoulders and a black fringe of longer hair below the neck. On either side he bears a conspicuous gray saddle-mark, which some have supposed that nature intended as a target. If so, it is like the false portholes painted on iron forts to deceive the enemy—too far back and too high. The belly is a pure white. His meat is excellent when well hung, but in February very lean. I saw no herd of more than twelve. The old rams were sometimes solitary, but more often in small companies by themselves. The young rams were often in the company of the ewes. It seemed to us that there was a preponderance of males, and we were told that the shepherds who bring their flocks to the hills in the spring, kill many ewes and kids at that season; but this disparity may be only apparent, as the ewes are easily missed with the glass.

He stands about the height of a Southdown sheep, but he carries a head that seems large, out of proportion to his body. The following are the measurements of our two best heads :

Length round outer curve	29 & 28 inches
Span across horns .	17 & 21 ,,
Girth of horn at base	9 & 10 ,,

It will be seen that as regards length and span they are not far inferior to big-horn sheep, but the girth and weight are much less. I had no means of weighing those we got, but our chamois hunter thought the weight of the best about twice that of a large buck chamois, which would bring it to about 100 lbs.

I believe the mouflon, as I know him, is confined to the islands of Sardinia and Corsica. There are mouflon in Cyprus, and also in the mountains of Tunis, but they are distinct species from the Sardinian animal, and from one another.

Take 'him all round, the *Ovis musimon* is one of the best hands at keeping a whole skin of any wild animal that I have hunted. *Rusé* is not the word for him. He is up to all the tricks of the trade and several more. One writer states that to approach the rams is "not unaccompanied by danger." If to his other good qualities this sturdy little sheep added that of occasionally showing fight, he would indeed be perfect. To say that "they frequent the precipitous bluffs, where even charcoal-burners find it difficult to set foot," as another writer avers, conveys a wrong impression. Though he lives on ground more or less steep, it is easy, and he has no occasion for any remarkable feats of agility. On the other hand, his best safeguard lies in the dense *macquia* which covers the hills. At this elevation it is exclusively composed of the tall "bruyère" heather, from which the so-called "briar-root" pipes are made. This grows from two to six feet high. If this covert were continuous, it would of course be impossible to see an animal which stands little over two feet, but much of it has been burnt, and there are natural openings besides. It is in these openings that he must be sought when feeding. As all wild sheep are constitutionally restless, and never remain long in one place, it will be understood how difficult it is, even when they have been spied, to hold them with the glass. They are constantly disappearing in the *macquia*, and have to be refound again and again before a stalk can be successfully effected. When they are alarmed or "at gaze," they have a habit, or at least the rams have, of placing themselves in the middle of a bush of *macquia*, or in the shadow which it casts. The ewes, who are naturally less conspicuous, do this in a less degree. The mouflon are also assisted by the wonderful alertness of their eyes. I do not think that they see at a great distance, but they detect an exceedingly slight sign at a moderate range. On one occasion I got up to a small band at so high a level, that there was no covert at all except that of rocks. They were two hundred yards off at least, and feeding away, and, the ground being bare, I could see that there were no outliers—that fruitful source of unaccountable alarms. Yet the moment I looked over with all the usual precautions, my cap, which closely matched the rocks, was "picked up," and the alarm communicated to the whole lot. No deer or chamois that I am acquainted with would have detected so slight a movement at that distance. This experience was repeated on several occasions. The Sards have a fable relating that a hair, which fell from the head of a hunter, was *smelt* by the wild boar, while the stag *heard* it, and the mouflon *saw* it. When startled they whistle as a chamois, and as a Highland sheep occasionally does.

One of their favourite devices is to seek for spots on the lee side of a ridge where the currents of air meet. Here, in otherwise favourable positions, they are quite unapproachable. And the worst of it is, there is no means of finding it out until the stalker, after surmounting all other difficulties, arrives within two hundred yards, only to find the treacherous wind tickling the backs of his ears. Well he knows that he will presently find their couches warm but empty. I also fancy, though I cannot prove this meanness against them, that they practise an artful dodge which is not unknown to red deer. This is to circle round an object which has excited some suspicion until they get the wind of it.

Many of our longest and most interesting days were spent in vainly trying to defeat craft of this kind, and to circumvent some strategical position that ultimately proved impregnable. At last they begin to feed; fading light compels us to do something, a flat crawl through thin *macquia*, a suspicious old ewe in the way, who will keep looking back instead of attending to her supper, finally a long running shot in the failing light without result—some such record was a frequent experience, but such days are not failure.

The ground on which we found them may be described as broken rather than mountainous. The valley in which we chiefly hunted is a wide tract bounded on either side by considerable ridges, and containing quite a maze of shallow corries, affording excellent shelter in all weathers, but where the wind was most aggravating for the stalker. Most of the valleys hereabouts contain groves of fine old ilex in the hollows. These ilex woods contain splendid timber of that species, as well as oaks. I saw one of the former in the hollow of which four men could easily have lain abreast. But the destruction of them is most melancholy. The *pastorali* or shepherds seem, out of pure wantonness, to build their fires under the finest trees of the grove, and it was a common sight to see such giants thus done to death and stretching their gaunt arms to the sky, or overthrown by the wind. On the day following the one above described, I went some miles down the road and explored carefully a valley thus wooded. The ilex were splendid to look upon; but though I tramped for many miles through the snow, there was not a single track of mouflon to be found, and the reason was sufficiently obvious. The ilex produce an immense crop of acorns, and large droves of tame pigs are brought into the woods under the charge of *pastorali*. The mouflon therefore quit the neighbourhood of these forests. Now our pet valley was free from such woods, with the exception of some small groves too remote for it to be worth while to bring the pigs so far, and which were given over to the wild boar. They had trodden the snow like a farmyard.

These boar lie too close in the daytime to stalk, and, as a rule, can only be driven; but on several occasions we caught glimpses of them, and once, by a fortunate chance, bagged one while stalking mouflon. We were all together on that day, and were spying for mouflon from some high rocks. One of our men was at the bottom of the slope four or five hundred yards off, and started a fine boar from a bunch of scrub. He came out into the open and stood half-way down the slope, unconscious of our presence as we were of his, until Enricetto jumped up, yelling "*Cinghiale! cinghiale!*" (wild boar) at the top of his voice, and waving his arms. This was the Sard notion of the best way to get a quiet shot. The boar started at his best speed, and tore across the slope below us as if he had forgotten something, his stumpy black body ploughing up the snow at every stride. F——— was the first to get hold of his rifle, an American repeater, and began "pumping lead" with it. I rushed back and laid hold of the first rifle I could find, which happened to be G———'s. He was twenty yards off and could see the fun, but not having his rifle could not get a shot in. When I got into position the boar was straight below us, going at a great pace through some burnt *macquia*, where he showed plainly against the snow among the black stems. I fired a length ahead of him. Some one said "*E ferrato*," and the beast seemed to slacken his pace. Before I could load my single barrel again, F——— got in two more shots, and at the last, as it appeared, piggy rolled over among the *macquia*. When we got down to him he was still sitting up, champing blood and foam. I got Celestin's big alpenstock firmly planted against his side, so that he could not charge, and F——— gave him the *coup de grâce* with his hunting-knife. He was a fine boar, about as big as they make them in this island, though less than the size they attain on the mainland. Only one bullet had struck him, and passed clean through. Of course we assumed that this was F———'s last shot, but after the "grallock" we followed the track backwards and found that the blood began one hundred yards from where he fell. It was therefore plain that the fatal shot might have been fired by either of us, and the question would have remained for ever unsolved if it had not been for a curious piece of evidence. We carried the boar to the top of the ridge, and, some further cleansing being necessary, a small battered piece of copper was found in his liver. Now

F—— shoots with a solid bullet, whereas I used an express, the bullet of which carries a copper tube in the hollow. The bullet had passed through, but it had left behind this unmistakable "certificate of origin." Poor cowboy!

We were obliged to bow down in the house of Rimmon, and, for the satisfaction of our Sards, devote a day or two to the *caccia grossa* which they esteem so much. A motley band of peasants, accompanied by a variety of dogs, appeared at an early hour one morning by agreement. Some who came from a distance had camped for the night in the woods. They were very keen and confident, and expected no pay beyond a supply of wine and a share of such game as might be killed. All had guns, but in a more or less rickety condition. The barrels of some were badly cracked, which was not to be wondered at, for the muzzles were "stoppered" with plugs of grass when not in use, and doubtless these trivial obstacles were occasionally forgotten. I was told of one man who shot with an ancient piece which had a distinct elbow in the barrel. This slight blemish, he said, had been made by his grandfather, so that only the owner should possess the secret of shooting with it.

Before each drive there was a great deal of voluble discussion, not to say quarrelling, as to how the drives were to be taken, and who were to act as beaters. About a third were told off for this purpose, while the remainder, with ourselves, occupied the "posts" on the ridge above the drive, or on the slope which was to be driven. I confess I envied the beaters, for we were soon chilled to the bone at the posts. They did not appear to attach much importance to driving down wind. The beaters kept up a discordant din, but the dogs did most of the work. We made four or five drives that day; boar or mouflon were seen in most of them, but only one or two snap shots were obtained, and the result was *nil*. They say a small pig passed within twenty yards of me without my knowing it. The following day we drove down to the little village whence most of these men came, and took some likely-looking places on another range. The result was no better. If we made any sceptical remarks as to any drive, we were greeted with, " *Cerri—altro!* " (with emphasis) " *Anche moufloni—Anche cinghiale—Suro, suro!* " (crescendo). This indeed was a formula with which we grew very familiar while we remained in Sardinia, but after this experience, we did not pursue the native form of sport, if such it can be called. Perhaps we were unlucky; certainly many boar are killed in this way, but I believe very few mouflon. This is borne out by the following, which is given by Mr. Tennant as the average annual bag on the Marquis of Laconi's estate, one of the largest and best-preserved on the island:—Mouflon, 5; red deer, 10; fallow deer, 40; boar, 85; partridges, 500; hares, 150; rabbits, 300; woodcock, 160; snipe, 125; duck, 100; quail, 50; plover, 30; bustards, 5. There are a few red deer on these ranges, and the Sards would occasionally point out an old mouflon track in the snow which had been enlarged by the sun, and assert that it was a red deer. I saw no genuine fresh red deer's tracks myself, but the exceptionally severe weather had, perhaps, driven them away from the high ground. Fallow deer must also be sought at a lower level.

Returning from that expedition in the evening in the little waggonette we had hired, we had an object-lesson in the obstinacy of Sard horses. Such a pair of jibbers I never saw before. After a series of tremendous struggles, during which we progressed about a mile in an hour, we gave it up and walked home. The driver arrived there at midnight leading his horses. The next day he made another attempt, but ultimately he was beaten, and had to walk twelve miles to fetch another pair.

After this we returned with renewed zest to our own methods, thanking our stars that we were not dependent upon a mixed rabble of Sards for our sport. It was not all plain sailing, however, for the weather again turned abominably rough, and remained so, almost without intermission, for the rest of our stay. One does not expect to find the Arctic regions within one hundred and fifty miles of Africa. Daily we had to face heavy falls of snow and hail, which condemned us to a voluntary imprisonment for hours together under some hospitable rock, waiting for such a clearance as would make it possible to use the telescope. But our worst enemy was the wind. So thrashing, hammering, persistent a gale I never tried to stand against. The windows of the *cantoniera* were partly blown in, and the fine powdery snow poured in through the broken panes for several days continuously, while outside nothing was to be seen but whirlwinds of snow and columns of spray one hundred feet high, literally torn up from the surface of the little river. Even when the snow ceased to fall, the wind was so high that it caught it up in wreaths, and filled the air with the fine particles like a fog, so that no use could be made of the glass. Nor was this the worst of it;

for, though we faced the weather, and by patience succeeded in finding the game, some shuddering current of air, whirling round the corries and rebounding from the cliffs, would carry a warning to their senses, from whatever quarter we attempted to approach, and time after time good stalks were spoiled. Still we were often reminded of our latitude, even on the worst days, by distant visions, as through a veil, of gleams of southern sun bathing in golden light the low country which lay beyond the influence of this centre of storms. More rarely we enjoyed a whole day's respite, which we thought heavenly by contrast, and in some sheltered corner we would pretend to take a midday siesta after the manner of these parts, with the head pillowed on a bunch of wild thyme, and its scent filling the nostrils.

On such a day we had one of the prettiest of stalks. We had spied from the top of a ridge two old stagers—rams of quite exceptional quality—on the slope below us. They were thinking of settling for the day, and the wariness with which they sought a retreat was highly instructive. After trying several spots they ascended the opposite slope, and at last lay down within shot of the top of it, but so carefully concealed that though they lay on snow and where the scrub was thin, if three powerful telescopes had not watched every move, we should certainly have lost them when they "couched." We had now to get down our side of the valley, which was, naturally, in full view; but the *macquia*, which generally favours the game, sometimes helps the hunter. Lying on our backs, and pushing ourselves down through the snow with our elbows, we slid in and out among the low bushes, as well concealed as our quarry, and reached the bottom in safety. Thence a shallow ravine led us easily to the top of the ridge under which the mouflon lay, and following it along to the well-noted point above them, and finding the wind there sure and steady, we felt pretty safe of a fair shot. I crept down the hill till I was nearly level with the rams, and could just make out a pair of horns. G——, who was to take the shot, got straight above them and much nearer. We stayed like this for twenty minutes waiting for them to rise, when suddenly, without warning, rhyme, or reason, they sprang from their beds and bounded down the slope without a pause. G—— got in a futile running shot. I was too astonished even to do that. The cause remains to this moment a mystery, but there is one hypothesis which fits the case. We had left Gigi forty yards behind on the other side of the ridge with strict injunctions not to move. I hope I am not doing him an injustice, but it is just possible that, as we had so long passed out of his sight, overcome by curiosity, he came over the ridge to see what had become of us. If he did so, it is certain that the rams would see him before he saw them. When we returned to the spot where we had left him, he wore an exceedingly innocent expression, but he did not inquire if the shot had been successful.

The *contoniera* was not attractive by daylight. Even at the worst of the weather we went out on the off chance, and by sheer perseverance sometimes got a stroke of luck and conquered fortune against odds. On one of the most unpromising of days we struggled against the gale to our favourite spying-place. On the ridge we found that, even if the falling snow would have allowed a clear sight, the wind was too high to hold the glass steady. So we descended into a deep valley at right angles to the course of the wind, and sought a big rock. Here we built a huge fire, and, baking alternate sides of our bodies, waited to see whose patience would first give out.

For five hours we waited for a chance, and then gave it up, and followed the stream homewards, but kept a bright look-out as we passed certain deep hollows on the sheltered side, well knowing that, in weather like this, all the living things in the valley must be concentrated in such spots. We had passed several of these, and were nearing the high road when Celestin, who was in front, dropped on the track. We followed his example and felt for our glasses, now almost useless from damp. High up the slope he had seen a mouflon, and we now made out four cunning old rams, the same, as we believed, whom we had seen on previous occasions, but who had always eluded us. They were sheltering under a steep slope where the patches of heather were quite six feet high, which accounted for their choice of the spot. Getting into a hollow we went straight up at them, with very faint expectation of getting within shooting distance. Perhaps they thought that nobody would be fool enough to be hunting on such a day. At any rate they were less vigilant than usual. Though the wind seemed to be whirling about in every direction we got right up to them before they were "jumped." It was impossible to tell exactly where they were, and the first sign I saw was a pair of horns describing a series of arched curves. I had just time to shout to G—— to look out, when they bolted up the hill across a patch of open ground.

The leader had his heels in the air before he could cross it. G——'s shot also seemed to tell. Then I tried to get into a sitting position for a steady shot when they should reappear in the next opening, but I forgot how steep the hill was, and rolled clean over backwards, heels over head, and only recovered myself to fire a futile shot. Again I got into position with the bead on the sky-line, feeling sure that one or another would turn there to look for his scattered companions. Exactly so! A massive pair of shoulders and horns clear cut against the sky! Click—I had forgotten to put a cartridge in. Egregious duffer! fat-head! tender-foot! Pile on the epithets—you will never have such another chance. Casting a hasty glance at the dead mouflon we followed up the trail, and soon found blood on the snow, which quickly led us to the body of another. We had two beauties at any rate, but we ought to have had the lot.

These two had heads which are not easy to beat, but there were two or three veterans about, with heads as wide and strong, and, in addition, with the outward turn of the tips of the horns, which gives such a character to some of the Asian sheep, and, more rarely, to the American big-horn. We were greedy for one of these, and for many days counted all else as "trash;" but they set quite as much value on their trophies as we did. One day we spied such a one, well placed on the opposite slope of a deep valley. He had others nearly as good in his company as well as some ewes, but we recked not of them. A solemn resolution was agreed to, to spare no time or trouble to get this fellow; and having so resolved, we immediately broke it. The first difficulty was to get down the slope below us, which was in view. We ought to have returned along the ridge for a mile, to where a hollow would have covered us, but to save a quarter of an hour we clipped it. I fancied there was a little ravine below us, but the slope proved painfully smooth, and the covert was unusually thin and the snow abominably white. Having got a third of the way down in safety, slithering *dos-à-terre*, we could not slither up again, and had to risk it. Now these crafty sheep practised a dirty little trick, which we observed on more than one previous occasion. They really saw us all the time, but *pretended* that they did not, and remained apparently unconscious until we disappeared from their sight into the gully of the stream, when they instantly departed. Fortunately we had left Benjamin on the top of the ridge with a telescope to guard against such a contingency. Finding them gone we now signalled him to join us. He had seen that their heads were turned towards us, but they did not even rise from their beds until they thought their departure would be unobserved. They then separated into two parties, but Benjamin had kept his glass on the patriarch and two or three others who accompanied him. He reported that they had passed over a shoulder of the mountain towards a certain deep corrie which we knew to be a favourite sanctuary. We now made a big detour, as we should have done in the first instance, and at length reached the rim of this basin. From here, after a long search, we again discovered them. To approach was a different business in this concave hollow. For several hours we wound ourselves about among the low bushes, and horribly cold work was this flat crawling in powdery snow; but it was impossible to get nearer than a quarter of a mile. We had left Benjamin at the point where we had refound them, with instructions to hold them with the glass. Once he thought they had discovered us, for all their heads went up together; but, turning his glass towards the quarter at which they were looking, he discovered the cause in a large boar snouting about the scrub. In the meanwhile there was nothing for it but to wait till they fed into a more accessible place. This they at length did, feeding down the stream till a friendly shoulder hid them. Then we jumped up and ran along the hill as quickly as our stiffened limbs could travel, till we got right above them. The supreme moment seemed to have arrived. They were quietly feeding through some tall *macquia* towards a clearing. We slid down a hollow which faced this opening, and waited seventy yards from it. First came a suspicious old ewe gazing about. Now they were all in the open except the big one. Last of all he trotted out, and turned to graze on the edge of a steep bank, the whole length of his broad back exposed to us. What a grand trophy he will make set up in Ward's best style! It was just the loveliest chance I ever saw, and after such a stalk too! I whispered to F—— to take him so. There was a crash of lead on splintered rock—twenty bounds, and he was gone. Alas that the minute trembling of some superfluous erratic nerve should squander all that labour, forethought, endurance, and science! Well, I know whereabouts he is, and—I hope to look him up again some day.

It would be extremely interesting to me, but I fear tedious for the reader, to describe other stalks, successful or the reverse. I will content myself with saying that notwithstanding quite an epidemic of misses, we secured nine mouflon and one boar, all by fair stalking.

I will conclude this chapter with a suggestion or two that may be useful to any one who may follow in our footsteps. If he understands stalking, by all means let him take a telescope, which must be used with industry and perseverance. Nor let him be content with looking the ground over once or twice. In such covert an animal may be hidden one minute and exposed the next. If he must drive, let him avoid surrounding himself with a tribe of natives. Two or three are enough to drive a wide area for sheep. Let them drive, while he puts himself in the *best* post. His individual chance will be as good or better than if the ridge were lined with impetuous natives. The headquarters should be as far as possible from a town. A few Italian cigars carried in the pocket are the best passport. The best season for stalking mouflon would probably be the summer, when they are high up on the peaks where the rocks are nearly bare; but there may be danger of fever until October. Supplies should be fetched every two or three days from the nearest town by a man on horseback. To avoid the necessity of carrying much money, a sum should be deposited with some agent there, and everything paid for through him. If the sportsman carries a good stock of wholesome incredulity, and relies upon his own judgment, he will enjoy himself. If he discovers my particular preserve, I hope he will move on to some other equally good, or, should I find him in my quarters, there might be a bad case of *vendetta*.

II

RECOLLECTIONS OF CHAMOIS HUNTING

Of the various forms of stalking which I have tried, none, in my opinion, will bear comparison with the chase of the chamois—*Antelope rupicapra*, the only representative of the species in Europe.

The main element in all forms of sport is that the interest should be sustained. This is not possible with any game that lives chiefly in dense covert. If the sportsman is so fortunate as to get a chance at such *feræ naturæ*, it comes suddenly, without warning, and often without generalship on his part. Chamois, on the other hand, live on ground which, as a rule, can be thoroughly surveyed with a telescope. Spying is in itself an art, the perfection of which is only attainable by long practice, combined with excellent natural vision, but considerable proficiency may be attained by an amateur possessed of a good instrument, and who is not content to look over his ground but *searches* it minutely and patiently. When he has attained even a moderate degree of skill, he has qualified himself for one of the highest pleasures of hunting. Moreover, he will not have reached finality, but will find that he can improve himself almost indefinitely, until he performs feats which he would have previously thought impossible.

It should be remembered that a chamois, even when at rest, always places himself where he can look out, and, as he can see, so he can be seen. I used to be astonished at the ease with which some of my hunters have, at a distance of two thousand yards or more, detected a chamois by the gray marks on its face—the only visible part of its body. Yet I have myself, when in good practice, accomplished the feat.

So great is the power of a good spy-glass that I do not remember ever to have had a blank day's chamois hunting, *i.e. without seeing anything*, except, of course, when the mountains have become shrouded in mist early in the day. This diligent spying is to my mind one of the most inspiriting features of the sport. Many a delightful hour of anticipation have I spent in watching a herd, or perhaps more than one, while waiting for them to settle for the day, discussing the best line of approach, and impressing upon the memory the salient features of the ground in their neighbourhood; and this is not wasted time, for these animals are so restless that it is often necessary to wait till noon before the real labour of the day commences.

The delight of overcoming rock difficulties—one seldom has any ice work in chamois hunting—adds another charm, and the Alpine Club is a standing proof that healthy Englishmen are fond of clambering for its own sake. At the same time it is a mistake to suppose that the conventional pictures that are written and painted, of *gemsjägers* in difficulties [1] are often realised. Chamois are, as a rule, found at an elevation of from six to eight thousand feet, and do not affect the tops of peaks, or very break-neck places unless they have been alarmed. Some *mauvais pas* are encountered, but as a rope is a hindrance, and is seldom carried, no one but a fool would court really bad places which might be turned.

Neither is the sport a very arduous one. The distances to be traversed are not really great, and though there is always a sharp burst of climbing of from one to three thousand feet—for the approach has almost invariably to be made from above—the ground must be

---

[1] I may be permitted to cull a few specimens from the literature of the subject, which accounts for the glamour which surrounds it in the public mind. One old German writer says that "the most dangerous chase of all is that of a chamois. The hunter must manage all alone, as neither man nor dog can be of any service to him. His accoutrements consist of an old coat, a bag with dry bread, cheese, and meat ; a gun, his hunting-knife, and a pair of irons for the feet. He then drives the chamois from one crag to the other, making them always mount higher, climbs after them, and shoots them if he can, or if he finds it necessary ; but if that should not be the case, and he has driven one so far that it is no longer able to elude him, he approaches quite close, puts his hunting-knife to its side, which the chamois, of its own accord, pushes into its body, and then falls down headlong from the rock." There is nothing impossible in the following, and I should be sorry to deny the truth of it, but I have not had the good fortune to observe such a game of "leap-frog" myself. We read of chamois crossing a snow-field, "that they hasten their flight in the following manner. The last chamois jumps on the back of the one before him, passes in this way over the backs of all the others, and then places himself at their head. The last but one does the same, and the others follow in order ; and in this manner they have soon passed over such a field of snow." Such writers do, however, occasionally hit upon the truth, as, for instance, where one of them says, "It is their inner heat which impels them to seek those places where snow is to be found." A friend of mine once took the temperature of a freshly-killed chamois, and it stood at 130° Fahrenheit. I am ashamed to say that I have never verified this experiment.

constantly re-surveyed, and the position of the game ascertained afresh, so that halts are frequent. Personally. I find the yielding bogs of Sweden, or even the long heather of Scotland much more trying to the wind and muscles.

The shifting scenes of Alpine peaks, forests, and glaciers form another inspiring element which is totally wanting, say in the leaden-coloured slopes and peat bogs of a Scotch deer forest. No doubt Scotch deer stalking has some of these charms, or had them in the days of St. John and Scrope, but those seven-strand fences have taken the flavour out of it. It seems a work of supererogation to circumvent an animal which you have already circumscribed with an impassable wire enclosure.

Then there is the real skill required to hit so small an animal. The vital part of a chamois is scarcely larger than this book. That may seem to the reader a sufficient mark, but when it is exactly the same misty colour as its background, and you know it is about to run away, I can assure him that it is remarkably easy to miss. It is no consolation when you hear the exclamation at your elbow, "*G-r-r-r-at über*," and your hunter shows with his finger and thumb how you wanted only half an inch to make an excellent shot. There are some people who never miss. I have encountered a few, and read the books of many. I am always sorry for them. It must be so monotonous. I once met an old sportsman returning from stalking, after missing a stag. He assured me that he had a private enemy who must have tampered with the sights of his rifle. That is about the tallest excuse I ever heard, but in chamois hunting a man must be bolder even than that to find reasons for all the misses which he is certain to make. When his invention is at fault, it is best to go and shoot at a stone till he has restored his confidence.

Another attraction of chamois hunting is that it takes you to the mountains at the time of year when they put on their most gorgeous raiment. At the latter end of September the corridors of the hotels are empty. Yet it is not till then, when the mild sunshine, even at mid-day, casts those wonderful purple shadows, that the infinite variety and delicacy of form of the everlasting hills stand revealed in clearest definition, often rendered yet more clear by a soft powdering of fresh snow resting on every ledge. Then who can measure the glories of an Alpine sunset, when the pink snow flush is framed in golden birches? Large patches of these clothe the hills—acres of them together—and out of them tower the great Arolla pines, black by contrast. The larches have hardly turned, but at a lower level on the Italian slopes, the beeches, though still green for the most part, carry fiery points; and under your feet, that close-growing bilberry-like plant which is, I think, the *Vaccinium*, burns to a scarlet so pure and brilliant, that I have often mistaken it for the blood of a chamois of which I was in search. It is not surprising then that, when the pursuit of new peaks and passes—the craze of my salad days—began to pall a little, I adopted with enthusiasm the chase of the nimble mountain antelope, which combines a mild form of mountaineering with all these delights.

Most of the chamois hunting which I have done has been within easy distance of the Engadine. The people of Graubunden are jealous of their sport being shared by foreigners, and they have a local law which forbids even a Swiss of another canton to hunt under heavy penalties. I have known them to send out spies to watch an Englishman who had gone out with a local hunter, and to see that he did not fire the shot. A trustful American once persuaded a hunter of Samaden to take him out for a *gemse-jagd*, but, as the risks of detection were so great, this guileless mountaineer demanded a high tariff—not less indeed than 100 francs. After an arduous day, the stranger returned with one small marmot, and was immediately mulcted in another 100 francs' penalty, having been informed against by his own guide, who took half the fine. This exclusiveness is of long standing. Von Tschudi mentions one, Colani, who lorded it over these valleys at the commencement of this century, and at whose door was laid the disappearance of not a few Italians and others, who had trespassed on his preserves never to return. Personally I doubt the authenticity of these bloodthirsty deeds, a belief in which was perhaps fostered by himself to keep off intruders from his domain; and I am inclined to think that his worst crime was inordinate lying. At least that is my inference from the following history of one Lenz, who bearded the lion in his den, and begged permission to accompany him on a hunting expedition. He seems to have been in a terrible fright of this monster of Frankenstein, who acted the part to perfection all the time which he passed in his company. I quote only the cream of the horrors which he underwent:—

"At one time Lenz and Colani were both lying down and leaning over a precipice of a thousand feet, in order to spy out the game below, when Lenz suddenly heard a loud rushing sound, and at the same time a cry burst from Colani. Lenz drew back and saw above him an enormous Lämmergeier, which in another instant would have shoved him down the precipice. Colani's shout had saved him from certain death. Soon he spied out five chamois in a spot, one of the most difficult and dangerous that can be conceived. Colani had only been there once before in his life, he said. However, straightway he buckled his gun on his shoulder, and reached the narrow gallery of a vast perpendicular rock, which sank to immeasurable depths below. The loose earth slipt from under them at every step. The ledge became narrower and narrower. Objects beneath appeared like the smallest specks. As they went on, vast chasms intervened from time to time, giving them sudden glimpses of the world below, and at last the path seemed to disappear altogether. 'Now, look sharp,' shouted Colani, and catching hold of a jutting tooth of rock, he swung himself over to the opposite side, leaving his companion to do the same. Lenz imitated him with the courage of despair, and rather, as it would seem, to the astonishment of Colani, who quietly remarked, 'I did not think we should both have stood here together. And now,' he said, 'for the chamois; we have got round them famously.' In half an hour they reached the top of the mountain, where they had seen the animals. Two were lying at their feet among the Alpine roses, on the brink of a precipice. Lenz's heart beat as he fired over Colani's shoulder. One of the animals sprang into the air and rolled backwards down the precipice; Colani's shot missed, his gun being poised on a tottering piece of rock. Lenz wished to go down and secure his prey, but Colani withheld him, adding, with what Lenz thought a guilty look. 'Whatever descends into that grave is buried safe enough.' Many years before, a hunter of the Grisons had disappeared there, leaving no trace behind. Lenz declares the spot seemed to him to smell of human blood.

"They next reached a valley full of blocks of stone, and shut in by perpendicular rocks. In clambering over some fragments, Colani caught sight of some object, threw himself down behind a stone, and motioned to Lenz to do the same. He made no answer to his companion's inquiries, but looked up through his glass and muttered an imprecation, at the same time clenching his fist convulsively. Lenz perceived at length a human figure high up among the rocks. The fierce expression and angry words of his guide filled him with strange misgivings. 'Remember I am come to shoot chamois and not men,' he remarked sternly. After a while the strange hunter disappeared. Up jumped Colani. 'Follow me,' he said; and they rushed at full speed up the hills, taking only ten minutes to accomplish what was usually the work of half an hour. They sank down exhausted for a moment, but presently the stranger reappeared, and Colani deliberately cocked his gun and took aim at him. 'Halt,' cried Lenz, pushing the weapon aside, 'I allow no murder before my eyes.' Colani cast a terrible glance at him, but presently gave him his hand and said, 'We will not quarrel with each other.' Meantime his destined victim had disappeared."

The Engadiners have still the reputation of—shall I say—great independence of character. Perhaps by this time the attrition of all the nations has put a polish on the surface, but thirty years ago, it sometimes took the form of rather masterful self-assertion. I remember Herr G——, who afterwards blossomed into a wealthy hotel proprietor, but who did not then wear a black coat, exhibited his dawning civilisation by announcing, in the course of the *table d'hôte*, that beer was not to be drunk at dinner, and that if any one wanted it he must take it in the public beer saloon. Now we Britishers did not all want to drink beer, for his Valteline "Montagner" was excellent, but we declined to be coerced into consuming it. We rose *en masse* from the table after soup, and adjourned to the tap-room. There we solemnly drank our beer and returned for the next course. This form of strike was successful, and the bloated capitalist, who by the way was a very good fellow, was brought to his knees.

On account of the local jealousy which I have hinted at I have generally hunted on the Italian side of the frontier, but my first expedition was near Zernetz. It was a sudden thought. We were not properly equipped. We used borrowed guns of the country, and naturally we came back after two days, having caught nothing but bad colds. There had been a heavy fall of snow; the tracks of chamois were everywhere, and though I failed to get a shot, I was badly infected with the buck-fever. This result was contributed to by the stirring reminiscences of my excellent friend Herr S—— of Pontresina, formerly President of the Graubunden, who accompanied us on that occasion. His large collection of chamois heads testifies to the zeal with which this fine old sportsman hunted them in years gone by.[1]

---

[1] I can only remember one of these tales. He was following with one companion, in the depth of winter, the bloody trail of a wounded chamois.

AN OLD CHAMOIS HUNTER.

from Pontresina, which was not the fashionable resort it

The track led them across a steep *couloir* filled with deep loose snow, into which they plunged up to their middles. When half-way across this the mass parted just above them, and moved downwards with ever-accelerating speed, sometimes covering them deep with a surging mass, and then again tossing them in the air. At last S—— felt himself suddenly and violently arrested by some protruding substance, which afterwards proved to be a broken stump of a tree. After a time he recovered consciousness and succeeded in shaking himself free. His first thought was for his friend, of whom nothing was to be seen. But as he gazed over the waste of snow, he saw at a distance a twig, which had been pressed downwards, recover itself and spring up. Thinking it might be the sign of some life he made his way to the spot, and close by it found a boot protruding from the surface. Scraping the snow away as best he could with his naked hands, he at length uncovered the body as far as the face. The man was apparently dead, and his face almost black; but presently he came to, and was little the worse, while S—— himself, in turn, fainted from the injuries he had received, and was laid up for six weeks before he recovered.

now is, for there was only an old-fashioned, wooden-walled inn. I made, in spite of the regulations, a preliminary canter in the well-known Val Rosegg. For the past ten years or more this valley has been constituted a sanctuary for chamois by the wise provisions of a Federal law. At that time they were scarce, but after a long search we spied three. The day was stormy, and under these circumstances the wind is always uncertain, and our stalk failed in consequence. However, I established, by a fluke, a reputation as a shot, which many misses never completely effaced. Returning along the mule-path, a marmot was observed outside his hole. As I sat down to shoot, he scuttled into it, but presently reappeared, cautiously showing his head and shoulders—a small mark—but I took pains with the shot and slew him at the door of his house. Presently the same thing happened again among some rocks, but this marmot showed only his head as he watched our movements. Besides, the shot was a long one, but by a fortunate accident this bullet also sped true. Ever after, my hunter attributed my misfortunes to anything but the true cause.

The valley of Livigno is a wide open pasture, with rounded green hills on either side, very fat and productive, and maintaining a considerable population. In its upper portion there is much high ground and some excellent corries, but the best ground is below the village. Here the river enters the wild Spöl ravine, the lofty sides of which are composed of dolomite, which produces rock scenery of the most contorted and bizarre character—isolated columns, terraces, mysterious hollows and clefts, flying buttresses, like those on Milan Cathedral—though the ruin of rocks is so great, that a closer comparison would be found in the remains of the temple of the Sun at Karnak. Most striking of all, water spouts out in certain places in full-bodied streams from the face of sheer cliffs. Then this kind of rock is stained with ochre and russet, and lights up strangely under the mysterious glow of sunset. The slopes are clothed with dense patches of the *Pinus mughus*, or *leg-föhren*, the tangled thickets of which are a favourite haunt of chamois. Owing to the inaccessible character of this ravine, the whole valley of Livigno, though geographically on the northern side of the watershed, and in the map projecting like a peninsula into Switzerland, has always belonged politically to Italy.

At the time of which I write there were many Lämmergeier in Livigno. It is nowadays a very rare bird in the Alps. It is easily distinguished from the more numerous eagles by its great size, and a tail longer in proportion to its body than theirs, as well as by more pointed wings.

There are always rumours flying about of bears in the Lower Engadine. Two or three times we came across tolerably fresh tracks in snow or on soft ground, and I once saw the skin of a newly-killed one, a dark pelt with a tinge of gray on the tips of the hairs, but I never encountered one in the flesh.

For a series of years I visited this valley almost annually, and always had good sport. Sometimes we approached it from Pontresina, across the mountains from the Bernina Pass. Sometimes we ascended its lower extremity from Zernetz. If the weather was very rough, we put up at the little *locanda* in the village. It smelt of cheese and required heavy dustings of " Keating ; " but its hospitality was of the heartiest, and indeed the whole community regarded us as their guests. Sylvestre, the landlord, was especially genial in his greeting, though

THE LÄMMERGEIER.

I am bound to say he tried to make hay on the rare occasions when strangers chanced to shine upon him. The result of this was that each year, as the day of our departure drew near, a slight coolness arose between us owing to the consciousness, which both of us had, of the inevitable row over the bill. To put up at the village involved a long walk to our hunting ground, and we generally camped in one or other of the goat-herds' refuge huts, supplemented by a small ridge tent.

Our favourite camp was about six miles down the ravine, on a little green platform raised somewhat above the river, in which there were some very nice bathing pools. Close by was a bridge, which was convenient, as it enabled us to spy both sides of the valley from the neighbourhood of camp.

In those early days my principal hunter was Spinas, a lean old man, who lived on the Julia Pass, with long black hair, a shrivelled face stained to a dark chocolate colour, and a great hooked nose like some bird of prey, which was strictly in character. He was very poor, but that was owing to his passion for hunting, which he preferred to more profitable occupations. In the winter he would sit up on moonlight nights to shoot foxes. Sometimes he set fall-traps for marmots. He was always catching something, but he once told me that the hardest work of all was trout-fishing. To my surprised inquiry he replied that the hotels will only buy them alive, and that involved carrying on his back a large enclosed trough, shaped like a coffin, which had to be constantly replenished with fresh water. He was a past master in the science of chamois hunting, but a terrible tyrant to his Herr, and very severe when the latter missed, on which occasions he would sometimes refuse to work any more ; for, like most of the Engadiners, he was very independent, not to say boorish. Fortunately for me he had a touching faith in the accuracy of my shooting, but combined with a profound distrust of express rifles. "*Zu viel pulver*" was always on his lips after some fatally bad shot on my part. On a question of wind, or the proper line of approach, he scouted all advice. Indeed he would allow of no difference of opinion in his own department.

I think his success was mainly due to his patient, or what sometimes seemed to me—when boiling over with ardour—his dawdling ways. "*Sempre lentano*" was his tantalising answer to all my urgent suggestions of prompt action: for he talked a mixture of German and Italian as well as a hybrid *patois* called Romansh, which is supposed to be debased Latin. I remember once finding chamois quite early in the day in a very good place. He had not seen them, and kept mooning around all day at a low level. Quite late we mounted, and of course found them where I had indicated. I missed them, and my temper was not improved by his sententious remark: "See what a good thing it is to wait. You are sure to see them at last." For all this I am bound to say his judgment was generally correct. He had a great hulking son, who was also an able hunter, but was even a gruffer and a rougher cub than his father.

Another of my favourites was old Bernardo, a tall, lantern-jawed, and clean-shaven native of Livigno, who, of all the Italians I ever met, was the slowest of speech and the most preternaturally grave. I never could divest myself of the idea that he was a Methodist preacher, and this was borne out by the dark clothes which he habitually wore. He was inferior in skill to Spinas, but the natives of this valley hunt but little, and leave it to the more enterprising Engadiners, who frequently cross the mountains to try their luck there.

The incidents of every stalk, whether successful or not, which I made in the company of one or other of these men, remain graven upon my memory; but to set them all down here would make a very monotonous chapter.

I will endeavour to describe a single successful day: and to present a faithful picture I must not omit all mention of the other sort, however painful the task may be. It was the first day of the season. We had reached over-night the little *wirthshaus* on the Ofener Pass, which is within reach of the ground I have described. We started soon after 3 A.M. and were far along the path before the day actually dawned. As it got light, the man with our baggage horses pulled up short, and pointed out to us a buck, which I could not see without a telescope, feeding on the opposite side of the stream, about five hundred yards off. It seemed strange that he should remain there so unconcernedly, but he was doubtless accustomed to people passing that way.

We attempted the stalk, but had hardly started before those who remained on the path signalled us back. He had got tired of being looked at, and with a shrill whistle had quietly walked off into a thick wood. Leaving the baggage to proceed on its way, we left the path and climbed the opposite mountain. As we neared the top of a steep *couloir*, another solitary buck jumped up above us, within fifty yards, and gazed at us, but not quite long enough for a shot to be snatched. Spinas now said that from the next ridge we should certainly see more " *Cammoche*," as he called them, as they would have come down for the salt. I did not then know what he meant. Sure enough when we cautiously looked over, there, on a wide green plateau, four hundred yards in diameter, was a herd of no less than twenty-four chamois. Some were chasing one another at full gallop round this park-like space; others butted one another, or in sheer exuberance of spirits sprang into the air and pirouetted on their hind-legs; while grave seniors, too old to dance, looked on with the same air of supercilious approval which grandfathers like myself assume at a ghillies' ball in Scotland. It appeared that earlier in the summer, goats are herded on this open space, and, after they have been driven down, the chamois are attracted by the remains of the salt which is spread for them. Sometimes such *salzlächener*, or saltlicks, occur naturally. It is not on my conscience that I disturbed this family party, for while we were making the necessary detour, they betook themselves to the woods for their mid-day siesta, we knew not whither.

I have several times been the witness of such a *gemsespiel*. They generally choose a wide patch of snow, in an open valley where they cannot be easily approached. Once, I am ashamed to say, I successfully stalked such a party. They were so occupied, that I succeeded in crawling down to them in full view. Chamois hunters do not understand this kind of flat crawling, and generally will not attempt it, as there is in most cases such abundant rock covert that there is no need for it; but it is often effective when chamois are feeding, and the light is not too good, if you let yourself downhill on your back, feet foremost, and only move while their heads are down.

I often found chamois, again, on the above-mentioned green plateau; and on one occasion I spied among a small herd a young buck with a curious deformity. One of his horns curved forwards instead of backwards. I was very anxious to possess myself of this trophy, but Spinas took me up too close. They got notice of our approach, and in the confusion of their departure I could not distinguish the one I wanted. The horn of a chamois is supported on a core of bony substance which rises from the skull. Some accident among the rocks must have wrenched this horn round on its pivot.

To return to the day in question—while Geof and Spinas continued to look for the big herd, Johann and I went farther up. We now found ourselves on the edge of the deep trench of the Spöl ravine, and proceeded to search, with great care, the chaos of rocks, gullies, and fir scrub, which faced us on the opposite slope; for the day was now well advanced and very hot, and the greater the heat, the more do chamois withdraw themselves into concealment, creeping into bushes and holes in the rock. Upon the thoroughness of this work depends our hope of sport for the day. Not only is it necessary to find the game, but to make sure that there are no others near them who might be started in the course of the stalk, and so disturb them. The occupation is absorbing, and there is dead silence, till after half-an-hour Johann says: "Now I see three in the *leg-föhren*." "Where!" "By the great rock under the little cliff." As there are millions of great rocks in view, and a thousand little cliffs, this is vague, and shows that Johann has not hunted much in company, for there is a certain art in describing the exact position of a chamois which you have found. The proper way is to take some conspicuous object which any one can identify in a moment, and lead up from it by a chain of minor objects to the precise spot you wish to indicate: something like the following:—" You see the green alp at the top of the wood. Follow up the *couloir* to the left of it till you come to a dead tree. To the left of that is a cliff with a black shadow shaped like a camel, and just below the camel is a rock with a narrow gray streak. They lie ten yards to the left of that." In this way one is led by the hand as it were, step by step, to the presence of the chamois. "See," says Johann, "I will show you with my stick." But the stick is useless as a pointer, for it is bent by Johann's fifteen stone of weight. "Stay, I will point the rifle," and he draws a bead on them, and puts his head on one side so that I can look along the sights. Now I see where he means, and pick them up with the glass—a doe, a kid, and a two-year-old. Presently we find six more: then another lot of three. The last were low down, and as it was getting late we chose them for attack.

It was a long and rough descent into the ravine, and we had to go down stream to a bridge. After half-an-hour of ascent at Johann's pace I began to be sorry I had come, but I was not really pumped till the *leg-führen* was reached. The flexible stems of this curious dwarf fir (the *Pinus mughus* is, I think, its correct name) are every winter bent flat under the weight of snow, and never quite recover their erect position, but remain partly recumbent and interlaced, each stem growing down the slope. It is easy enough to go straight down through it, and not very difficult to climb straight up, but to cross it diagonally is a trial to one's temper. It is a perfect net-work of interlaced branches, too thick to push aside, too thin to bear your weight. If you try to get over them, they fly up at the wrong moment, and if you crawl under them they pull your cap off, and catch the rifle which hangs at your back. In a thick grove of it you cannot see three yards in any direction except towards the valley. I suppose it was some instinct, which lower animals like myself do not possess, that guided Johann to the right spot, but we found ourselves at last at the top of the cliff under which the chamois had been lying. They had moved, and for some time we had to crawl about through the branches, peering down through peep-holes in the deep fringe which projects beyond the upper edge of the cliff. At last Johann signed that they were below us. I struggled to his side, and through a gap I saw one of them for a moment, but he had moved before I could get the rifle into my hand, and the branches hid him from me. Then Johann pointed out another right under me. I had to stand up and shoot straight down. As I fired he gave a shiver and bounded off, so that he was at once hidden. We pushed through the thicket to a more open place, and, as we reached it, I caught sight of the brown flank of another which was making off through the covert, and knocked over a second, stone dead. Quickly we found a way to descend and let ourselves down by the branches. There was the bloody track of the first chamois. The poor beast had not gone far, but had life enough left to get away once more. Following more cautiously, I got a sight of his head, and finished him with a bullet through the neck.

I hate carrying my rifle, and never do so if I can help it; but the exception is when my hunter is otherwise well loaded with the results of a successful stalk. Then it feels as light as a feather. The *leg-föhren* no longer ruffles, and you step airily over the *mauvais pas*, which you distinctly funked in the morning. In a hurried shot like the above I do not pretend to be always able to distinguish the bucks. I am guilty of the death of many a *geiss*. In the above case my second beast was only half grown, but his cutlets served with cream—make a note of it— were enough to make one devote oneself to shooting nothing but kids.

Along the broken gorge of the Spöl there is a mule-path, but the difficulties of the ground compel it to cross and recross the torrent, if I remember rightly, no less than six times in four miles. These bridges are an important aid to chamois hunting, as it is necessary to survey the flank of the valley which it is designed to hunt from a spying-point on the opposite side. This route is supposed to be practicable for the roughest kind of *berg-wagen*, but on one occasion, when we were driven by bad weather to escape by some means, and had loaded our possessions on such a vehicle, we went very near to losing the whole of them, and the horse into the bargain. The actual torrent bed is so deep and narrow in places, that a moderate spate will raise the surface of the water forty or fifty feet in two or three hours. It was in such a place that wild shouts were heard in front, and on rounding a corner, we saw the hind wheels of the *berg-wagen* already on the water-worn slope of rocks below the path, while the body of the machine literally overhung the gorge. The foremost man

TWO TO ONE AGAINST THE HORSE.

was tearing at the horse's head, and madly shouting to it to make fresh efforts to save itself from destruction, while the terrified brute, fully aware of its danger, was struggling on the brink. The second charioteer had got his feet planted against a rock, and was holding like grim death by a rope to the hinder part of the waggon. One shaft was over the horse's head, and the whole was at such an angle that all our goods, including our weapons, must, even as it was, have tipped into the glacier torrent, wholly past recovery, if we had not taken the precaution to cord a big mattress on to the top of them. Rushing forward, we seized every available guy rope or holding-place, and presently by main force hoisted the crazy thing into stable equilibrium.

To show the abundance of chamois in those days, I may make an extract from my journal of the history of two successive days, which also happened to be the first days of the expedition of that year. We left Pontresina at some unearthly hour, and drove to the entrance of the Val del Fain. There was a sharp frost and the little stream was frozen nearly hard. We walked to the head of the valley, seeing nothing on the way till we had crossed the frontier, when we almost immediately made out two little lots, of two and three chamois respectively. As they were in different directions, R—— and Spinas went after one, while G—— and I with Johann tried for the other. Before we had gone very far these disappeared, but about one o'clock I saw a lot of ten at a greater distance. Just then, however, our attention was taken off by seeing the other party, who had come round the other side of the mountain, and were signalling to us that there was something on the cliff below us. We climbed cautiously down, peering about, but could see nothing till we got nearly to the bottom, where we came upon them lying right below us. G—— had the shot, but, unfortunately, for some reason which I cannot remember, had Spinas's rifle instead of his own, and missed clean. These native weapons are mostly furnished with a hair trigger, which is very puzzling to any one who has not practised with it. They came right up past us, and gave me a good running shot which I ought to have done something with. Returning, we again made out our herd of ten on the top of a hill, and a single one in another direction. The herd being on the best stalking ground, we went for them. The stalk was a simple one, and we arrived within a hundred yards of them. To creep forward into position I had to show myself on the sky-line, which should always be avoided if possible. The *corgeiss*, or doe sentinel, instantly saw me, and twisted sharp round to have a better look. A buck, which lay nearer, stood up, but the next instant he sprang into the air and fell dead. My second shot, as they ran, glanced from a rock with a "ping" just in front of the nose of one of them, and I heard it buzz across the valley; but I got in another cartridge just in time for an outlier who had been feeding behind the ridge. He galloped up, stood for a moment, giving me a capital chance, so that I dropped him dead almost on the back of the first. In the meanwhile R—— had also had a good chance, and knocked over a chamois with a bullet through its body; but even a ·450 express is not always enough, and this one managed to recover itself sufficiently to reach covert, and the darkness coming on, it was lost.

Herr S——, who was always most solicitous for our welfare, had on this occasion—this was after Pontresina had developed, and when his son had begun to keep a hotel—lent us his leading *chef*, a very smart young man, whose ability with the saucepan was beyond question, and who was supposed to be fired with ambition to distinguish himself in *la chasse*. We camped that night in a hut which was decidedly draughty. Alphonse's courage seemed to be evaporating, and our supper was not a success. The next morning there was no appearance of breakfast or cook. He had decamped in the night, and the following evening was discovered in bed at Pontresina. Another cook was despatched to us, with less artistic soul for sauces, but with more pluck. He had served in the French army, and was great on his feats of arms and venerie. Soon after his arrival, he borrowed, unknown to us, an old fowling-piece from the curé. There was an air of repressed mystery about him as he prepared us for our evening meal, and the climax was reached when he set before us, with a tremendous flourish, a tom-tit and a chaffinch on toast, and exquisitely garnished.

The day following the one just described was, I think, the most disastrous I ever experienced; but I look upon the reader as my father confessor, to whom I am bound to make a clean breast of it, whatever the result may be to my reputation. At ten o'clock I saw a chamois looking at us a quarter of a mile off. He thought we were not pleasant company, and went over into the next valley with three others. We followed, and found them again lying down straight below. I crawled up to the edge, and thought I was going to distinguish myself, but, owing to my clumsiness, they saw my head and jumped up. Thinking they were about to start, I was in rather too great a hurry, and was guilty of a most annoying piece of *gaucherie*. I was shooting straight down, and did not grasp the rifle tightly enough with my left hand, so that its weight pulled off the trigger before I had quite aligned the sights. I am ashamed to say it is not the only occasion that a similar act of carelessness stands recorded against me. The shot disturbed a lot of eleven and another of two. The latter went and lay down in a good place, and we made an excellent approach. There they were, not more than fifty yards off, one feeding and the other lying down. I was determined I would not be in too great a hurry this time, and lay watching them over the ridge, with my legs in Switzerland and my rifle in Italy, waiting till the biggest turned a little. I felt that he was bound to roll over. He was, however, of a different opinion, and galloped off unscathed. It would have been difficult to make a worse miss. At two o'clock we spied a big buck lying on the top of a narrow rocky ridge. We had a difficult stalk down the ridge itself, crawling sometimes on one side, sometimes on the other. The wind was uncertain, and he got a whiff prematurely, and was off before I looked over. I had a long and dim shot, and did not know whether he was hit or not, until, following the track, we found some spots of blood. We traced it till it got too dark to follow it, and we had to come to the conclusion that he was only scratched. I am reminded of the sensible utterance of a young friend on a similar occasion, "Regardez ici! tout ce que puis dire c'est ceci; que si un izzard doesn't tomber within fifty metres of where he's tiré'd at, he's aussi bon que manqué'd."

The valley of Livigno is so cut off from the rest of the world, that the village priest is physician of the bodies as well as the souls of his flock. More than once I have had to call in his services. My companion in 1874, who was rather inexperienced, was suffering from an ailment familiar to Alpine climbers fresh out from England. Unknown to me this had continued for several days. Our remedies were not sufficiently potent, and prompt measures were necessary, or our hunting ground must be abandoned in search of medical aid. I sought the tonsured apothecary, who received me with delightful *bonhomie* in his den, which smelt, about half and half, of old books and rhubarb. In my finest Italian I furnished the learned man with a diagnosis of the case. Seizing my hand, the curé assured me that I need be in no further anxiety; that he had the very thing, a remedy which was *suro, suro*.

I suppose that the present generation has advanced beyond Seidlitz powders and knows not that ancient remedy. For the benefit of *fin-de-siècle* youths, I may mention that the powders in question were contained in white and blue papers, and that it took one of each colour to make a draught. This was what the Padre produced, but in parcels of so portentous a size as were never seen before, doubtless designed for the iron stomachs of his mountaineers. One would say that such a mass of ebullescent material could not be administered to an ordinary mortal without something happening, but if this double-barrelled remedy failed, I was to try another shot at 3 o'clock in the morning. At 6 A.M. I think half the inhabitants of the valley had assembled outside. They were no doubt anxious for our own sakes that we should remain, but they were chiefly concerned for the efficacy of the Father's remedies, to which I think they attached something more than mortal qualities. They could not come to Lord's or to Epsom; why should they not assemble to watch this contest between the priest and the devil? There was something like a cheer raised, when, at 6.30, I announced that the priest had exorcised the devil.

The next occasion when I consulted my reverend friend was a more serious one, but that is a long story. My brother and I were camped at the lower end of the Spöl Ravine, and went as usual in different directions, though on the same side of the valley. Young Spinas and I had a long walk over the hill without seeing anything, and rather late in the day spied a splendid buck close to the top of the Piz Diavel, the highest peak hereabouts—too far away if it had been an ordinary chamois, but this beast was worth an exceptional effort. To cut a long story short, after a tremendous climb we lost him, then refound him, but came upon him suddenly in a position where he must inevitably smell us in a few seconds; ran as hard as we could to get the shot before this happened (for a chamois when he gets the wind goes off full pelt, without raising his head or looking back as a stag will do), and consequently, being blown, I all but missed him, but not quite. Burdened with his body, we made slow progress home, and it was nearly dark when we reached the edge of the cliff which overlooks the valley, and came in sight of the camp. At sight of it Johann raised a view holloa, and, to my surprise, it was replied to by a faint and distant response to our right, and still higher than we were. "That is your father with the other Herr." "Yes, they are very late, but they will get down an easier way." The way down this part of the cliff is extremely intricate. It is composed of what I can best describe as hard-baked slopes; that is, shoots of mud and shaly material, so baked by the sun as to afford very insecure footing, and without big hobnails they are decidedly dangerous. In this case the slope was divided by several horizontal lines of low cliff, only to be negotiated here and there, and the scrub made these spots difficult to find. In the fading light we lost the way more than once, and it was pitch dark before we got to the mule-path. As we tramped along it, I fancied I heard another shout behind us, and then I saw a light glimmering in the woods above the line of our descent, and where no light should be. Johann said it must be made by some woodcutters, and that the other party would be surely back in camp before us. A two-mile walk brought us there, but they had not returned, and I now felt sure that they had tried for the same passage as ourselves and failed to find it; and it was clear that they could not get down safely without a lantern. As a matter of fact they also were burdened with a heavy buck. They had given up the attempt to descend when I first saw their light, and were now making the best of it under a rock, where I should have done better to have left them; but that I could not tell. Snatching up the lantern we hurried down the valley again. At the bridge we again saw the glimmer in the wood, and a distant answering shout assured us that we were not mistaken in the identity of the party. Lighting the lantern, Johann and another man started to pick out the difficult way while I waited anxiously. At 11 o'clock it began to pour, and I retreated to the camp. Hour after hour passed and they did not return. At the first glimmer of light, I was down at the bridge again and soon after saw them appearing.

In the meanwhile our two men had reached them, but, though they had succeeded in finding the way up, they could not hit off the clue again, and after struggling for some hours in the dripping *leg-föhren* at an angle of 50 degrees, they found their way to a woodman's *gîte*, where they sat, soaked and shivering, for the rest of the night. Twenty-four hours later, my brother was seriously ill, and developed a severe attack of dysentery. This was beyond the healing power of the priest, and, making an ambulance of a *berg-wagen*, I got him with some difficulty over to Pontresina, where for a fortnight I nursed him until he was well enough to travel home.

The next time I visited the valley the poor priest was dead—died of *ennui*, they said. For that he had no remedy.

I never had anything approaching an accident in chamois hunting, though I once hurt myself rather badly. We were stalking some chamois in a difficult position when they took the alarm. By running hard for three or four hundred yards we were able to cut them off at a pass, and arrived just as they crossed, at a distance of twenty yards. I knocked over the leader, and then ran forward again to try to get a second shot. I had to descend a short but steep slope of snow, and did so by a standing *glissade*; but, as I was carrying a rifle, I could not steady myself as usual with a stick. The bottom of the slope was converted into hard ice, and upon this I slipped up, my foot striking heavily against a rock at the bottom. I felt that I had received a very severe blow, but it did not bring me down, and I still ran on, but at last was brought to a standstill by the sharp pain in my foot, and looking down, I found a cut extending literally from the toe to the heel of the boot, as clean as if it had been done with a razor, and the blood streaming from it. Fortunately for me this happened on the watershed, between Italy and the Engadine. With some difficulty, after binding up the foot with handkerchiefs, I was able to hobble down to a path and send for a horse. It was nearly two months before I could use the foot properly, and though it is eighteen years since, I still carry the scar.

While I am upon the chapter of accidents, I may mention an adventure which befell me some thirty years ago in this neighbourhood, though it had nothing to do with chamois hunting. We had made a successful first ascent of one of the peaks of the Bernina Range, and were returning down its northern slopes, which afford a grand series of *glissades*. There was a hot south wind blowing, and the snow was exceptionally soft and wet, so that only the steepest slopes gave sufficient impetus. One, of the necessary pitch, was soon found. As we careered down the slope, a cushion of snow was raised under our knees and in front of our feet, and this gradually extended till we were carrying along with us quite a considerable avalanche, of the consistency of a bran mash, which surged round us up to our waists, but instantly solidified when we came to a halt.

One of our guides was in the habit of carrying a large

nautical telescope in the side-pocket of his coat, and in his struggles to keep his head uppermost, it fell out, and now lay buried at an unknown depth in the congealed heap. We probed in all directions, and scraped away the surface, but digging with an ice-axe is slow work, and it became evident that the matter was hopeless. Slushy snow is the coldest of mediums, and patience was soon exhausted, as well as animal heat, besides, worse weather appeared to be brewing. Our three guides still persisted, another instance of Engadiner obstinacy, and when repeated expostulations had failed, we five tied ourselves together, and left them to their fruitless search. Presently we came to another slope which appeared to be even longer and more inviting than the last. Owing to a light haze, the end of it was not distinctly visible, but as far as we could see, its surface appeared quite unbroken, and we started in full confidence that we had only to keep our heads above water and go ahead. I led, and suddenly I saw that it was not all right. The slope curled over ominously in front. I pulled up as quickly as I could, but it was too late. Those behind me were not equally practised, and before I could warn my immediate follower, he came into violent collision with my back. I was not proof against such swift bowling, and was driven over the edge at an ungovernable rate. Then followed the unpleasant sensation of resting on nothing, and I fell straight through the air, completely clearing the *berg-schrund*. With a thud I penetrated the soft snow, and then it seemed to me that each of my companions in succession fell on the top of me. We were followed by the snow, which came down in a cataract on our backs, and when I righted myself we were far down the slope, slithering away still, the centre of a great wave of snow. As soon as I could get my head up, I counted the heads of my companions, and, to my horror, there were only four of us. However, the suspense was not of long duration, for, looking back, the face of the missing member presently appeared, looking benignly down on us from the edge of the *berg-schrund*. Our impetus had carried us over it, but he had stopped himself against me and dropped straight into the chasm, which was fortunately choked nearly to the brim with snow that had preceded us. The height of the drop was some five-and-twenty feet, and the rope was broken in several places, but happily the pulpy condition of the snow prevented further mischief, except a few abrasions and black eyes.

One of my expeditions was spoiled by an incident which, though not so serious, was scarcely less annoying. I had handed my single Henry rifle to a group of peasants in a *wirthshaus* who were anxious to examine it. Somehow or other they must have loosened the screw which retains the striker in its place. The next stalk I had I made a beautiful approach, got within fifty yards of the wholly unconscious herd, and, as I pushed the rifle forwards for the shot, I noticed a blank hole where the striker should be. Carefully withdrawing myself, for an hour I searched the ground I had passed over, but in vain. I was obliged to retire leaving the chamois undisturbed. I had brought with me a spare striker which Andreas, another of my hunters, who is a blacksmith by trade, as well as a most skilful and patient stalker, spent the next day at the local forge in ingeniously fitting into the place. Unfor-

ANDREAS.

almost immediately stopped, offering a capital chance, when the rifle missed fire. We were able to keep him in view with the glass till he lay down far above us, but it was then too late to follow and we never saw him again. While we were thus engaged, another buck had seen us, and taking us, I suppose, for a rival, as they will sometimes do at the end of September, had approached within shooting distance. The whistle of alarm he gave when he discovered his mistake was the first warning we had of his presence, and even then he was not quite sure of

HE TAKES US FOR A RIVAL.

us, and stood whistling and stamping. Once more—click —but no explosion except a maledictory one. The next day I went to the Val del Aqua, so called because there is scarcely any water in it, only a waste of loose stones. Even the little glacier which fills its head is covered with them and looks inky black. Near the foot of it we spied eight chamois. It was necessary to descend and cross the valley below them, and then mount the slopes till we were far above them, and try to come down a gully; but this was a noisy proceeding, as stones kept hopping down in front of us. They became suspicious and began moving up the edge of the glacier, we skirting along high above them on the look-out for a chance to cut in in front of them. At last a favouring *couloir* took us down to within a little of the glacier. But by this time a light mist had driven up, and we had a difficulty in making them out among the rocks. Chamois, however, can see through anything less thick than pea-soup, and the moment we looked over they picked up our heads against the sky and began whistling. For the life of me I could not make them out, so that they put fully two hundred yards between us before I got a chance. Then one of them ran a little way on to the glacier to get a better view of us, and gave me a clear sight of him against the snow. It was an almost impossible distance, but it was my last chance. The hammer fell—click, bang!—the cartridge hung fire again. I think it was a hundred to one against that shot. What was my astonishment, therefore, when he reared up on his hind-legs, ran a few yards, and fell dead.

The old "solitaires," who are males of an unsociable

disposition, and are always the best beasts, are often to be found quite low down; but as they are experienced old hands, they know well what precautions to take to save their skins. One especially noble fellow, with a very fine head, lived on a scrubby slope of the mountain within easy shouting distance of the châlet of Campoggiolo. He had frequently excited our covetous instincts, but he was very crafty and we never got a shot at him. The natives were almost inclined to regard him superstitiously, as we were by no means the only hunters who had tried in vain to outmanœuvre this crafty old general.

One day in the year in question I had not left the bottom of the valley for three minutes, to make the ascent of this hill, when I heard the shrill hissing whistle which sends the heart into the mouth of every chamois hunter, and my shaggy black friend, whose form I knew so well by examination through the glass, sprang away not twenty yards off. Hoping for another sight of him, I threw myself on the ground into shooting position. I had scarcely done so when he sprang on a rock thirty yards off, and surveyed us for several seconds. There could be no doubt of him this time. I could lay the bead against any part of his black neck or shoulder which I chose, and I even think that, in that brief second, I made up my mind on what part of my walls I would hang his head. A mocking click was all that followed. I was near enough to this old buck to see him wink, and I believe he did wink, before he slowly turned and sprang out of sight. I will conclude this chapter with the memorable words with which Bernardo consoled me on that occasion—"*Ma che volete? e diavolo!*"

III

THE ROCKY MOUNTAINS

For years I had nursed the project of a hunting trip to the Rocky Mountains, and derived endless excitement and pleasure from the contemplation of what I could hardly regard as more than a vision. At last a favourable moment arrived, and with my son fresh from college I started in the *Arizona*. We did not let the grass grow under our feet. My friends thought that I was going to study educational problems in Boston, but during our absence of eleven weeks from London we only passed two nights in a civilised bed —one in New York, the other at a far-away Fort in the foot-hills of the Great Divide.

Neither the length of this flying visit, nor the extent of our bag, entitles a " tender-foot " like myself to speak of those regions, or the big game which inhabits them, with the authority and experience of those past masters of the chase who fill large galleries with heads and skins which have taken years to collect, but we did manage to bring back, besides some handsome trophies suggestive of delightful memories, a stock of vigour from the most bracing climate in the world, which many toils did not exhaust. Across the Atlantic we sailed a time race against the *Servia* and *Austral*. We won by half an hour, which was inspiriting, though the speed was not comparable to that attained nowadays. For the continental journey one makes a good start in the "Chicago Limited," but it gradually diminishes in speed and civilisation as it approaches the watershed. We passed through a "hot snap," but there was an antidote to the intense heat, by help of which we not only endured but even enjoyed it. This was to sit in the smoking saloon of the train in a cane-backed chair, with both feet out of the window, so that the fifty-mile-an-hour breeze, entering by the boots, passed in a soothing current up the legs, permeated the small of the back, and escaped behind the ears. All the passengers did it, at least all the male ones, and every window was decorated with these patent ventilators.

Arrived at Rawlins, a station on the "Union Pacific," at 3 A.M. of the fourth day, we found that the mail for Fort Washakie started four hours later. A rapid series of transactions with the local banker, who had to be roused from his bed for the purpose, and we were ready at seven. The vehicle, locally known as a "mud waggon," was a small edition of the "Deadwood" coach which burned so much powder a few seasons ago at West Kensington. It was not showy, but had need to be very tough. Our course of thirty-six hours, or thereabouts, over sage-bush plains and ridges, was not dictated by any consideration of gradients. Dry watercourses or gulches were taken at a canter, with a swoop of which the Switchback Railway gives a faint idea, and a bounce which drove the tops of our heads against the roof, fortunately made of nothing harder than canvas. At sunset a respite from this bone-shaking process was given us. On the way we had borrowed the driver's old muzzle-loader—and, from the box seat, had annexed certain over-confident "sage-hens," or rather poults, for the old ones are almost uneatable, and these made a welcome addition to our supper, after which for two blessed hours we stretched our cramped limbs under the stars.

Anglo-American friends had been very sceptical about our accomplishing the distance to the confines of civilisation in the fourteen days which I had allowed, but we reached Fort Washakie in a fortnight, almost to the minute, from Liverpool. At the present time this record could doubtless be easily beaten.

In the last stage of groaning stiffness and dislocation, but otherwise ready for whatever might turn up, we were driven up to the strange settlement—half traders' camp, half military compound—where the U.S. Government, with a handful of soldiers, overawes, or mercifully controls, the Red man, and administers its well-intended system of out-door relief. The theory of it is that the precarious living which the Indians gain by hunting is supplemented by Government rations, and that in the meanwhile the savage, restrained within his reservations, will change his nomadic nature, and learn the steady arts of peace. In practice the meat-hunter is accomplishing his work more rapidly than the schoolmaster. The game is dying out, and all that the Indian is learning is to rely on eleemosynary aid, while the steam ploughs and other expensive implements, with which it is in vain sought to tempt him to scratch the teeming soil, are broken up for firewood in the first cold winter. This at least was, as I gathered, the result with the

Shoshone Indians, on whose reservation we were; and yet under this fostering system this tribe are actually on the increase. One of two things. Either a great and industrious nation must be content to have on its hands, in perpetuity, a weak and thriftless race as a pensioner at full wages, or when, as has recently happened at Pine Ridge, the pinch comes, there will be cattle-stealing, reprisals and a final massacre. Doubtless there have been pilfering, blunders, misunderstandings, and cruelty on the part of some of the American agents, but against these should be set the persevering efforts of the Government to reclaim a treacherous and untameable race. The Indian question is one of the few "small grits," in the vast American wheel.

The centre of activity was not in the so-called "Fort," which consisted of a railed-in enclosure and the officers' quarters, but at the traders' store, which was constantly surrounded by a group of squaws and ponies, while their lords inside bartered their "ration certificates" for all sorts of articles, useful or otherwise—but never for whisky. The sale of that article is an offence visited with the severest penalties on the trader, and here at any rate the law seemed to be rigidly obeyed.

Here also we found our "outfit"—an elastic term by which, in this case, I mean the *personnel* of our expedition—loafing around. They had started with our pack train nine days before from Rawlins, and had arrived two days since. They consisted of Bob, the "boss" hunter, Madden, the packer, and Cris, the cook. In addition to these I engaged "Shoshone Dick," a local hunter, as guide, as none of the others knew the country where we were going. English hunting parties who are compelled to rely on the guides which they can engage at short notice must be tolerant of such men, and not expect that those who will undertake this temporary work are the cream of the population. We were not exempt from this experience.

Bob was an excellent horseman and careful of his cattle, but not a lively companion; nor did he seem to think it of such vital consequence as we did whether we found game or not. Madden was a good-natured giant, whose duties were to round-up the horses in the morning, and pack the beasts of burden when we were on the march. He lost his horses often, but never his temper.

Dick was of a more mercurial type. He was said to have been the only survivor of the famous Mormon massacre of emigrants, and being then a baby, was taken by the Indians, who were believed to have been prompted by the prophet of Utah to that shameful deed, and had lived with them ever since. This, at least, was the story as it was told to me. As might have been expected, Dick had little of the varnish of civilisation about him, but though his vocabulary was limited, he made free use of it. He copied in every particular the gait and manners of his foster-parents, his white skin and high spirits alone contradicting his bringing-up.

Cris was supposed to be the cook, but he was the worst cook of the party, not excepting myself; and, as the sequel proved, we could have well spared his services.

In the struggle for existence, which is the necessary condition of life in a new country, every man is expected to "boss his own portmanteau," and if he comes to grief it is not the business of those about him to help him out.

It is at first a little startling when this principle is observed by your own servants, whom you pay to look after you; but an Englishman who wishes to enjoy himself out West had better fall in with this view of life, treat his men on

INDIAN DICK.

equal terms, and expect no personal service. His clumsy efforts to fend for himself will be openly ridiculed, but secretly respected.

They had pitched our camp a mile beyond the Fort, on the banks of one of the numerous forks of the Wind River, for the sake of better feed for the horses. Thither, after paying our respects to the commanding officer, we presently cantered out, full of the first glamour of expectation, on "big buckskin" and "little buckskin" *anglicé*, light bay horses. It was rather a cold *douche* to our spirits to find no palatable food in camp, and our men in a condition of surliness, which was perhaps to be accounted for by the dearth of whisky. As usually happens on these occasions, at the first start, there was much to improve in the camp, and the arrangements were not so complete as they should have been. The waggon, which was to accompany us for ninety miles to the edge of the thick timber, had not been engaged. Madden, who had informed me he had " made his pile" but lost it in mining speculations, had not provided himself with a horse, as it was his business to do: and, in fact, was waiting for my arrival to borrow money to buy one. The tents, of which we had two, were wanting in bottom flaps, and, though ventilation is desirable, an open window six inches deep all round the bottom of your house is trying to city-bred people when the thermometer sinks below freezing-point, as it does every night in those regions, for no part of Wyoming is less than five thousand feet above the sea.

These and other deficiencies involved a delay almost intolerable to impatient spirits, and perhaps led us to think that our men were not so eager to leave the fleshpots of Egypt as we were; but by the timely help of the garrison officers, and some drafts on Government stores, they were all made good on the following day. The next morning I was up before sunrise to try to hurry up the men for an early start. But saddling up the packs is a long business. First the horses have to be " rounded up," and driven into a bunch, when one or two are lassoed and the rest allow themselves to be caught. Then the packages have to be carefully apportioned, and, after they are fastened on with the "diamond" hitch, examined, to see that the balance is right. After three hours' hard work we pulled out and took the shortest cut to the Wind River, which we were to follow to its source, and beyond.

Mexican saddles are universally used, and are comfortable riding when you get the knack of it, which consists in lengthening the stirrups and straightening the knee. In ignorance of this "tip" the "tender-foot" soon finds himself tender elsewhere. I was slow to learn to carry my legs like an inverted V, and suffered accordingly. Nor were my raw places soothed by the remark: "You fellers should learn to ride afore yer come hunting;" but it would take worse experiences than this to spoil the keen delight of the first few days' ride in the crisp air, and above all, of the first camps. One of the earliest of my minor misfortunes was to crush the life out of my watch with my knee, when I thought I was only squeezing my air-bed. Thenceforth there was only one sound timepiece in the party, and that had lost the minute hand; but it is astonishing how soon you can dispense with the fringe of civilisation when you try. Our train consisted of four riding horses for ourselves, five pack horses, two pack mules, and six horses belonging to our three men—seventeen in all.

Our plan was to cross the ridge which constitutes the backbone and watershed of the continent, and thence make a rapid dash, lightly laden, to the Geyser Basin in the National Park, which, at that time, had been but rarely approached from the south. Afterwards we proposed to return to the basin of the Wind River to hunt.

I had studied the account of the official survey of these parts by Dr. Hayden, and some excellent maps, which that explorer had given me, and had decided upon the To-gwo-tee Pass at the head of the final source of the Wind River, which, though not previously traversed by more than two or three parties of whites, promised the most direct route and the best game country. Most English hunting parties, visiting a tolerably open country, are accompanied by a waggon, and can thus afford to carry many luxuries not possible with a pack train, except one of very unwieldy dimensions. But, owing to the fringe of dense timber with which this part of the Main Divide is belted, its passage was at that time impossible for wheels, and all we could do was to send up the heaviest of our stores in this way, a four days' journey, to "Clarke's"— the farthest ranche up the river—and there make a depôt to which we could return later on.

We had laid in some excellent provisions from the Washakie trader (the Americans are ahead of us with preserved eatables, which are a necessity of existence in a newly-settled country), but for some reason fresh meat was not at the moment to be had there. We had not troubled ourselves much about this, knowing that we should soon be in a game country, but after a few days we all began to loathe salt ham and tinned meats boiled to strings, even though it was supplemented by plenty of trout, and longed so much for fresh venison steak that we determined to diverge at once from the main river valley, into the mountains, for a preliminary skirmish. This course would also allow the waggon, which travelled slower than we did, time to arrive at Clarke's. Striking off to the right on the third day out from Washakie, we rode for a dozen miles up one of the numerous forks, and camped in the heart of the hills.

Now, at least, we hoped to reap the first-fruits of our long journey. In the morning we started in two directions —Gerald with Dick, I with Bob. Boiling with ardour as I was, it was rather trying that my man, in a fit of obstinacy, declined to follow me at a greater rate than a walk. As our chief aspirations were for "big-horn" sheep, we made for the top of a high ridge in front of us. But there were no traces of them, at least, none of recent date, and indeed at that time—28th August—they must generally be sought for much higher. Some few fresh traces of elk were enough to raise my spirits, but I soon made up my mind that deer-stalking on horseback was a mistake—or, at least, that I did not like it. It was all very well when game was "very plenty." Then, if you disturb nine-tenths of it, it matters little. Enough remains. But, when it becomes scarce and shy, the heavy tramp of a horse, and, if in timber, the frequent crash of a dry snag, disturbs everything for a mile in front. Of course if you want to hunt at a distance from camp, it is well to ride out to your ground. A good hunting horse, if the reins are thrown over his head, will remain where he is left, or thereabouts, and, while he quietly grazes, will avoid entangling his feet in them. As Bob always remained glued to his horse in spite of my expostulations, I generally, after this, took Dick, or stalked alone; which, though I did not pretend to their knowledge of woodcraft, is infinitely more interesting. On the present occasion, too, I discarded further assistance, and sending Bob back with my horse, took a line of my own.

The timber grew in thick groves, on the slopes of spruces, chiefly of the *Douglas* kind, and, in the hollows, of *cotton-wood*—a sort of poplar. Here and there were "parks" of grass, now burned to a light brown. Apart from hunting it is always a delightful experience to stroll for the first time through such pathless woods, and make acquaintance with the things that fly and run—the *wood-chucks*, a little beast like a marmot, the *squirrels* and their miniature striped counterparts, the *chipmunks*, who squeaked at me from every fallen tree. I found large stones and stumps, which had been overturned by bears for the grubs that lie under them, but saw nothing larger than the above-mentioned animals till rather late, when, from a high ridge, I spied far below a herd of prong-horned antelope. They lay well on the way to camp, and would at least afford fresh meat, even if theirs was not the trophy that I desired most keenly; so down I went for an hour through the pine forest, during which time they were, of course, out of sight; but emerging from the covert I discovered them again, feeding on a slope of sage brush. Flat stalking in sage brush is not pleasant, but the sun had set and there was no time to lose; and after a close crawl, most of the way in view, I rolled over a good buck. It was too late to do more then than grallock him and carry off the liver for immediate consumption.

Arrived at camp I found I had not been the first to draw blood; Gerald had forestalled me in the matter of meat, having killed a bull wapiti or "elk" in the vernacular. He had had his ups and downs, however. The bull he had actually secured was not the first. The first had run away after he literally had him in his grasp.

A FLAT CRAWL.

The stalk had been successful. The monarch was laid low. With all the exultation of youth at a first successful shot, he had carefully laid down his rifle to gloat, with the more freedom, over its grand proportions, and, counting the points, he drew his knife in orthodox fashion, and leant over the fallen tree against which the elk lay to cut its throat. But at the first touch of the knife the animal rose slowly to his feet, made a lunge at his enemy, which must have had serious consequences if it had not been for the barricade between them, and made off. Fancy the cruel revulsion from triumph to despair when it was realised that the rifle was ten yards away and unloaded! Of course when Dick came up an attempt was made to track him, but in vain. The poor beast had been shot too high and had gone off to die elsewhere, or perhaps not to die at all. Fortune, however, took pity on the young hunter, and showed him another bull on the way home, which he easily stalked and killed. So at supper that night we were not despondent.

As camp was now well supplied with meat, we determined for the present to do no more hunting, but to proceed on our journey. In two days we arrived at Clarke's. This was the farthest ranche on this side of the Main Divide, from the top of which it is distant only a three hours' ride. Indeed it was then the only abode beyond Washakie inhabited all the year round. To call it a ranche is flattery, for it consists of a single log room. Here old Clarke had led a completely solitary existence for seven years, and yet he was no misanthrope. He gave us a most hospitable welcome, and proved a genial host, with more information, and more ability to impart it, than is usually found among the rougher Westerners. There were various stories of how he came to settle here. One was that he thus got out of the way of drink; another, that he was the "Jack the Ripper" of those days; but I did not invite his confidence. Apparently he supported himself exclusively by trapping, which art he told me he had taught himself out of books. He certainly drew no income from his gold mine, which was his special hobby, and which was for ever in his conversation. This was a claim which he had secured a short distance above his house, and to work which he tried to persuade us to invest our capital and bring out a company. There is gold throughout the Wind River mountains, and to "show the colour," *i.e.* tiny flakes of gold, it was only necessary to wash out the first handful of river gravel in a tin basin; but to do this on a large scale and profitably, in "placer" mining, it is necessary to find not only a good gold-bearing bed of gravel, as Clarke had done, but a great fall of water which can be brought in iron pipes and directed against the face of the gravel in a jet sufficiently powerful to break it up, and to wash away the superfluous stones and mud. These and other necessary conditions were wanting in this case, so I was not tempted, nor by other discoveries of his, which he imparted to me in solemn secrecy, and which afforded him a great amount of innocent satisfaction.

Arrived here, to our dismay we found no waggon. It turned up, however, the following night. The way is an uncommonly rough one, and one of the horses becoming entangled in the harness had been so injured that he had to be killed. We used the delay to pay a visit to Clarke's mine, and also to climb an outlying peak, where we hoped, vainly as it proved, to find sheep, but from the top of which we caught our first glimpse, over the top of the Main Divide, here at its lowest, of the Teton Peaks far on the other side of it. To reach the Union Pass, which is that most usually travelled from the upper part of the Wind River, takes only four hours from Clarke's, but the top of the To-gwo-tee Pass is a long day's ride.

THE TETONS OVER THE DIVIDE.

Taking Clarke, who had been to the top, to show the way, we left his house on September 2. We rode for several hours along the Wind River, now reduced to very small proportions. At mid-day we began to rise into the thick timber, and for the rest of the day it was a continuous struggle with a maze of snags and fallen stems.

This bane of pack-trains is caused by forest fires, which have burnt out the life of the trees, leaving only gaunt stems and blackened ground, followed by tempests which have whirled these tottering giants in heaps to the ground. In places the stems lie parallel to one another, and piled to the height of many feet as though they had been laid in sheaves. Elsewhere, while some have stood the shock and are still erect, their neighbours lie prone at every conceivable angle to one another, and their branches pierce the air as weathered snags. This ghastly waste, whether brought about by natural causes, or the recklessness of man, will have to be paid for some day, for are we not within measurable distance of the inevitable worldwide timber famine? The present low price of timber is no proof of unlimited abundance, but is rather caused by the eagerness with which the merchants' yards are being glutted and the supply exhausted.

But the equanimity of the traveller is more likely to be disturbed by the immediate difficulty of penetrating this *chevaux de frise*. The horses are clever at clearing single trees. These minor obstacles are surmounted with the minimum of effort, and without much displacement of luggage, by a slow standing jump; but from time to time the cavalcade gets so pounded that there is no release without the axe. However well trained the horses may be to keep their burdens clear of accident, a rending sound is a frequent accompaniment, as some bundle, perhaps the tent, is caught by a snag, and suggests draughty nights thereafter and evenings spent in darning.

To such mishaps, and the frequent attempt of one or another of the horses to break the line and find a way of his own, there is a running comment of Western language. This and the tramp of horses and snapping of dead wood keeps up a chorus which is rather inspiriting to the man who manages not to lose his temper every time his hat is swept off, or his last pair of stockings snagged. It may be imagined that the course is a devious one, and that progress is slow; but, however time may fly, a halt is out of the question in such ground. There is no space to pitch a tent, and the absence of feed would inevitably cause a stampede of horses in the night. It was late before we

THE CHALLENGE.

reached the top of the pass and camped in a small open park. This was at a height of fully ten thousand feet, and, when I returned from an evening stroll, ice had already formed in the bucket. All our blankets and every available garment were wanted that night, and the streams were frozen to the bottom in the morning. The descent proved much easier than the ascent. It lay through open parks of grass with patches of cotton-wood, which became thicker and more frequent as we drew downwards. Passing one of these I caught a glimpse of a large animal lying down with something like a young tree on the top of his head. I pulled up sharp, and a big bull elk, the first I had seen, sprang up. He got behind some trees before I could get off to shoot, but at least I had had my first sight of an elk, and I envy any one that moment. Half an hour later we jumped two others. This was too much, and, as we again wanted meat, we elected to make a short day, and go into camp at once in a wide grassy hollow, on a chain of hills between " Buffalo Fork " and " Black Rock Creek," the waters of which ultimately find their way to the Pacific. After a feed I started out with Clarke on foot. We had hardly gone a mile, and were walking along a bare ridge with cotton-wood groves on each side, when he pointed out what he said was a bull elk among the trees below us. I got out my field-glasses and made out a narrow perpendicular section of some large animal, which was all I could see for the tree-stems. It was a long shot, but I felt pretty sure of him if I could only avoid the trees. When I fired he of course disappeared, and Clarke said I had missed him, but I fancied I saw the top of a thin tree shaking about as though something were struggling below, and sure enough when we went down there was my first elk quite dead, and the aspirations of many years ought to have been satisfied. Yet I am afraid I was not content, for though young and tender, and carrying more than enough meat for our outfit, and to load down Clarke's horse on his return journey as well, his head was a poor one, and I could not resist the temptation of trying for a better one. So while Clarke went for a horse to carry the meat to camp, I went on with bloodthirsty intent, but was only rewarded by jumping another and much better bull, who was too quick for me, and this had the effect of making me keener than ever. It is astonishing how silently these great creatures dive away through the thickest timber. There is a crash, a sound of muffled steps, then dead silence; but if you follow the wide-spread footprints show that speed was not relaxed. What they do with their horns when the stems are close ranked is a mystery.

In the next day's march we should have reached the Snake River and Jackson's Lake, whence we hoped that a three days' ride would bring us to the Geyser Basin; but we were not destined to proceed far in this direction. As we broke camp the weather began to break too, and the snow to fall in soft melting flakes, which quickly whitened the upper ground, though for a time they melted as they fell among the timber. Gerald and I started on foot to hunt along the ridge between the two streams, agreeing to meet our followers at their junction, which might be five miles down. There seemed no room for a mistake on their part, and my maps had proved so correct that I never doubted my ability to find the way to the trysting-place in two or three hours. After we had walked a mile or two we saw a bull staring at us a hundred yards away. The snow was falling thickly, so that he could not make us out plainly, and while we made a careful inspection through the glass—for we now determined to be chary of shooting at anything that did not carry a good head— he continued at gaze. As he appeared to come up to the required standard I fired, but, owing to the dim light, hit him too high, and missed him altogether the second barrel. He went off—alas! badly wounded—into the thick wood, where the snow did not lie, and we vainly tried to trace him. I have no justification to offer for firing this shot, for we had meat enough at the moment, but I suppose there are few Western sportsmen who have not been similarly tempted by a fine head, and Englishmen are not the worst offenders. While I continued the search I sent Gerald down to Buffalo Fork, where I made sure he would encounter the pack-train, for the purpose of stopping it. We agreed that he should hold a due northerly line by the compass, so that if I followed in the same course I should strike the river at the same spot. At length I had to abandon the search, and went down the steep slope, compass in hand. Arrived at the bottom I could neither see nor hear any signs of Gerald or the men. In vain I shouted. The whole valley, except for the swirl of the stream, seemed as silent as a mountain top. I waded the river and crossed the valley, which was here wide and swampy. It was cut up by numerous stagnant lagoons, and covered with a dense growth of willow, but game trails, of which there were plenty, afforded a clue to the labyrinth, and in due time I got across. Here I found a big open game trail, parallel to the course of the river, which I made sure the caravan must have followed if my directions had been understood; but there was no sign of anything except wild animals having passed that way for a thousand years. In no pleasant frame of mind I wandered, now a mile down stream, now a mile up, shouting myself hoarse, and occasionally firing my rifle till I had nearly exhausted my cartridges. I cared nothing for losing the men for the time, but I was quite unable to account for my son's disappearance. The intense solitude was oppressive, and my imagination conjured up all sorts of terrible contingencies.

After two or three hours, to my great relief, I heard his voice, now as hoarse as my own, on the side of the river from which I had come, and after a long struggle with the willow brake he rejoined me in a panting condition. He had been several miles down to the junction of the streams, but had no more news of the pack-train than I had. We were utterly mystified, but, after once more walking down to the appointed meeting-place, late in the afternoon there was an answering shot to one of ours, and in a quarter of an hour the missing band appeared, looking very much bedraggled and rather ashamed of themselves. My directions to Bob had been explicit—to go straight down to the stream to his right, and follow it to its junction with the other. It was obvious that that was the easiest slope for the horses, but he was in one of his obstinate moods, and had followed our track in the snow along the ridges, and when he arrived at the end it was too steep to get down, so that he had to return on his track nearly to the last camp. It was now 4 o'clock, and farther progress, soaked and tired as we were, was out of the question, so we went into camp at once, and there were destined to remain for some time.

The weather now for a time completely broke up. Owing to the dense timber, which we knew covered the ranges that lay beyond, through which there was, at that time, no known track, and the serious delay which this involves with heavily-laden animals, we had intended to leave most of our horses and equipage, with two of the men, hereabouts, and to make a forced march from this point to the Geyser Basin, with little besides the clothes we stood in and the horses we rode, afterwards returning on our tracks. But with snow lying deeply, an unusual circumstance in the first week in September, it would have been hardly prudent to traverse the high-lying intervening ranges thus lightly equipped, and, our time being strictly limited, we could not afford a slower rate of progress. The Park was therefore struck out of our programme, and we consoled ourselves by the reflection that that region has become sadly vulgarised. After all, the wonders of nature that abide with a man are not those which he has read of in guide-books. These are half stale before they are seen. It is one's own casual discoveries, the unexpected, some mountain glory or vision of cloud and water, which paint the lasting pictures of which he never tires.

My chief trouble was that, at the Geyser Basin, we should have touched the fringe of civilisation, and we lost the only opportunity of posting a letter. I therefore bribed Dick to undertake the journey and to be my postman. He returned to us in a remarkably short time, and said he had found two miners going that way, to whom he had entrusted his charge. He had a bedraggled aspect and wore the expression of a dog who has paid a surreptitious visit to the larder. I am inclined to think he found the weather too much for him. At any rate the letter was never delivered.

We had arranged with Clarke, who had left us to return home, to meet us on a certain day at the head waters of the Gros Ventre, another tributary of the Snake River, which we believed would be good game quarters, so we could now afford to take it easy. The delay was not without its compensations. Buffalo Fork is a lovely valley and had at that time been little visited by whites. We drew this inference from the entire absence of the remains of slaughtered animals. Indeed, at the time of our visit this was true of the whole of this part of the basin of the Snake River, sometimes known as "Jackson's Hole," and is due to the difficulty of the passes leading into it, and the enormous quantity of snow precipitated here by the lofty range of the Tetons, conditions which were said to make it impossible of residence in the winter. The tameness of the smaller animals told the same refreshing tale. I remember a pine martin—surely one of the shyest of animals—which remained at a distance of four or five yards to gaze at me with an expression of amused curiosity, yawning the while in my face, as much as to say—" Wall, stranger, what do you think of our country? I find it a dull place." Great hawks would sit on the boughs overhanging our heads, screaming defiance, but not deigning to offer to the power of man the homage of fear.

A few hundred yards off a lovely little lake reflected the full height of the Teton Peaks—separated from us by the wide flat of the Snake River valley. This was the only mountain which I saw which could be described as Alpine in character. Indeed, this double peak is described by visitors to the Park, from which it is distinctly visible, as the Matterhorn of America. There was not another of the so-called peaks which came in our way, to the top of which I could not have ridden a horse with little trouble. On the lake in the foreground waded and paddled a great quantity of wild fowl—cranes, ducks, the beautiful green-winged teal—and a tiny white mark on the very imperfect photograph which I took represents two wild swans which lazily swam almost within gunshot, though my camera was on so small a scale that my friends are sceptical.

This camera helped to pass the time, though it did not produce satisfactory results. We could not carry so fragile an article as a dark lantern, and as there was a faint light in the tent even at midnight, a change of plates had to be effected by the sense of touch inside a sewn-up blanket. On our return some strange results were developed—such as a picture exposed on the back instead of the front of the plate, and thus reversed. We tried to keep strict account of the slides which had been exposed—not always with success. Gerald, returning to camp, and fired with artistic ardour, would superimpose a great visionary horse, or cooking pot, on the sky of a lovely landscape which had taken my fancy an hour before.

In spite of the weather we did some hunting, but

THE TETONS FROM BUFFALO FORK.

not much. It is nearly as easy to lead pack animals, loaded with wapiti horns, through such timber, erect and prone, as lay behind us, as to drag a flight of hooks through a knitted stocking, and we could only afford to devote a single horse to this kind of luggage. There was therefore little temptation to hunt, except to keep ourselves in meat, for we could not carry off our trophies except to a very limited extent.

But though we did not burn much powder, some interesting days fell to our lot. During the whole of one day, we together followed an immense herd of wapiti, which the snow had apparently compelled to herd together and migrate to a lower level. It had also the effect of hastening the "whistling" time, and the woods resounded in this first week in September with the strange note. It was as if all the steamers, big and little, in New York harbour had got into a fog and were trying to avoid a collision. The guttural old hero of many fights was answered by the impudent squeal of an aspiring youngster. Hoarse or clear, deep or shrill, all combined to swell the chorus of many throats, amongst which, after a time, we fancied we began to recognise the characteristic note of certain individuals. The snow, as we followed in their tracks, was ploughed like a cattle-yard. We hoped to "get in" and slay the monarch of the herd, but it was constantly on the move and covered a large area. In our attempts we were more than once baffled by some outlying young stag or cautious old cow, who barked her alarms. These warnings did not seem to quicken the pace of the main body, who at length gathered and halted on the top of a low hill, partly bare of trees. Now was our moment, and we crept up *ventre-à-terre* right amongst them. Every minute we would see a tawny flank among the trees within a few yards, but I do not think we were detected. We could hear much pushing and fighting going on on the bare top, where the big ones were assembled; but though we now and then caught sight of a fine pair of horns over the intervening hedge of undergrowth, we could not see enough to pick and choose. Perhaps we ought to have run in among them and taken our chance of picking out the biggest, or, as I have sometimes thought since, so great was the preoccupation of the herd, we might have climbed one of the fir-trees without being observed, and so commanded the serried mass in front; but we hoped that in the frequent rushes of the old bulls to drive off the young ones, the "master" would come our way, and we lay low. At last one, bigger than any we had yet seen, showed himself in hot pursuit of a youngster. It was his last charge. Into the jaws of death his blind jealousy carried him. He was a good bull, but I am convinced, though I never got a fair sight of his rivals at close quarters, that he carried by no means the champion head of such a herd. I afterwards got to the top of a hill which commanded the country, and made out the whole herd about three miles off, gathered in the flat river bottom. They were too distant to count, but there must have been quite two hundred of them.

It is very interesting and instructive, though, owing to the restlessness of wild animals at such a time, seldom productive of a tangible result, to follow their tracks in the snow. I have a vivid recollection of a day I spent in such solitary diversion. Early in the day I hit the fresh spoor of a heavy bull, a cow, and two smaller ones, and lazily followed through all their wanderings. well knowing that I should almost certainly be "picked up" by them as they lay at mid-day. After following the trail for some distance, I found there were the tracks of two bulls instead of one, though I had not noticed where the second had joined the company; and when, farther on, one of them diverged, I followed that. He took a circuit of a mile or more, then rejoined his own track and followed the rest of his family. In fact, it was one and the same bull whose double track had puzzled me, and who, like a wise general, wanted to make sure of his rearguard. Perhaps he had caught a distant sight of me. At any rate, when the party lay down for the day, they were so placed as to command their own track without being seen. The bull had taken even greater care to hide himself, and when his consort was at last jumped, I failed to get even a glimpse of him. But, taking up his track again, I followed it, and found that, at this alarm, he had made a short circuit till he got my wind, and then off at full speed. Retracing my steps, I found that the stalker had himself been stalked. A wolverine, an animal that is fond of doing his hunting by deputy, or rather contents himself with the scraps which he thinks the two-footed hunter will leave him, had been cautiously tracking *me*, step by step. His footprints, which are like those of a small bear, were very distinct in the melting snow, and showed that he had kept almost close to my heels, but had slunk out of the way when he saw me coming back. The intelligence of this animal is remarkable. In fact, according to some of the histories I have read, he must be quite the smartest character in the States. He follows the trapper on his rounds, and springs all the traps with a stick before he eats the baits. When they set a spring gun for him, he *half-cocks* it before he steals the meat!

Subsequently, I followed the equally fresh track of a gray wolf, who appeared to have been watching me for some time from behind a fallen tree before he had slunk away. It is hardly necessary to say that snow tracking is not the surest method of filling the larder, but it is an eminently suggestive way of spending a happy day.

In the course of this walk I came upon a bare hillside facing south, on which were large numbers of shed elk horns, some of which were of grand dimensions. Many had lain long enough to become partially decomposed. I suppose the warmth of the situation must tempt the elk to come here in the shedding time, which is the month of April for the old bulls. I do not know whether the wapiti is less anxious than other deer undoubtedly are to conceal these evidences of their presence. They are certainly more frequently found.

The extraordinary phenomena of horn growth would be beyond the scope of this chapter, but it may be well to remind the unlearned that these antlers are completely grown each year in a period of ten or eleven weeks, and become almost as hard as ivory in another month. As every sportsman who has sawn a wapiti head in half for transportation knows, to the cost of his muscles, the skull which supports this structure is extremely massive, having a minimum thickness of nearly an inch. One of my wapiti was struck as he fell by my second bullet full in the middle of the horn, between the bay and tray points, but such is its strength and elasticity that even a solid ·500 missile failed to penetrate, only scooping out a cavity about a third of its diameter in depth, and, springing to one side, carrying away a great cantle of horn.

While on the subject of horns, I should like to say a word on the setting of them up. Many heads are to my mind somewhat marred by the habit of mounting them with the horns nearly upright and the nose tucked in close to the neck, as if he were trying to see the top of his head in a looking-glass, or had adopted the detestable fashion of bearing-reins. This is no doubt done for the purpose of showing the full height of the horns, and also to avoid contact with the wall, but it is not natural. No stag could pass through brushwood in that attitude. He habitually lays his horns back over his flanks. Thus the facial angle should never be steeper than 45 degrees, but the truer attitude is with neck sloped a little downwards and the head nearly horizontal.

Among other ills to which flesh is heir the wapiti are occasionally attacked, and ultimately killed, by a very virulent form of scab. I believe it is contracted from the big-horns, who probably first took it from some herds of tame sheep. Once Gerald and I found a large stag, so freshly dead that the wet foam still lay on his lips. The ground and the surrounding scrub was trodden and torn by the poor tortured beast in his dying agonies. The disease must have been of rapid progress, for his horns were very fine, and could have only been grown by a healthy animal.

Many cotton-wood trees near our camp on Buffalo Fork had been felled by beavers, and on a still night we could hear the sounding smack with which the animal hits the surface of the water with its flat tail.

They tell tall tales to tenderfeet about beavers. One of our men was never tired of arguing that the beaver, when constructing or repairing his house, loads that spade-like implement with mud and carries it in front of him like an apron, while he walks erect. I am reminded of a Hibernian tenderfoot, who, seeing a beaver's skin in camp, remarked—"Begorra! what a *tongue* the craytur has!"

We had with us a single beaver trap, which we occasionally set. The lure is a minute portion of the powerfully-smelling gland of a beaver. Pliny tells us that beavers, well knowing that they are pursued for certain organs, will mutilate themselves when hard pressed. The essence is rubbed on to twigs overhanging the water. The scent is carried far down the stream: the beaver follows it upwards to its source, and gets caught in the trap, which is set under the surface and firmly pegged. Only once were we successful in securing a specimen. Being short of meat at the time we cooked him. He was greasy eating, especially the tail. No animal has been more mercilessly harried for his coat than the beaver, and the skilful pelt-hunter, following up every creek in the country, clears them one by one of their inhabitants. Even this individual had lost one leg in a past encounter.

There are, or were in 1884, a few moose in this part of the Rocky Mountains, though I had not at that time heard of any sportsman who had been successful in obtaining them there. Once on Buffalo Fork my son got a distant glimpse of a cow with his spy-glass. I have no doubt he was correct, as we several times saw the tracks, which are much larger than those of a wapiti, and a moose, male or female, is unmistakable.

We were snowed up for eight days in Buffalo Fork, but, in spite of the fact that we were seldom dry, we only once lost our tempers. That was when we could get no breakfast because Cris had left the axe out, and the snow had effectually hidden it in the night.

From Buffalo Fork we travelled south along the valley of the Snake River, with the Tetons towering above us, and then turned eastwards again up the Gros Ventre River towards the Main Divide. Here we encountered two gold prospectors, the only human beings, unconnected with our party, that we saw for a month. They rode into our camp in a very dilapidated and half-starved condition. They had lost their way, and one of their horses was dead lame. The snow had driven the game from the country which they had passed through. Notwithstanding their poverty-stricken aspect, one of them proved to be a highly intelligent gentleman, who told me that he was Sheriff of Leadville, and was making this trip more for pleasure than profit, though always hoping to strike a good thing, stake out his claim, and make "a pile" on the mining market. As scores of wanderers like himself had even then prospected nearly every creek in the Rocky Mountains, it is not likely that much remains to be revealed, and what there is can only be made remunerative with heavy machinery.

As I lay one day *ventre-à-terre* a bright object within two inches of my nose attracted my attention. It was a beautifully-formed arrow-head of transparent agate, and must have lain there, at least since the general adoption of iron by the Indians two hundred years ago. This and a small gold nugget which my mining friend presented to me at parting, were the only trophies I carried off from the Gros Ventre. The snowstorm had cleared the game out, and we were driven by the exhaustion of our stores to move on to meet Clarke, who was to join us at a certain trysting-place with a fresh supply.

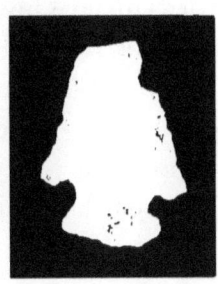

The Main Divide here forms a broad hog-back at a great elevation, from which rises the Union Peak. This is not quite the highest point of the continent, but it is the very crown and centre of the watershed, and from it the three great river-systems take their rise, so that it would not be impossible to find a point whence three snowballs might be thrown, of which the first, melting, should ultimately find its way to the Gulf of Mexico, the second would reach the Pacific by the Gulf of California, while the third would enter the same ocean two thousand miles farther to the north.

The wooded plateau on the Divide was charmingly broken into open parks, and here and there were lakes, surrounded by tall Douglas firs. With a long pole, cut on the spot, and a piece of bacon, Madden caught a trout in one of these tarns, which must have scaled fully 7 lbs. Inside it was a full-grown water-hen. It was welcome, for at this time we were again short of meat. With the smallest foresight this need never have happened, but the Western palate abhors any meat which is not "bloody flesh." The reader will perceive that this expression conveys a literal description. Our depraved appetites often longed for meat in a less crude condition, and we tried to save up for our own consumption what had been killed a reasonable time; but we were always informed that the "stinking stuff" had been left behind at the last camp, and no expostulation availed. Owing to this improvidence, we were sometimes needlessly sharp set when our larder just before had been overflowing.

CRIS.

Another of the amiable weaknesses of Cris, our cook, was to purloin the best of our stores for his own private consumption; but his most objectionable characteristic was a very violent and dangerous temper. One morning towards the end of our trip, I was peacefully eating my porridge, when the ruffian set upon me in so insolent a fashion that Gerald knocked him down. This increased the blind rage of this Caliban, and he picked up a large knife and came on again like one distraught. It looked serious, but Snell, now thoroughly alive to the situation, sprang upon him. I was told afterwards that I should have received nothing but gratitude if I had then and there rid the territory of the pestilent "rustler," but lynch law is out of fashion, and I took the simpler course of paying him his due, and bidding him "slope." From a comparison of notes with my friend, Mr. Theodore Roosevelt, I have some reason to think that this miscreant is now doing his ten years, having been one of a band of thieves whom that gentleman overtook and captured, and brought down in the depth of winter, after guarding them day and night. The tale is admirably told at length in Mr. Roosevelt's charming book on Ranche Life, but as that work is not very generally known on this side of the Atlantic, I may be permitted to give a brief sketch of the incident as I had it from the author's lips.

At his ranche on the Little Missouri, Mr. Roosevelt kept a boat, the only craft of the kind on that part of the river. Three bad characters, for whom the country had become too hot, came down one night in a flat-bottomed "scow," and, seizing the boat, proceeded down the river. The loss was soon discovered, but pursuit in the depth of winter seemed hopeless. But these were men who were not easily to be denied, and they set to work, and in three days built another flat-bottomed scow, and started down stream in the wake of the thieves, a task all the more critical because the ice was just breaking up and the river full of floating masses of it. Indeed, this ice had formed a lofty barrier across the stream, which had ground down past the ranche a few days before, ripping the bark from the cotton-trees on the bank and leaving banks of ice stranded along the edge. On the third day's voyage, on rounding a corner, they perceived the smoke from the camp of the marauders, who had not reckoned on this determined pursuit. Cautiously landing and creeping up, the one man in camp quickly yielded to a call to "throw up his hands." Then, lying in wait for the other two, they also, on their return from hunting, were in turn "beaded" and secured.

Now the average Westerner would probably have used a short and sharp method with such evildoers, but that was not Mr. Roosevelt's way. The real difficulties of the capture only now began. The problem was to bring three wholly reckless and unscrupulous ruffians down to town in the depth of winter, guarding them day and night.

The first and perhaps the most effectual measure was to remove their boots. In those parts the ground is frequently covered with a cactus, so dwarfed as to be almost invisible, and covered with sharp spines, which will bring a man, who attempts to walk unshod, to the ground with an involuntary yell. It was impossible to face the current, and the voyage had to be resumed down stream; but an unexpected obstacle was encountered in the before-mentioned *jam* of ice, which they overtook, and which was slowly creeping, like a ploughshare, down the bed of the river. Thus the party was forced to dawdle down for eight days in the wake of the ice, with dwindling stock of provisions, at length reduced to a little flour without yeast; and never for a moment could the anxious watch be relaxed. At length a ranche was reached whence a rough waggon was obtained, in which this precious freight was conveyed to the town of Dickinson. For thirty-six hours the gallant captor followed the vehicle on foot with loaded rifle in hand, for by that means only could he command his captives and ensure himself and his companions against the risk of a sudden attack, or attempted escape.

Without endorsing Mr. Smalley's opinion that for high breeding the best Americans beat the best Englishmen, it must be admitted that, for humanity combined with pluck, this feat is calculated to make an Anglo-Saxon proud.

We now camped close to the Union Peak in the hope of finding big-horn sheep, but the weather had driven them all down into the timber, in which it was all but impossible to come upon them unawares; and though we found some tracks, we failed to get a sight of them. We could do nothing at such a height, and therefore dropped down on the east side of the Divide to Clarke's ranche, which we found occupied by a considerable number of rats. They were about the size of our common rat, but with long fur and of a light gray colour.

On one of the affluents of the Wind River we found game in plenty, and the wapiti were now in the full swing of the "running" season. We camped in a grove of cotton-wood, over which a fire had passed some time before, leaving them sear and dead. This was well enough for a camping ground in still weather, but somewhat critical in a wind, as under these circumstances such poles are apt to fall without warning. The first evening I heard the whistle of a large beast, and, hurrying in that direction, got within two hundred yards of him, when we were stopped by a small *cañon* with perfectly sheer sides. There appeared to be no means of crossing without a detour, for which there was no time, but on the way home we hit a practicable crossing. There was scarcely light enough left, but we hurried back along the opposite bank on the chance. My friend had stopped whistling, but suddenly we caught sight of him, and at the same moment he saw us. In the heat of his jealousy he mistook us for a rival, and instantly advanced towards us. We crouched perfectly still among the pine stems, in full view, but saved from detection by the dimness of the light. On he came with a most insolent and overbearing demeanour, challenging all the way, till he was within ten yards, when he gave me a certain shot.

This was a good head, but I improved upon it a few days later. My best I got with a penny whistle. In company with Dick I reached at mid-day the edge of a bluff overlooking a splendid basin a mile or two in diameter. It was so densely timbered that stalking was difficult, but the "calling" was in full swing, and we counted on finding our game by the tell-tale signal. We had been late in starting, and the day was hot, and even the most amorous bulls had "quit" whistling to take a siesta. Dick said he would wake them, and proceeded to gather the dry stalks of a plant, out of which he extemporised a whistle, and sitting down with his legs dangling over the edge of a low cliff started a very passable imitation. I doubt whether any one can produce the exact thing. The choking, pig-like grunt which follows the whistle takes more wind than human lungs can produce. But they were not particular in these parts, and the challenge was instantly answered by a good but not first-class bull, who presently showed himself in an opening, impatiently squealing defiance. Immediately afterwards another animal with a much deeper and more sonorous voice opened on the left. Then began a very lively trio, which we kept up in the hope of drawing the big one from his cover, for I was sure, from the volume of the note and the unwillingness of the first elk to approach him, that this was the boss. But he wouldn't show, and Mahomet had to go to the mountain.

Marking the position of the sound as well as I could, I dived into the timber. When I had gone as far as I dared, I sat down, for fear of jumping him, and gave a low whistle. The bull came straight towards me suspiciously, and without uttering a sound, and keeping himself so much under cover that I could not see him plainly. He stopped about twenty yards off, but completely hidden, and, after a pause, calmly turned tail and walked slowly away without once giving a chance. Another cautious whistle must have stopped him, for when, a few minutes later, I followed, in spite of every precaution I jumped him from behind a group of young trees, and though a snap shot at the yellow mark on his stern quickened his trot, he got off with a whole skin. It was rather a bad miss, but it was better so, for if I had hit him I might have lost him, and I had seen enough of his points to be keenly disappointed and to long for a nearer acquaintance. Dick, who of course had a clear view of him while I was away, said he was an "old time bull," so I determined to lie low for him. But I was too impatient, and began badly, overrating my woodcraft. Dismissing Dick to take the horses back to camp, I followed the elk's track on foot. He appeared to be accompanied by a single hind only. Several times I heard his now familiar note, but I never seemed to get to close quarters, and he was probably again jumped without my knowing it.

Early were we in the saddle next morning. As the particular kind of dry stalk available for whistles was not always to hand, I borrowed a tiny tin whistle from one of the men. Riding out for an hour or so, we tethered the horses and climbed to the top of a ridge which commanded the basin from another point. Our puny note, favoured by the stillness, was carried far over the tree-tops. Instantly came back the deep-chested challenge, muffled by the trees, but loudly and confidently expressed, as though he had no doubt at all about this strange thin-voiced rival. A minute or two later it sounded again, and then again, each time nearer. Evidently he was coming rapidly in our direction. The timber below our perch was dense. It is always difficult to look down into a wood, and clear patches were rare, besides which he now ceased to answer. It seemed that he could not get up to us, for our ridge fell away in a steep cliff on that side. Clearly, the only chance was to go down and find him. Dick said I couldn't get down, but I was in no mood to stick at trifles. Leaving him there, with instructions to whistle cautiously at intervals, I started, and, with the help of a projecting tree or two, was soon at the bottom. Pushing through the thicket to the nearest open patch, I instantly saw what was up. Three hundred yards off the ridge was broken down into a slope. My elk had made for this to get at his imaginary rival, and there he was, still accompanied by his single faithful hind, laboriously making his way up it. No wonder he had not answered, he was too blown to do it, and he was reserving himself for the encounter. He was already close to the top, and in a few minutes it would be all over, for he would come from behind on Dick, whom I could still hear cheerfully tootling above. At whatever cost of skin and shin I had to get back to him first, for the elk would surely detect the spurious sound as soon as he came to close quarters. How I did pound up that cliff! I came down it on a pretty straight course, but I went up again straighter. As soon as I came within sight of Dick I commanded him in a whispered shout to "stop that whistling," and then drew out to a more open spot to receive the monarch. I was only just in time. He was already approaching, and in the same cautious way as the day before, advancing a few steps and then pausing to listen. He was already within a hundred yards when I caught sight of him. I was ready to take the first chance, for I didn't mean him to show me his tail again if I could help it. But that rush upstairs had set my heart a-thumping, and the muzzle of my rifle oscillated like a pump handle. Under such circumstances, a bullet is very fond of the open air. At last he stood rigid, with every sense on the alert, and fairly showing his shoulder between two trees. As often happens with elk, he did not seem to flinch to the shot, but I knew it was well planted. He stood for some seconds without moving, then his legs trembled, and down he came, driving his great brow antlers into the ground. I may fairly say that I got him with a penny whistle, and I strongly recommend any one going to the haunts of the wapiti to arm themselves with at least one lure of the same kind.

The same day Gerald secured a remarkable head. It had no brow antlers to speak of, but the horns were spread

I

into a fine palmated top, a variation which sometimes occurs with the wapiti, but never, so far as I have observed, with any other red deer.

On one occasion I had sent Dick home with the horses, intending to try for a bull which I had heard in the morning, and I was confident that he would speak again before sunset. At last I heard him, and the depth of his voice indicated a heavy animal, but before I got near enough to sight him, six shots were fired in rapid succession, and when I came up to the place, I found the animal dead but no hunter visible. I knew very well what had happened. It was Dick who could not resist the temptation. When I charged him with spoiling my sport, he excused himself by saying that he wanted "sinnus" for his squaw. The Indian women use nothing but sinews for all kinds of sewing; but in this case it was only an excuse, for the carcass remained untouched till we left.

We soon tired of pursuing the wapiti, for, with a small outfit, frequent kills mean wasted meat. We were still most anxious to secure some big-horns, the *Ovis montana*, the great wild sheep which is closely allied to the *Ovis ammon* of the Himalayas.

No trophy is more coveted by American sportsmen than a big-horn ram. He is a true sheep, but like a deer, clad in a dense coat of hair instead of wool. He carries a provision against cold which I have not observed in any other animal. The hairs of the neck, though presenting outwardly a smooth surface, are *crinkled* one over the other, so that each separate hair follows a zigzag line, thus enclosing more air in the folds, and affording a very non-conducting "comforter." A bold rock-climber, yet so far as my observation goes, he cannot approach for agility the chamois, and still less the ibex. Most Rocky Mountain sportsmen have heard of the delightful manner in which the big-horn transports himself down a mountain. A cowboy once related to me, with Western energy of language, a personal experience of this kind. He had circumvented a herd of twenty-one rams, and when fourteen of them had fallen to his rifle, the remainder had sprung over a perpendicular cliff several hundred feet high, and, alighting comfortably on their horns, had proceeded calmly on their way. To my mind nothing shows the true frankness of the American mind more than the simplicity with which the Westerner believes that you believe his taradiddles.

Not many English hunting "outfits" succeed nowadays in bringing back the heads of good big-horn rams, but I attribute this to the fact that the Western hunter, who generally thinks first of meat and how to get it most easily, is apt—at least that is my experience—to discourage his employer from hunting on foot; and from the rough nature of the ground where this animal generally, but not always, abides, this is the only effectual way to get at him.

On our way up, a month before, we had looked from a distance into an upland basin of one of the forks of the Wind River, surrounded by high and broken peaks which looked likely. Two days' journey took us thither, but at the first attempt to get into it we were completely beaten by fallen timber and intricate cañons. The next day I rode out by myself and succeeded in finding the clue to the entrance. On the way down again I heard the squirrels chattering in front of me, and, by the tracks in the snow, found I had started an unusually large bear. I never got a sight of him, and I am not sure that I should have cared to tackle him if I had. It is all but impossible to walk silently in snow that has melted and frozen again. I think we were rather unfortunate in that neither of us got a chance at a bear on this trip. Nor were any of the remains of kills which we revisited touched. Perhaps they were temporarily scarce in that part, for bears shift their quarters a great deal. But with the best opportunities very few are killed by ordinary sportsmen in fair hunting. The great majority one hears of are obtained with the assistance of a 60-lb. iron trap.

On my return to camp I found that during the temporary absence of our men the fire had spread to the surrounding grass. The men were just in time to save their blankets, but one of the tents was burnt, and for the rest of the trip they had to shelter under one of those make-shifts which Westerners so readily contrive. Another two minutes and every article which we possessed, except the clothes we stood in, would have gone up in smoke.

We now moved camp into the basin, determined to leave no stone unturned to secure a ram or two; but till the very last, though we saw some ewes on more than one occasion, and were frequently tantalised by fresh tracks in the timber, we got no chance at a big one. The last day before our intended departure had arrived, Gerald had searched in vain for most of the day, when Bob, by a fine piece of spying in the bright interval between two snow-storms, made out a band of old rams feeding in a cañon on the opposite side of the valley in which our camp was pitched. A quick descent and a toilsome climb brought them to the spot, and though the search was difficult, owing to the snowstorms, they at last got even with them, and Gerald in a succession of quick shots managed to bag two fine old rams and severely wound a third, which he recovered the following day. This change of luck induced us to postpone "pulling out" for two more days, in the hope that the good fortune of the son might be extended to the father. Next day I was once more tantalised by jumping some rams whose track I had followed into a timbered cañon. I did not see them, but the bounds with which they had sprung from their beds, which I found in the snow, left no doubt as to the cause of their departure.

And now the last day and my last chance had arrived. Three long days with the pack-train, thirty-six hours in a mud waggon, and finally the continental express, would barely leave two or three hours of margin before the sailing of the "Cunarder," which we must catch to keep public engagements and private promises. It was now or never. The best chance seemed to be to try high, and we determined to go straight to the top of the serrated ridge, which rose three thousand feet above the camp, and divided our valley from the next creek. This had some craggy ground on its slopes, which looked likely for sheep if only the weather had not driven them all down. Riding up till we had passed through the timber, and the slope became too steep, we left the horses and took to climbing. In three hours from camp we had reached the top, seeing some encouraging "sign" on the way. We proceeded along the ridge, carefully spying on both sides, but a piercing wind swept across it and made it hard to persevere. Fine hail and cubes of hoar frost blown from the rocks smote our hands and faces, and now and again one had to pause on the lee side to take breath. During one of these halts, on looking back along the ridge, we saw a band of ewes and small rams about five hundred yards off, and apparently following in our track. Some whiff of our taint had disturbed them. Aware of danger, but not seeing us, they bunched up, and I tried the shot as a last chance, but without result. But its echoes disturbed another lot of eight or nine, this time all old rams, at the very bottom of the next valley. After a bit they disappeared behind a rise, and, failing to see them reappear, we assumed that they had remained there. There seemed to be nothing for it but to tramp to the bottom, and this we did reluctantly, as it lay right away from camp. Down we went for half an hour as hard as we could go, but when we reached the foot of the slope the sheep were nowhere to be seen. Glancing upwards, there they were, outlined against the sky on the top of the ridge, within a hundred yards of the point where we had left it, so that we had not only had our tramp in vain, but lost a fine chance into the bargain. On our way down they must have passed pretty close to us, concealed in a hollow. Up again we had to go in the worst of tempers, but consoling ourselves with the assurance that we should be able to follow their tracks in the snow. Alas! when, after an hour's severe grind, we reached the point where they had disappeared, not a "sign" remained. Though the weather was clear the wind had smoothed away every trace. We commanded a wide area, but the band had wholly

THEY MUST BE HEREABOUTS.

disappeared. Gloomily we turned downwards and campwards.

However, luck must turn, and the usual reward of perseverance was yet to be ours. At the upper edge of a curious castellated cliff, which formed a conspicuous feature from our camp, we came upon the tracks of another band, so burning fresh that it was obvious they must be immediately below us in some broken recesses of the rocks which we could not command from above; and, in fact, while we peered about, a backward curl of the strong wind which was beating against the face of the cliffs must have carried a message to some of them, for one, fortunately a ram, marched out into full view on the opposite side of the amphitheatre, with deliberate step, but evident signs of uneasiness. The next minute he was spinning backwards through the air with a bullet through his spine. Then—oh, glorious luck!—out stepped another ram, wholly unaware of the fate of his companion, and stood on the same identical shelf, and he also was "my meat." The third ram now appeared lower down, and making off at his best pace; but he was so inferior to the two which I had secured that I let him go. As long as he was picking his way down the rocks his movements seemed to me slow and clumsy, but the moment he cleared them how he did stretch himself out, and "dust" down that mountain! And now a curious thing happened. The remainder of the herd were all ewes or little ones, and being deprived of their leaders, and apparently bereft of sense, gathered on a buttress just below us, and for some minutes, though I stood up, shouted, and threw stones at them, they seemed glued to the ground as though they were under a spell. Such want of resource I never saw in any wild animal.

It was no light matter, in our exhausted and half-frozen condition, to secure my trophies. My first ram had fallen quite three hundred feet into an almost unapproachable *couloir*, where the powdery snow was literally up to my neck; but it was done at last, and the head and such meat as we could carry conveyed to a point accessible to horses. Then home to the camp fire and mutton cutlets; and the next morning "eastward ho" with contented minds.

SUNDAY DINNER.

IV

ON THE RIM OF THE DESERT

The recent opening of branch railways through the Atlas Mountains into the desert of Sahara has brought within reach of London a winter climate, almost as superior to that of the Riviera, or the Algerian littoral, as these are to our own; indeed, if time-tables were strictly adhered to, it is even now possible by landing at the port of Phillipville, one hundred and fifty miles east of Algiers, to reach the oasis of Biskra, which is well out in the desert, in little over three days from London. If the Algerian trains could be persuaded to travel at the modest speed of twenty miles an hour, this would be accomplished with ease. Although Biskra is not much more than a hundred miles from the coast, the traveller has there left behind him the mountains which attract and condense the moisture of the Mediterranean, and, after the beginning of January, he can count on perennial sunshine, except when— and this is seldom— a high wind fills the air with a dust-fog almost as impermeable to the rays of the sun as a watery cloud.

The climate was not, however, the chief attraction which drew me thither with two companions one January.

On the arid side of the ranges which immediately overlook the desert, there exists, the whole way from the Atlantic to Tunis, a certain wild "Barbary sheep," called by naturalists the *Ovis tragelaphus* or the *Aoudad*, by Arabs the *Aroui*, and by the French the *Mouflon à manchette*, from the long pendent mane, if that be the correct term, which the animal carries on the under side of its neck and shoulders down to the knees. It is a large sheep, scarcely inferior to the "big-horn" of the Rockies, and of a dull rufous-yellow colour, well calculated for concealment on the red and yellow cliffs which it inhabits. Though not extremely rare, it is, for reasons which will subsequently appear, exceptionally difficult to find. True, the kids are occasionally caught by the Arabs, and, as the *aroui* breeds freely in confinement, it has been distributed from the Jardin des Plantes to other zoological collections, including our own.

Why not, then, be content to examine him at the Zoo? Why should one want to kill the poor beast? I have no defence to offer, except that rather mean instinct which forces up dodo's eggs, uncut folios, and foreign postage stamps which have ceased to be useful, to fabulous values. After numerous inquiries I had failed to hear of any English sportsman who had successfully stalked the animal, though I know of two, one ten years and one twenty-five years since, who had tried in vain.[1] A French book in my possession, *Renseignements sur la Province de Constantine*,

---

[1] Since the above was written a friend, who is one of the best rifle shots in England, followed almost exactly in our footsteps. He and his companion hunted the same ground for five weeks, and secured three specimens, but two of them were much better trophies than any of ours.

which professes to give a description of the fauna of the province, does not mention the animal. An accomplished traveller told me that it was scarce, "but not quite so difficult to get as an Algerian lion." A friend who had travelled through the southern ranges of the Atlas admitted that he had never heard of it. Can it be wondered at that I desired to secure so rare a trophy, and incidentally to use it as a peg upon which to hang a fresh series of experiences.

to wander among mountains rarely visited, to pitch or strike my camp when and where I pleased, among a people who daily do the same?

Our expedition began with some misfortunes. A great January storm in the Channel had blown down some telegraph posts, and so delayed our arrival in Paris that we missed the Marseilles express, and consequently the Algiers boat. At Marseilles we received a telegraph from my dear old *chasseur* Celestin, who, on his way to meet us there, was seized by the fashionable complaint, and lay halfway from his mountain valley, helpless as a log. He did not join us till ten days later, but I had a second very efficient string in Andreas, a blacksmith and chamois hunter.

Our first point, reached after two days spent in the train, was El Kantara, sometimes called "the Gate of the Desert." Here a ridge of red rock, nearly the last outwork of the mountains, rises for eight hundred feet above the plain. Through this ridge the little river, at times a rock-shaking torrent, has opened a gap, admitting the passage, for many ages past, of the converging caravan routes from the south, and for the last few years the railway from the north, which now terminates at Biskra, thirty miles farther.

As we took our evening stroll through the gap, its contorted red rocks were lighted on the east side into a fiery glow by the setting sun. At the far end of the gap one comes suddenly on the first oasis, a wealth of gray-green foliage, and the waving plumes of sixty thousand palms, finely contrasting with the thirsty rocks. A few of these have established themselves in the very gorge itself, as though struggling for the first drink. Some of the palms are tall and upright as a ship's mast, others bending over the stream which has undermined their roots. Among the black columns and shaded aisles white-robed figures flit about—for you never *hear* an Arab walk—or lie coiled under mud walls. A month later the greenery was varied by pink clouds of apricot blossom, but this was not yet. That which strikes one most is not the sight of the palms, but the sound of them. The waving plumes respond to the breeze by a low monotonous hiss, as distinct as possible from the rattle and quiver made by the clashing of deciduous leaves. Seen from an elevation, these oases look black on the plain, like nothing so much as huge leeches sucking at the juices of the mountain.

But we were not thinking much of these things that night. What sportsman does not remember the first eager hope with which he examines the new hunting ground? Are the wild animals we have come so far to seek still to be found in those cliffs? I knew that they were there ten years ago, but men of knowledge had assured me that the railway must have driven them away, and that I must go farther afield. We had yet to learn that it is not the habit of this old-world sheep to run away from civilisation. He has other means of protection.

Behind the little inn at the north end of the gap was a sandy ridge, which offered a good spying-point. From this our telescopes presently scanned the cliffs of the Jebel Metlili, the highest point in these parts, which rose to the north from a little plain to the height, I should judge, of five thousand feet. There was no doubt about the broken character of its cliffs. Their appearance, at any rate, justified our hopes.

Two very dirty and ragged Arabs, Ali and Abdullah, had been fetched from the mountain itself with a view to being retained as guides, and, while we supped, they interviewed us, squatting on their hams on the tiled floor. These ragamuffins gave an edge to our appetites by asserting the undoubted presence of *feshtal*, as they call the old male of the *aroui*, in the cliffs we had been examining, and the more eager we showed ourselves, the higher rose their terms. We finally settled with them for three francs a day, at which price they proved distinctly dear.

Gerald started at a very early hour with Andreas and

old Ali to try the nearest and most precipitous part of the range. The rest of us, after the delays which generally accompany luggage, got off an hour later with the mules and camp train, and had not gone far across the plain when we saw my son and his companions still on a neighbouring rise. We went across and found a somewhat mixed altercation proceeding, which, as none of the three could speak the language of the others, was not surprising. Old Ali was at the bottom of the mischief. He declared that it was impossible to go up the mountain except by the path, but as there was obviously no difficulty, he was made to understand that he could take his choice between going as he was bid, or returning to the tents of his fathers. This imp of mischief elected to go, and it would have been better if he had never been born, for on this very first morning such a chance offered as did not soon recur, and he spoiled it. They had scarcely got well into the ravines with which the range is seamed, when they spied some mouflons, one of which, a large ram, lay in a position most favourable for a stalk. They were so eagerly engaged in determining the best line of approach, which was by no means difficult, that they did not pay any heed to their follower. Looking round, to their horror they found that he had gone off on his own account. His intentions were no doubt innocent, but the result was disastrous. He probably thought that the Englishman could not possibly get near the game unaided, and would be much pleased if the game should come to him. It was about a hundred to one against this happening; still he would try, and, slipping off, he succeeded, in about ten minutes, in showing himself and giving the wind at the same time. Twenty minutes later he arrived at the rock where the quarry, which was now far away, had been lying, and began to throw rocks down. He finally rejoined the strangers, and appeared to think that he was being congratulated on his spirit. Later on, yet another was spied lying favourably placed on a cliff, but when the spot was reached it had gone, having probably heard the nailed boots on the rocks. This was a difficulty which we afterwards found it very hard to avoid.

In the meanwhile the rest of us, with the mule train, followed a well-engineered path constructed by the French to give easy access to a tower of observation which they have built on the highest point of the mountain. After three hours of steep ascent, we halted at a convenient plateau a little short of the summit. This was a most attractive camping ground, but I saw at a glance that, with uncertain weather, it would be far too exposed, especially as one of our tents had been temporarily lost on the railway, and our men would be very imperfectly sheltered by the make-shifts which we had brought from El Kantara.

It commanded, however, a marvellous view. The Metlili is the highest point for many miles, except to the north, in which direction we were slightly overtopped by the cedar forest ranges near Batna. To the east, but at a distance of many miles, the great mass of the Aurès, crowned by the highest point in Algiers, the Chellia, now white with snow, rose perhaps three thousand feet higher than where we stood. But to the south who can describe the wonderful expanse of the desert which lay four thousand feet below us? To my mind there is no panorama so interesting as a

THE DESERT FROM JEBEL METHILI

bird's-eye view over a plain from a considerable height. The plains of Lombardy from Monte Rosa, of Spain from the Brêche de Roland, have this human interest, but in both these cases subsidiary, but still lofty ranges serve to break the contrast. But here we were on the top of a great craggy wall which rose straight from the plain. True, the latter was seamed by three low, rocky ridges which lay parallel to one another between us and Biskra, but they were completely subordinated and looked like small purple islands rising out of a golden sea. Over them one took in the whole plain, every inch of it, to the very horizon, clear cut and level as the sea itself. To the east, perhaps thirty miles off, lay a large *chott* or salt marsh, but whether its shining surface was due to water or half-dried salt I could not determine. The sunsets and sunrises from this and similar elevated camps were of marvellous interest and beauty, especially when a sea of cloud clung to the mountains, as sometimes happened in the early morning. In the foreground ragged-edged peaks, with deep purple shadows, pierced the luminous mist ; beyond, the shadowless, illimitable plain. The nights were not less beautiful. In still weather the air was so clear that the stars shone with scarcely diminished brightness down to the horizon itself, and one seemed even to look down on them.

All the southern slopes of the Atlas are singularly waterless, and the Metlili is no exception to the rule. Every drop for our use had to be brought up in barrels on mule-back. I wanted to send the barrels back so as to have a fresh supply the next day ; so I poured the water into two of my canteen baskets which are lined with

waterproof canvas for the purpose. Now the wear and
tear of many camps had told upon this lining, and no
sooner had the mules departed with the barrels, than we
found that the baskets were leaking badly and would
presently be empty. Here was a pass, for, though we had
some wine, the Arabs would of course not touch that, and
for ourselves cooking would be impossible. Willie, who

WILLIE.

adds to his other good qualities as a companion a resource-
ful habit, sharpened by many "round-ups," suggested my
waterproof cape. Hastily fetching it, we pushed it into
the third basket so that the edges hung over the side.
That held a part of the water. Another inspiration; the
vaseline pot! I smeared the yellow grease about the
chinks and angles of the now empty basket, and lo and
behold! it held the rest of the water splendidly. True, the
colour was repulsive and the flavour pungent, but the
Arabs were not deterred by their scruples from drinking

it. Indeed, the climax of nastiness was reached when the ugliest and dirtiest of them on his arrival at camp, hot and thirsty, plunged his whole face into it and drank freely.

As soon as we had squared this and other matters in camp and pitched our only tent, Willie and I started for an exploration on our own account. Though the best of the day was gone and we saw nothing, we found some fresh tracks; and the tracks of the *aroui* are calculated to rejoice the heart of the hunter, for they are as large as those of the red deer; and as Gerald arrived late in camp with an account of what he had seen, our expectations were raised to the highest point. We had not yet realised that it was one thing to catch a glimpse of the animal, and quite another to put salt on its tail.

The next morning I went with Andreas to the steepest part of the mountain. It is cut into a series of deep ravines which score the slope from top to bottom. At right angles to these run long lines of vertical strata from which the softer limestone is worn away, leaving enormous slabs; the biggest slab of all forms a cliff several hundred feet high and two miles or more long, which runs along the face of the mountain. Just outside this is another similar slab or series of slabs, only a few yards in front of it, and almost as tall as the cliff itself, and seeming from a little distance to form part of it. Between the two is a deep, narrow trench, barely accessible here and there where the outer battlement is broken down. Lesser plates of rock project all over the mountain side, and afford splendid shade and hiding-places for the *aroui*. Here and there are ragged bushes of thuja and clumps of *alfa* grass, like the pampas grass of our gardens but of smaller growth. So rough and broken is the ground that only a minute fraction of the surface can be covered with the glass. We traversed the ravines, spying each with great care. At mid-day I heard a shot in the adjoining hollow and hurried to the ridge which commanded it. After a long search I spied an Arab with a gun, far below and on the other side of the valley, evidently lying in wait for something. Presently he began signalling to another who was below us, but invisible. I thought they must be after partridges, and did not pay any particular attention. I was just settling down to luncheon and had laid aside the rifle when I saw the head of a moufflon passing along the rocks not more than twenty yards from me, and wholly unconscious of our presence. Before I could get the rifle in hand he had passed, offering a splendid chance if I had been ready. I ran forward, making sure that I should get another view, but he had succeeded in putting one of the above-named upright walls of rock between us, and I never saw him again.

The experiences of these first days had given us a tolerable notion of the appearance and habits of the animal which we hoped to secure, and the difficulties of the pursuit, and I will now endeavour to describe them and to impart the secrets of the craft, together with such "tips" as subsequent adventures suggested. Herodotus mentions "asses with horns" which inhabited these ranges. True, in the same sentence he describes "monsters with dogs' heads, and others without heads who have eyes in their breasts"—I should like to possess trophies of some of these—but asses with horns is a description which aptly fits these wild sheep, with their long and rather dull faces, like most African animals, and in marked contrast with the bold and high-bred expression of their smaller namesake of Sardinia and Corsica. Pliny describes the animal as the "goat hart," which is also rather apt. The pendent mane and sandy colour I have already referred to. On the knees he has patches of bare callous skin after the manner of a London cab-horse, which I suppose enables him to kneel and reach his food on steep places and in the crevices of the rocks. The Arabs say that these animals do not drink more frequently than once in five days, and this enables them to traverse long distances on these thirsty slopes. They are unknown nearer to the coast, as, for instance, where the climate is moist enough to support the cedar forests, nor do I believe they are ever found out of sight of the desert.

The knack of keeping himself out of sight, and getting out of it when surprised, is the most obvious characteristic of the animal. The habits of the Arabs, continued through countless generations, have helped to form the habits of the *aroui*. These nomad tribes pitch their tents necessarily within reach of one of the scanty springs of water. Here at night, within the circle enclosed by their black *geitouns* and a small *zareba* of loose thorn bushes, they herd their flocks of goats. In the early morning numerous thin columns of blue smoke mark the positions of such camps, generally placed for shelter in dry watercourses. With barking of dogs and shouting, the flocks move off up the mountain, and as the day advances they work up and over it, so that no cliff or corrie is safe from their intrusion. The wild sheep have no means of escaping from them, as every mountain within reach of water is similarly

THE BARBARY SHEEP.

infested. They are thus constantly within sight and hearing of the Arabs and their goats, and, having no means of escaping from their neighbourhood, have developed the art of hiding themselves to an extraordinary degree, and their confidence in their own invisibility is unlimited. A practical illustration of this occurred to me one evening when I had sat in one place for twenty minutes carefully spying the surrounding country. My coign of vantage was a knoll which commanded a small shallow hollow, in which there was not a vestige of cover except the few thin thuja bushes, which looked as if they could not hide a rat. It was not till I rose to shift my position that a female *aroui* and two yearlings started from these bushes. They had been lying within sixty yards of me, and must have been fully conscious of my presence. In this and other respects the *aroui* is very like the Pyrenean ibex, which lives in similar steep, broken rocks and scrub, and which also relies on concealment in preference to flight. It has, moreover, the same inward turn of the tip of the horns to enable it to push through the bushes. The horns of the Alpine ibex, which lives among bare rocks, curve in one plane.

This habit of observing you while he believes himself hidden, is highly inconvenient to the sportsman. If he thinks himself unnoticed, he remains till the coast is clear. If a bolt is necessary, he watches for the most favourable opportunity, and, like a woodcock, puts a rock or a tree, in a trice, between himself and danger. From this it arises that one views the game much more frequently than shots are obtained, and many of these are snap shots. My own experience is suggestive. I hunted on twenty-three days, being nearly always out from before sunrise until sunset. During that time I saw sheep about a dozen times, but I got shots at only four—two of which I secured and lost a third. It was quite a rare event to discover them with the glass, and this sickened our chamois hunters. Celestin was constantly exclaiming, as he closed his glass with a snap, "Cela n'amuse pas de rien voir," while the more phlegmatic Andreas in despair would dreamily search for camels on the distant plain. But if one did happen to get a view of a band in an undisturbed condition, the difficulties were not over, owing to the fact that the animal is constantly shifting to avoid the goats and their Arab owners. Nor is that the only reason for their restlessness. Though it is forbidden to the Arabs to carry firearms, we frequently saw them prowling about with their long flintlocks, which seem to have run to barrel at the expense of the stock. They are seldom successful, but the game is not the less disturbed.

Of another difficulty we very early became aware. Visitors to Egypt will remember how many of the ancient monoliths ring like bells. So here the dry rocks are resonant to a degree of which I had had no previous experience, and to walk silently in nailed boots is almost impossible. The Arabs who wear sandals of *alfa* grass move noiselessly, and Andreas, for a time, adopted the native fashion with tolerable success, but our Alpine nails clashed and rang, step one never so delicately. The difficulty is, except for one defect, completely met by thick india-rubber soles. Indeed, not only are they very silent, but they give quite a new sense of power and security in climbing rocks at a steep angle, *provided these are perfectly dry*. The defect is that these sharp-edged rocks ruin the best attachments in about two days, and repairs are not always possible. Boots were not the only article of attire which suffered. A single flat crawl downhill made ribbons of the toughest Harris tweed. I was very soon scarcely decent, but Gerald, with true filial piety, abstracted two large patches from one of Willie's coats, and sewed them on to the sitting place.

During the first few days the weather was treacherous, and it was clear that our first camp was untenable as long as our men were so badly protected. The poor linen-clad Arabs looked especially miserable, and it was melancholy to see them scrape a small hole, fill it with hot ashes, and squat over it, making a sort of open-air Turkish bath by spreading out their burnouses, and this at the best could only have cooked one end. So we had to make arrangements to remove camp to the foot of the mountain until the weather improved, and we could recover the missing tent. It was well we did so, for even three thousand feet lower, and well under the lee of the mountain, our tent pegs with difficulty held the ground. The wind drove the dust through the flaps, and snowstorms were frequent. The mountain was covered with wreathing storm-clouds, and the position at the moment was so hopeless that we again sent for the mules and pulled out for El Kantara.

Ali and Abdullah took this opportunity to strike for higher wages, which was not surprising under the circumstances; but, as we had no hope of hunting that day, it was a badly-chosen opportunity, and we told them to go to the —— landlord and be paid off. They went with their burnouses between their legs, and returned crestfallen to their *geitouns* on the hill. I was not sorry to part with Ali, who was a radical and leveller, if not a Gladstonian, and had poisoned the mind of his companion; but we missed Abdullah, who was teachable. Like most Arabs he was gifted with wonderful eyesight, and a day

ABDULLAH.

or two later he spied me on the hill, and came racing across it, dragging his wife, who was rather a good-looking young woman, and these mountain Arabs have no nonsense about covering their faces. She came to plead for him—at least I gathered that that was the upshot of their jabber—and when I took him again into my service I was rewarded with grateful glances.

The weather mending we again moved to the mountain, and this time we determined to camp in the watch-tower itself. At the top a curious and tantalising thing happened. We were close to the tower, and the mules and nearly all the men had already reached it. Willie and I were nearly in the rear of the line, when two fine ram mouflons appeared within a few yards of the path. It was blowing a gale of wind, and I suppose that this, and the fact that the ground was covered with snow, had prevented their hearing the tramp of the mules. As usually happened our rifles were not to hand, and the animals passed, as we found by their tracks, within six yards of the tower without any one there being aware of it. Again, an hour later, just as it was getting dark, I saw from the tower another mouflon cross an opening scarcely two hundred yards off. I rushed out, but there were numerous bushes to hide him, and, the darkness coming on and clouds blowing up, I could not sight him again.

What light there was after our arrival we used in stuffing up the loopholes of the tower, as well as we could, with pieces of wood, tent covers, etc., as the wind literally screamed through them, and in sweeping out the snow which lay in fine powder on the tiled floor, with extemporised brooms of thuja bushes. This building was devised solely for observation and defence, but it has been disused by the authorities since they have carried the telegraph to El Kantara, and the Arabs have taken advantage of this to loot the place as far as they could, and especially to remove all the locks, so an entrance was easily effected. It is a solidly-built stone structure, two stories high, each of which is approached by ladders only, which can be withdrawn through trap-doors. At the top, angular projections of iron pierced for musketry command every side in case of attack. Each floor is also loopholed. On the top story is a little stove, and there we established our cook and canteen. We inhabited the first floor, and our dinner had to come through the trap-door and down the rickety ladder, which was rather critical for the soup. Our two Arab hunters camped on the ground floor, and made a good fire in the middle of it. As the bullet-proofed tiled floors were very cold to the feet, we spent a good deal of time by their fire, and watched them plaiting the *alfa* grass and weaving the plait into sandals. They turned out a good working pair in about twenty minutes. This tough grass constitutes one of the chief sources of wealth to Algeria, being used for many purposes, and exported as the raw material of paper.

From what I have described already, it might be thought that the *aroui* abound to such an extent that you could hardly throw a stone without hitting one, but, though one or other of us saw some almost daily, it was not till the sixth day that any of us got a chance. That evening, on his return to camp, Gerald got a very long shot in the dusk and severely wounded a good one. The poor beast lay down three times in two hundred yards, but finally got into such broken rocks that, darkness coming on, the search had to be abandoned. We scoured those cliffs nearly all the next day, but the maze of rocks and bushes defeated us. That he lies dead there somewhere I do not doubt. The truth was, as we discovered too late, the little ·360 rifle which Gerald carried was not powerful enough for so large and tough a beast. For a week we had worked hard and lived hard, and here was a crowning misfortune.

But our luck turned at last. It was in what we called the "Big Corrie" to the west of the tower that Gerald, who was accompanied by Abdullah that day, scored the first success. Quite early in the day he spied, at the bottom of the corrie, the head of a mouflon sticking out of a bush. The animal was so bad to see that, when he took his glass off the spot, he could not refind him for a quarter of an hour. Soon after this he made out four others with him. The approach was not very difficult if they could get over a certain space which had to be crossed in view. He himself went first, moving with extreme slowness and caution; but when Abdullah came to follow, the patience of that child of nature was not equal to the strain, and, when halfway across, he started up and ran the rest of the distance. The sheep of course saw him and moved to a far more impregnable position high up the opposite side. The hunters were, moreover, now fairly caught, being in full view, and there they had to stay for four hours till the sheep began to feed. They then slowly crept back the way they had come, and, making a great circuit of the corrie, came down upon them from above, and got at length within one hundred yards. There was a good ram with them, and Gerald thought he had picked out the very hair that he desired to hit. The beast, however, went off with the others as if nothing had happened, and the running shot, as usual, had no effect. Fortunately the hill was nearly bare in this part, and, as the ram followed the opposite face, he could be kept in sight. Seen through the glass, when he had run three hundred yards he showed signs of distress, and finally rolled over dead. The shot was exactly in the right place, having entered behind the shoulder and passed out at his throat; but this animal also might well have been lost if the ground had not favoured keeping him in view. As soon as he fell, Abdullah, after the manner of his kind, set off at full speed. Gerald, who was a university runner, wholly failed to catch him, and before he got up, the beast's throat was cut from ear to ear, to the great damage of the specimen. There was great rejoicing in the tower that night. Until this success, we had begun to think that we had lost our time and broken our hearts over Jebel Medjili in vain, and now that the mountain had yielded a single trophy, we were quite ready to try fresh scenes.

A low mountain of a light cream colour, halfway to Biskra, which our telescopes had shown to be of a singularly broken character, and therefore likely for sheep, had attracted our attention. This is generally believed to be the Salt Mountain of which Herodotus says:— "There is another hill of salt, and water, and men live round it, and near this salt is a mountain which is called Atlas. It is narrow and circular on all sides, and is said to be so lofty that its top can never be seen, for it is never free from clouds, either in summer or winter." It lies close to the small oasis of El Outaja, on the Biskra road, and though it seemed rather too near the haunts of men, we had already proved that this was not necessarily incompatible with the presence of our sheep.

Our first care on arrival at this place was to call on a certain wealthy Arab, Achmet Ben Driz by name, a retired captain of *Spahis*, reputed to be a mighty hunter. He courteously showed us, among other live animals, a pair of baby *aroui*, which he was trying to rear, and which settled the question of the presence of that animal in the neighbourhood; also a female *edmi*, or mountain gazelle, which had been snared by some Arabs when feeding at night in their barley-fields. It is about twice the size of the common gazelle of the plains (*Gazella dorcas*), and differs from it in the long, upright, and straight horns, as distinguished from the lyre-shaped horns of the smaller species. The *edmi* has long pointed ears, and very large and prominent black eyes. This beautiful animal excited us greatly, but, from what we were told of its rarity and the difficulty of finding it, we had not much hope of securing a specimen. I was, however, destined to become acquainted with it. Captain Ben Driz's enthusiasm for sport, as is the case with most of the better-class Arabs, was centred in hawking. Unfortunately we had no opportunity of seeing this characteristic pursuit.

Our movements were governed here, as elsewhere, by the scarcity of good drinking water, and we finally got leave to spread our mattresses in some spare rooms at the railway station, to which a fresh supply of the precious liquid was daily brought by train.

The foot of the Salt Mountain is distant about two miles across a stony tract of desert. We were told that its intricacies were so great that it was impossible for a stranger to find his way, but there was no real difficulty, and we should have done better without the Arab whom we took with us, as he was both stupid and lacked the keen sight of most of his race. The mountain, which is not more than three miles long, has the appearance of having been dropped from above, and broken in the fall. Its chaotic character is due to the solubility of the salt.

Every storm which washes it carries away a portion from the interior, so that it is honeycombed with hollows inside and out. The surface is disintegrated salt and earth, with a white saline exudation which makes the mountain contrast strangely with the red rocks and yellow plain round it. Once well into the mountain, the confusion of form caused by its huge trenches and fissures is remarkable. Circular craters abound where the soil has fallen in, and here and there we came, with startling suddenness, upon clean-cut perpendicular shafts with walls of green semi-transparent salt, closely resembling the "moulins" of the larger glaciers of the Alps. These were of all sizes from a foot to ten feet in diameter, and of many the bottom was lost in gloom a hundred feet or more below. They are dangerous places without care, as there is a crumbling verge which frequently overhangs. The ground gave back a hollow sound in many places, but it was easy to see where one could go with safety by watching for the gazelle tracks, which were frequent. Little grows on the saline soil except a plant like samphire, and another fleshy-leaved plant; but flocks of blue rock-pigeons, which breed in the clefts, gave some life to the scene. Bright-coloured earths, pink and purple, crop out here and there. On the top there is a less broken part, and something of a plateau, with a little vegetation, and here we hoped to find game, of which we soon saw plenty of tracks.

After our Arab had disturbed three gazelles by his noisy walking, we separated, Willie taking one side of the mountain and I the other. Soon after I made a good spy of three mouflons on a red cliff, which faced the other end of the Salt Mountain, at some distance. We had hardly started for the stalk when a curious and painful accident happened to me, which afterwards had unfortunate consequences. Slipping up, I brought my hand down on an edge of salt so sharp that it ripped the whole of the skin from the ball of my thumb, leaving nothing but bare flesh from the joint upwards. The mishap nearly caused me to faint at the time, and gave me great pain for several weeks afterwards.

It took us an hour or more to reach the top of the cliff, under a ledge of which we had seen the mouflons lie down, and creeping down with extreme caution, for the slope was covered with loose stones, we reached the edge of a little bluff which commanded the spot, and there we waited for them to rise from behind the rocks where they lay, and show themselves. For nearly four hours we lay broiling in the sun, but our patience was in vain; for they had really changed their position before we arrived. At last a great rattling of stones above us told only too well what had happened. They had moved to the left while we were making our stalk, but, a herd of goats entering the valley, they had returned, but above instead of below us, and getting our wind, quickly took leave of that range. We returned in a despondent mood over the Salt Mountain, and followed the most beaten track I could find, where I expected to see nothing. Going round a corner we nearly stepped on a splendid *feshtal*. I snatched the rifle from Andreas, and should have had an easy running shot, but the handkerchief which I had wound round and round my wounded thumb came in the way of the alignment of the sights, and, before I could tear off the miserable rag, he was round the corner, and though in three or four seconds I reached the spot, he easily kept himself out of sight in the maze of contorted furrows and gulches. Was there ever such fatal bad luck from so despicable a cause? After this I generally carried my rifle at full cock, hung by the strap on one shoulder—a perfectly safe position.

The next morning I partly retrieved my fortune by killing my first mouflon. Beating the ground like a trained setter and with rifle in hand, for it is impossible to spy the numerous hollows, we found some very fresh tracks, and following these came upon a small band of mouflons, who, as usually happened, had seen us first and were going hard. This was excusable, for they were in deep shadow while we were in bright sun. The shot was a long and doubtful one, but, waiting until they paused a moment, I picked out the one which seemed to be the biggest, and had the satisfaction of seeing it tumble backwards. Owing to my damaged thumb, and partially left-handed condition, I fumbled over the hammer and so failed to get the rifle reloaded in time for a second chance, which presented itself when they paused for several seconds on the sky-line. So exactly the colour of the rocks are they that when I went up, it was quite a long time before I could see my beast, though it lay there in full view within a few yards of me. To my disgust it proved to be a female, and there was a good ram in the herd, of which I should have been pretty sure if I had been ready for them on the sky-line. The chances of war had certainly been against us so far, and continued so to the end; but I think our mishaps reached a climax at the Salt Mountain. The sportsman who complains of his luck usually stands as self-condemned as the workman who complains of his tools, but I certainly think that all the bad luck which I ever deserved, and did not have, was concentrated on this trip.

While at El Outaja we made friends with the sheik of the village, a very dignified and courteous personage, who invited us to dinner, along with the stationmaster and a French gentleman who had lately arrived to try an experiment in vine culture. We were received in a windowless room, with a handsome carpet and a good deal of furniture of a plain kind. His secretary sat at another table writing most of the time, for the village sheiks exercise magisterial functions. After a preliminary course or two of rather highly spiced viands, served in European fashion, the *pièce de résistance* came on. The table was cleared and a flat iron dish, a yard in diameter, was placed there, after which two servants bore in a half-grown sheep, roasted whole, on a wooden spit. This was deposited on the dish and the spit withdrawn. The sheik then proceeded to pull off the choicer parts with his fingers and place them on our plates, after which we were expected to help ourselves in the same "go-as-you-please" fashion. It was not so nasty as it sounds, for it was roasted very brown and crisp. After this followed the great national dish of *Kous-Kousou*, signifying "generosity"—flour moistened, and rolled by the hand into tiny balls like sago, then steamed and served with different sauces or raisins. A wife is valued, to a great extent, according to her ability to make *Kous-Kousou*. We had lots of Algerian wine, which the sheik did not disdain to drink himself. Dates and pomegranates finished the meal.

The language was a difficulty, but we learned something

about the palm-growing industry. It all depends on the water-supply, and a water-right costs about £16 per acre, which is a great deal more than the land itself is worth, and conveys a perpetual right to a copious irrigation every three days. A palm-tree comes into profit about five years after it is planted as a sucker, and, when once it is in full bearing, may produce to the value of ten francs per year. The owner has then little else to do but to open his sluices and sit in the shade.

Our next move was to Biskra, which has been often described. It is redolent of the desert, for the Arabs from the country, which may mean two hundred miles south, come here to buy and sell. The sights and smells of the market-place are curious. Huge packages of dates jammed into one solid mass are the leading commodity. The public letter-writers sit in the sunshine, while their customers whisper their correspondence into their ears. Another functionary, who also performs in the open, bleeds the Arabs in the head, which they think improves their eyesight. The subject, wearing a solemn " having my hair cut " sort of expression, squats on the ground; the performer, similarly seated behind him, makes incisions, and " cups " him on the back of the head.

The flesh-pots of civilisation did not detain us, but we struck out again for the Ahmar Khadou range, a ridge of the Aurès mountains, two days' ride from Biskra. These mountains are inhabited by the *Chawia*, a branch of the Berbers, the original owners of the land, but dispersed by the invading Arabs and driven into these fastnesses. They are a stationary race, and build themselves stone villages, and wherever a hollow in the hill has accumulated a little soil they roughly terrace it and grow barley. To keep off birds and beasts they build a little pyramid of stones painted white, to represent a crouching Arab. Their villages harmonise so closely with the rocks that in a bad light you may stumble on one, and fail to see it is a village at all. On one occasion such a mishap did occur to two of our party. We had moved camp to the village of Hammam, of which they knew the approximate position, but they missed it, and slept supperless on the hill. We pitched our first camp by a little *ain*, or spring, the thread-like trickle of which was sufficient for our wants. Here, or hereabouts, we spent a week in a position even more commanding than the Metlili. Though we got two more sheep, our hunting adventures did not differ greatly from previous experiences. We varied our bag, however, by stalking a very large boar in the open, a somewhat uncommon experience, as those animals rarely leave the cover by daylight.

A goatherd, with whom we carried on a pantomimic conversation on the hill, after describing the way in which the *aroui* hide themselves, and then sneak away when you are gone, had told us there were immense quantities of boar in that part. "*Halouf bezef, beze-e-e-f!*" he repeated, screaming out the last syllable, and waving his arms.

As we were returning to camp I saw between us and the setting sun the dim outline of a large animal, which I took for a donkey, of which there were several about. Gerald confirmed my impression, as he said he saw it wag its tail. We walked on, but presently I thought better of it and took out my glass, when I found it was a large

boar. "Chutt! Sanglier!" and my companions dropped
like well-trained pointers. It was odd that he had not
seen us, but he was too busy with his supper, or rather his
breakfast. There was no time to lose, as the light would
soon be gone, and we crept towards him in full view, rely-
ing on his obtuseness of sight and preoccupation. At last
we lost sight of him in some rough ground, and approached
more quickly; then he reappeared, coming towards us, and
we again dropped to the ground. He fed down below us
into a hollow, and we began to fear that he would get the
wind. He was snouting about, and at last got his head
behind some bunches of *alfa* grass, though the rest of his
body was exposed. It was necessary to risk something,
and, trusting that he would not raise his head, we jumped
up and ran down into a little ravine, under the cover of
which we quickly got to close quarters. Gerald took my
rifle, as being more powerful than his own, for he really
was as big as a donkey in the body. The light was now
very dim, and all we could see was a great arching back.
I am inclined to think that the shoulder was mistaken for
the other end. At any rate the shot was *very* far back.
However, it knocked the pig clean over, but he recovered
himself with a loud "ouf," and made off. I missed him
as he ran, but he seemed to realise for the first time that
he had an enemy. He faced round towards us, and stood
with his head high in the air. A steady second shot from
Gerald laid him flat, and his death struggles made the dust
fly. Celestin and I hurried off to camp for a mule, while
my son completed the obsequies, and made a fire of dry
scrub as a beacon to show the spot. The brute was
enormous, and taped from the tip of the tail to the snout

6 feet 2½ inches, fair measurement, without stretch of string or imagination.

The Arabs, to whom he was the accursed thing, did not at all approve of having to handle him. One of them piteously exhibited to me a spot of blood on his clothes, apparently thinking that his injured conscience should be compensated. I told him to wash it—I mean his burnous. He seemed to think this was adding insult to injury.

One day we watched a curious phenomenon from this range. A high wind began to blow from the south, and columns of dust, hundreds of feet in height, marched in stately battalions across the plain. Though we were three thousand feet above it, the air surrounding us gradually thickened into a fog, dense enough to blot out everything a quarter of a mile off, but of dust so fine as to be quite impalpable. In a short time it began to settle as a delicate bloom upon everything in the tent.

Returning to Biskra, our next expedition was to the eastwards, to El Gattar, a pretty camp in a river bed. Although for the most part dry, a small stream rose a short distance below, and fell into a natural bath of white rock fringed with maiden-hair fern. Dense masses of oleander surrounded it, and were the nightly roost of countless desert sparrows. We pitched camp under a low white cliff, from the crannies of which miniature owls looked out. Our Arab followers thought there was something uncanny about the place, and tried to dissuade us by saying that the cliffs would fall upon the tents, or that the floods would come and wash us away. Nothing would induce them to sleep there themselves. The Arab whom we picked up here for a local guide was the best

specimen that we encountered, Achmet Ben Saäd by
name, a good-looking gentleman with a Scotch face and
courteous manners. I suppose that he had never been
in the company of Europeans before, for he took an
intense interest in all my proceedings. Whenever anything happened he seized my hand and bowed his head
over it; as, for instance, when I slipped and recovered
myself, also when I failed to do so; again if I understood
what he said, or equally when I did not. Most effusively
of all when I offered him some tobacco and thin paper
which I happened to have in my pocket; the climax
being reached when I lighted his cigarette with my sun-
glass. But this was a forbidden joy which he would have
piously refused if any of his friends had been by. When
luncheon time arrived I was very hungry and particularly
anxious not to share my store with Achmet. I knew he
had brought nothing with him, for they are the most
abstemious race, and I hoped that his scruples would
prove stronger than his appetite. With some confidence,
and with a great show of politeness, I handed him my
slices of meat, well knowing that he had seen them frying
in grease. This was of course rejected, and bread also.
A biscuit he nibbled with extreme caution, evidently in
terror lest some fragment of fat should poison his soul.
There remained the *bonne bouche* of my luncheon, a
handful of luscious dates. So far I had got all the credit
of my generosity, without having lost any luncheon.
Grown over-confident, I chanced it, and handed the
packet to him. To my horror his eyes glistened with
eager joy, his lean fingers outstretched and clasped the
whole brown mass, gathering it together to the last fruit.

These same dates of Tuggurt were a joy and consolation to us throughout the trip, but they had their troublous side. They had an awkward habit of getting loose among the clothes, and especially the blankets, and there dispersing themselves, till there was nothing left but the mere skeleton of a stone. There was no remedy except the Arab plan, to rub over the greasy stain with a handful of desert sand. Dry dirt is their only soap, and it is not ineffective.

From the adjoining range of Bou Arif we again took sportsman's toll, but the old patriarch ram for whom we lusted eluded us to the last. Only on the last day, on our way back to the railway and civilisation, did a real bit of unexpected luck fall in our way.

Once, on the Ahmar Khadou range, I had caught a glimpse of a herd of gazelles, which from the length of horn of the leader I believe to have been the large rough-coated mountain kind. I was shifting camp and riding one of the mules when twelve of these handsome animals crossed the track. Of course the rifle was behind, and, by the time I went after them, I found an Arab with a gun as long as himself in front of me. He had already succeeded in showing himself to them, and further pursuit was useless.

We thought there was little chance of obtaining this coveted trophy, but between our last camp and El Outaja there is a long red ridge called "Ben a Chouf," on which we were told there were some of these *edmi*. We were very sceptical, as the ridge was a low one, and there were Arabs all over it, for we could see their fires on it at night. Still it lay on the way, and we would try a drive.

Going forward to a point about two-thirds of the length of the ridge we climbed up it, and posted ourselves on the rocky crest, while our men drove it along. A small herd of the common gazelle were seen to take to the plain, but nothing came to the guns. Climbing a high point which commanded the remainder of the ridge, we sat down for a careful spy, and Celestin presently made out four gazelles, which were assumed to be the common kind, on a stony plateau far below us. An Arab woman was gathering brushwood for fuel in the same field of the telescope, and though really at a somewhat lower level of the mountain, it added a further spice of excitement lest they should get her wind. This was another instance of the way in which these wild animals frequent the immediate neighbourhood of man, confident in their invisibility and the acuteness of their senses.

My companions, as they always did, wished me to take the chance. They stayed at the top, and there are few more interesting things than to watch the approach from a station which commands both the stalker and the stalked.

Before starting we arranged a code of signals by which the watchers could indicate the direction of the animals if they should move during the progress of the stalk—a common practice with chamois hunters, but one in my experience often leading to mistakes.

We disappeared from their view, and, after the lapse of half an hour, were seen emerging from the gully, some hundreds of feet below, and apparently close to the gazelles. Our gallery of anxious watchers saw that we approached the appointed spot. We seemed to them to

THE MOUNTAIN GAZELLE.

be moving with unnecessary deliberation, for, from above, the ground looked nearly flat. In reality it was rather steep, and so covered with unstable rocks that we had to take extreme precautions not to set them rolling. At length we were seen to reach the little broken ridge we had previously noted. I edged myself forwards on my elbows, and laid the rifle for the shot, but no report followed. Had the cartridges been forgotten? An agonising idea! The fact was that the distance, foreshortened to them, was too great for a certainty, and I waited for the beasts to feed into the next ravine. This they presently did, and we, the stalkers, crept forward to a mound from which we hoped to see them reappear. Here we waited in suspense, and at length turned an inquiring telescope upon our companions. They were signalling that the animals had gone up the ravine. They had seen one do so, but the others really remained opposite to us. The mistake nearly cost us dear. Our steps on the loose rocks were heard. We saw three bounding forms, but the gazelles had heard and not seen us, and paused on the other side long enough to give me the desired chance. I thought I was steady, but to my disgust I heard the bullet clink on the stones.

There was a vision of yellow bodies rushing through a maze of yellow rocks, and my second shot went anywhere. They had run a hundred yards, when one lagged, and Célestin said, "Mais il est bien touché!" The next moment his heels were in the air, and a "whoop" went up to those on the top, to be answered by a similar pæan from them. When I examined my beast and found that it was a fine buck *edmi*, "scarce and little known," as an able naturalist describes it, the shouts expressed still greater triumph. My first shot had passed literally through his heart, and out at the other side.

This was a good finish, and made up our bag of large game to seven head; not a murderous one, but sufficient when the rarity of the trophies is considered.

Six days later we were in London.

THE ALGERIAN BUZZARD.

V

THE ELK

It is curious that the largest of the wild animals of Europe, or, indeed, of any part of the Northern Hemisphere, unless an exception be made of the almost extinct North American bison, should have received so little attention from that ubiquitous creature, the British sportsman. This is the more strange because many of this enterprising class do not count it too much trouble to cross the Atlantic to hunt the same animal, under the name of "moose," in the forests of Canada. It cannot, therefore, be the difficulty of his pursuit which deters them. Some faithful votaries there are who may be looked for with certainty on the deck of the *Eldorado* or *Angelo*, with their faces set towards Scandinavia, about the middle of August, and not even the sternest tones of the party whips will serve to detain them on the languid benches. The pairing time has arrived for them and for the elk. But these are the exceptions, and may almost be counted on the fingers. That at least was the case at the time of which I am writing.

I do not pretend that elk hunting is the prince of sports; that designation must be reserved for the chase of those animals which are to be found on open ground, like the red deer, and, above all, the chamois, because in that case the contest between the strategy of man and the instinct of the beast, the varying fortunes of the day, the complications of the scientific stalk, are visible and patent to the least experienced sportsman, and shared in by him during the greater part of the daylight hours. On the other hand, to the elk hunter the golden chance for which he has toiled, while it seldom offers, may occur suddenly and almost without warning. He must work on in faith and not by sight, and if for many hours his dog leads him on a not too fresh track of an old ox, he must bear in mind that all the time his quarry may be miles beyond his boundary, or may have come round to leeward and be at that moment sniffing the tainted air, in which case the hunter will find it out, when he reaches the spot, by the lengthened stride and mud-scattering hoof-marks of an elk that has been *skræmt*, to quote an expressive and only too familiar word from the vernacular.

On the other hand, some sportsmen have surprising luck. I heard of a novice, whose host sent him out on the opening day of last season. He had not penetrated a hundred yards into the forest before he disturbed a large bull elk, and fired a snap shot at its retreating form. Hurrying forward he obtained a second glimpse, and fired again, as he supposed, at the same elk. Laying on the dog, he presently came up to the animal in its last gasp, and, a few yards farther, a *second* in the same condition.

There are not many of us who have fairy godmothers, or carry such straight powder as this, and the very uncertainty and the rarity of obtaining a clear view of an animal whose tracks are everywhere visible, and the huge size of those tracks, so far larger even than those made by the wapiti or great red stag of the Rocky Mountains, gives the elk an air of mystery which adds a zest to his capture. His curious antediluvian appearance, caused by abnormally high shoulders and great bulbous upper lip, which was surely nature's first attempt in the direction of the elephant's trunk, adds to the impression that he is the forgotten remnant of a bygone period and of contemporaries who must be sought for in the coal-measures and Irish bogs. Old Bishop Pontoppidan credits him with such length of leg "that a man may stand upright under his belly," but this is of course an instance of the glamour which surrounds the animal.

The elk makes his home in the boundless forests of spruce and birch which clothe the central plateau of the Scandinavian peninsula. These verge on the monotonous, but are saved from it by the ever-varying views of lakes of all sizes, and countless number, which dot the woods, by the bogs which once were lakes, by the gardens of mosses and lichens, furnished forth by every fallen and rotting tree-stem; and, lastly, by the sound of bird-life which alone breaks the silence. The capercailzie, more often heard than seen, rises with heavy bustling flight, and flumps into a fir tree a hundred yards away, surveys the position, and waits for you to pass—at least that is his practice when you don't want him; or a covey of the beautiful white-winged grouse, which remind you by their crow that they are the near relations of the Scotch grouse, and which, when you want a change from "elking," will afford you a delightful day's gunning among the patches of dwarf birch on the adjoining fjeld. In the densest groves of spruce a rapid scuttling of wings will indicate the presence of a covey of *hjerpe* or hazel-grouse, the smallest, and, perhaps, the handsomest of the grouse tribe, and, as some think, the best eating. They only fly up into the adjoining spruce, where the brown bars of the breast, so

THE CAPERCAILZIE.

conspicuous when the bird is handled, harmonise perfectly with the twigs. On the bogs the double snipe, of slow and heavy flight, and other long-shanks, give a charming variety to the bag.

In the olden time the elk appears to have been hunted both by stratagem and with the assistance of dogs, for, in the *Gentleman's Recreation* we read that when the hunters "have found the trees whereunto they lean, they so cut and saw them that, when the elk cometh, he overthroweth the tree and falleth with it, and being not able to rise is so taken alive. When they are chased eagerly and can find no place to rest themselves and lie secret, they run to the waters and therein stand, taking up water into their mouths, and in a little time do so heat it that, squirting it upon the dogs, the heat thereof so scaldeth them that they dare not come nigh or approach them any more." [1]

In Scandinavia, at the present day, there are two legitimate methods of hunting the elk, and in each a trained dog is the essential coadjutor, but the principles of his science differ radically in the two styles. In one case the *bind-hund* is held on a leash, and depends exclusively on a highly sensitive nose to lead the hunter to the quarry, either directly, or by following the tracks. This method is generally pursued in Norway, and, indeed, is now, I believe, the only one allowed there. The dogs so used are generally of the Esquimaux breed, protected from the cold and the consequences of their pugnacious disposition by a splendid growth of hair, especially on the neck and shoulders. A friend of mine has trained a setter to this work, and he requires no lead at all. With this dog as his sole companion he has killed many elk, and this excellent sportsman scorns the idea of there being any science in any other method.

[1] This writer may have taken his information from the younger Pliny, who was possibly not a very good authority about hyperborean regions, but who has the following passage :—"Moreover, in the Island Scandinavia there is a beast called Macklis. Common he is there, and much talk we have heard of him. Howbeit in these parts hee was never seene. Hee resembleth, I say, the Alce, but that he hath neither joint in the hough, nor pasternes in his hind legs ; and therefore hee never lieth downe but sleepeth leaning to a tree. And therefore the hunters that lie in wait for these beasts, cut downe the tree whiles they are a-sleepe, and so take them : otherwise they should never bee taken, so swift of foot they are, that it is wonderfull. Their upper lip is exceeding great, and therefore as they grase and feed, they goe retrograde, least if they were passant forward, they should fold double that lip under their muzzle.'—*Pliny Secundus,* Trans. Philemon Holland.

On the other hand, the *lös-hund*, or ranging dog, is generally affected in Sweden. His business is to beat a tolerably wide area on each side as his master proceeds through the forest, but never so far that his bark will be out of hearing. He is often of a lighter build, and more calculated for speed than his brother who works in harness. The loose hound has necessarily a large amount of discretion left to him, for, although he knows very well where his master is, by his trail which he continually crosses and recrosses, he is frequently invisible to the latter for twenty minutes or half an hour at a time. When the dog finds elk, generally, in my experience, an ox, a cow and a calf, his aim must be to hold them by barking round them, but without getting too close; so as to keep them at bay, until the hunter, attracted by the sound, approaches near enough for a shot. If, as generally happens, the elk break the bay, the dog endeavours again to head them and arrest their flight—an exceedingly difficult thing to do if the animals have suspicions of a two-legged pursuer : and, indeed, success in this form of hunting is seldom attained, except after a run which tries the bottom of the staunchest wind. If the hunter possesses that attribute, I promise him some glorious experiences. On the other hand, the *finesses* of venerie and the intelligence of the hound are best observed in following the gentler method.

Elk have increased of late years under protective legislation, and large numbers are killed by both the above methods. A writer in the *Field* gives the official returns, which do not include those surreptitiously taken out of season, at 515 for Norway and 1782 for Sweden in the year 1889. In 1890 the number killed in the latter country was 1963, and 1679 last year.

My first attempt for elk was made in Norway. On the way out I revisited the Hevne Fjord, opposite the

WATERING THE "TORBA."

Island of Hitteren, in the hope of picking up the casual bear. The steamer landed us one Saturday afternoon at the quaint island town of Christiansund, and an hour later our party of six started in a launch which I had previously engaged for the remaining seventy miles of water journey. Steaming up the Sound between the islands and mainland, we were overtaken at sunset by a dangerous fog, and had to lie to under the island of Smolen, and make up extemporised beds on board, for the ladies. At 4 A.M. the haze lifted sufficiently, and, after watering the engines at a stream which fell over a cliff where the rocks dipped sheer into deep water, so that we could draw up alongside of them, we sailed up the still waters of the fjord. I shall not soon forget the lovely Sunday morning which greeted us. The sun shone brilliantly, and as we passed alternately barren cliffs, wooded hills, and green valleys, I pointed out to my daughters the scenes of past triumphs or failures. The glassy surface of the fjord was broken only by numerous boats loaded with family parties, converging from all directions on the little church and the red and yellow homesteads of Kirkesæter. On two previous occasions I had found bears numerous on these hills, and each time either I or my companion had secured one. This year my former hunter, Per Klonglevik, informed me that they had deserted the country, and two days' search confirming his statement, we sailed on to Throndhjem.

I had hired through a Norwegian agency an elk shooting near Levanger, of which more presently, but, having in the course of these preliminary wanderings encountered a Norwegian who knew the district and gave me an unfavourable impression of it, I changed my plan, and proceeded first towards the Swedish frontier to the south-west of Throndhjem.

Our first halt was at Selbo, at the upper end of the large lake of that name, where we put up at the "Sanatorium," in reality a capital hotel, where the landlady—motherly soul!—alternately hung over us with tempting dishes, and discoursed sweet music in the adjoining *salon*.

This was too civilised for me, but the landlord assuring me that there were elk in the woods, and that he had secured three "rights," I delayed two days to give it a trial. The latter expression requires explanation. In Norway every *bönder*, or farmer, has the "right" to kill one elk on his forest holding; but in the great majority of cases these privileges are like the advertisements of some Highland proprietors—"ten deer may be killed." It is only on the best ground that they are of any use, and, as the holdings are small, it is necessary, for any hope of success, to have a wide range, and to secure permission, by hire or otherwise, to hunt over many holdings. Indeed, unless the rights are let, it is a common practice for the farmers jointly to commission the most experienced hunter they can get hold of, or rather the one who owns the best dog, for that is the essential element, to do their hunting for them—the elk, when killed, being delivered to the fortunate man on whose land it happens to fall.

At Selbo I could hear of no good dog, but I had previously purchased one through a correspondent at Throndhjem. "Tump" was a splendid specimen to look at, with a magnificent "stand up" coat of black hair, especially on the fore part of his body. A broad head, prick ears, and narrow nose combined to give the foxy expression common to the Northern breeds of dogs, while the double curl of his tail, if it did not quite, as somebody has suggested, lift his hind-legs off the ground, gave an im-

pression of energy not belied by his performances. His short
legs and powerful build enabled him, when harnessed, to
drag his master uphill like a young cart-horse. He was an
able hunter too, and would have been worth the long price
I paid for him but for one physical defect. He was in the
habit of pulling so strongly at the rope, when on the track
of elk, that he had injured his windpipe, and had a chronic
cough, which could not always be suppressed at critical

TUMP.

moments, and he lost me some chances in this way. Morally
he was not a perfect character; at least he suffered from
green-eyed jealousy. The last I heard of him was in the
following laconic epistle received two years later: "Tump
is dead. He was with two powerful dogs, and he resented
them. One of the other dogs is very sick." The last
statement I can well believe. Dear old Tump! He was
as affectionate as he was quarrelsome, and his caresses
were as vehement as his onslaught.

I started from Selbo before daylight and drove nine

miles in a carriole, then struck into the fir woods with Paolus, who was supposed to know the boundaries of my rather narrow beat. Perhaps he did, but his account of their whereabouts varied according to the needs and expectations of the moment. Tump was of course harnessed, and led by a cord, or rather led us—at a handsome pace too. One of the first qualifications of an elk dog which I noticed is that he knows where his master can follow, and avoids low horizontal branches and such like obstacles. The harness consists of a broad strap along the spine, to which are attached two collars, one passing round his neck, the other under the chest. He pulls so hard that a single collar would choke him. There is another advantage. The cord, being attached to the hindermost collar, is much less likely to entangle the dog's legs.

It is a stirring moment for the elk aspirant when he first finds the tracks and other signs of his quarry. Not till then does he realise the huge dimensions of the beast. The merest tyro will not fail to mark the change in the demeanour of his dog when the latter gets the wind. It was not very long before Tump exhibited such symptoms. He paused, head in air, eagerly snuffing the breeze. The long hair on his back stood more erect than ever, and he gazed intently in the direction whence came the taint, while his body trembled with excitement. Then he started with a pull on the rope which threatened to jerk it out of the hand of the hunter, or lay him flat in the mud. In a few minutes he paused again, and laid his nose to the ground. There are the tracks, fresh enough, but only those of a cow and calf, so after following them for a short distance in the hope of catching a first glimpse of the coveted game, we struck off afresh, hoping to hit on an ox.

The elk lies down from 10 A.M. till about 3 P.M., and, unlike deer in this respect, he rarely changes his couch during those hours. At this time it is of little use to continue the search. He has some craft in his stupid old head, and one of his tricks is to return on the lee side of his track, so that any pursuer following is certain to give the wind. Besides, his hearing is very acute, and as he lies *perdu* in thick scrub, the hunter is almost certain to be heard before he is aware of the proximity of the game. These hours of waiting are very difficult to spend, and very trying to the patience. Sometimes a small pent-house of birch faggots, into which one can just crawl, serves as a refuge, sometimes a more substantial hay-hut, but most frequently the hunter must sit "just there" among the spruces, and keep himself warm by collecting dead wood for a big blaze. On the present occasion we had a little diversion. Paolus said: "We will have boiled trout for luncheon." I did not know what he meant, but presently he led me to a small rivulet running into a lake, and began working up it, scanning its miniature pools. Presently a wave and the protruding fin of a good-sized trout was seen, but the water was too shallow for him to escape, and after a short but exciting run we had him out on the bank. In a quarter of an hour we had two more, and the three averaged about a pound each. It was pleasant, but wrong. I only remember one similar hunt. That was after a large eel, which we dislodged while tickling trout under the stones in a Scotch barn. The ghillie called it a "sarpint," and squirmed with superstitious terror whenever its black coils showed near his boots. But nobody had any objection to eating the trout, and a haymaker's hut being handy, and the customary iron pot in its place, we soon had them before us, fizzing hot on the plank bed shelf.

In the afternoon we again struck *spör*, this time a bull, a cow, and a calf. They were travelling down wind, and I had little hope of any result, but I contented myself by picking up some wood-craft from Tump. It is not difficult to measure the degree of freshness of the track by the behaviour of the dog. He is not content with roading the track itself, but frequently stands on his hind-legs to smell at the twigs which have been nibbled. Now and again he pauses with head in air, and tries to catch the wind direct from the elk. If the scent was very hot Tump would utter a sound which I can only describe as a bark in a whisper. I have known other elk dogs to do the same.

Now the track takes a more zigzag course as the band search for their afternoon feed. Suddenly Paolus, who is in front of me, starts backward, and points along a narrow glade. I can see nothing but the vanishing flick of a yellow stern as they whip away into the deep shadow of a clump of spruces. I had at any rate seen my first elk, and my appetite was whetted.

The chief food of the elk consists of the leaves of deciduous trees, especially of the mountain ash, and one soon learns to regard a "black" wood, *i.e.* one of firs only, as a poor chance. From his length of neck he reaches his food to a considerable height, but, not content with this, he presses down the limber saplings by the weight of his body, and standing over them browses them to the top. In hot still weather the elk sometimes leave the dense covert and frequent the more open fjeld. Once, when my son was shooting grouse on such ground, his setter drew up to a bunch of young spruces, but suddenly leaving his point began barking furiously. As the sportsmen hurried up, expecting to find some wild cat, or possibly a bear, a large bull elk rose up and calmly trotted away. Of course it was the day *before* the opening of the season.

My first experience was all very well for a beginning, but we wanted a wider range and more unsophisticated quarters. My Norwegian servant had already been sent on with the luggage up the fine valley which here falls into the Selbo Vand. I was assured that the Tydal had not been visited by Englishmen for several years. The accommodation was said to be too rough for ladies, but they protested against the assumption, and we started in a *stolkærre* and three *karjole* on the following day. The road is in the old-fashioned style, that is to say, like General Wade's roads in the Highlands, it goes over hill and dale instead of contouring them. This means finer scenery with diminished speed. At the second station where we changed horses, we noticed the head and skin of a freshly-killed elk, shot, as we were told, by a Swede who was hunting in the valley. A few miles farther on we encountered a cart with the huge carcase of another, the handiwork of the same man, and the farther we advanced the thicker grew the rumours of the prowess of this mysterious hunter. At each station we found that Dahl, the

"Tolk," had continued his way, and if we put our noses inside we concurred in his judgment. It was not till the late evening when we were approaching the watershed which separates Norway from Sweden, that we found him established at Lovöen, a group of farmhouses, roomy and clean, with homely folk, to whom the sight of English ladies was a revelation. The river, even up here a fine torrent, thirty yards wide, ran past the house. The wooded hills rose on either side six or seven hundred feet to bare tops. Higher peaks stood farther back. We dined off a *seven-pound* trout. This was not taken out of the stream, but netted in one of the numerous lakes which dot the woods. Subsequently ducks, not mallard, but a dark brown kind, were brought to us, which were got in the same way. This kind are rather tame, and when they find themselves enclosed in the circle of the net, instead of flying, dive under it and get their heads into the meshes. Except milk products we could get no supplies from the farm, but there were many reindeer in the woods, which, though apparently wild, are all owned by Lapps. We sent up to their camp, fifteen miles off, and the next day they brought down a three-year-old, which furnished us with the finest meat in the world for a fortnight.

Our rooms were large; all round the bedrooms stood numerous "marriage chests" of past generations, and a great variety of reindeer coats, *sheepfeldts*, or sheep-skin rugs, which serve as sheets, blankets, and counterpanes to the natives at all seasons, and other garments hung from the rafters. The beds in Norway are a difficulty; they are too short for most Englishmen, at least those of my inches, and are generally inhabited. We were independent of them, having brought calico bed-bags. These are no weight to carry, and when stuffed with dry hay and laid on the floor make excellent lying. If not thus provided, a couple of reindeer skins form a mattress which is both elastic and free from vermin.

We arranged with the various owners that we might hunt where we liked, and if we killed an elk we were to pay twenty *krone*, or about 22s., to whomsoever it might belong, besides the meat, reserving the skin and head for ourselves. We also sent for the usual hunter of reputation. He came, but would only consent to enter our service on condition of carrying his own rifle. I knew what that meant, and allowed him to depart. Thrown back on Tump and the light of nature, we made a poor hand of it. Our want of success was partly due to still weather, which is fatal to this kind of elk hunting. Repeatedly we found burning fresh tracks of elk which had doubtless been *skræmt* by us, but we failed even to catch a sight of elk. After this it began to snow, and continued to do so intermittently for three days. It was terribly wet work forcing one's way through the birch saplings, bowed down and tangled by the mass of snow, but one learns more of the habits of an animal when hunting in snow than at any other time.

We sometimes took an off day at the birds, and on one of these occasions one of those incidents occurred which are *pour rire* afterwards, but very unpleasant at the time. The ladies accompanied us, and two of them went home at mid-day. An hour later the third followed, receiving instructions to keep the wind on her left cheek

SKREMT.

until she reached the edge of the valley, whence she would see the farm below. When I reached home at seven she had not returned. Calling a hasty council, for there wanted but half an hour of sunset, we organised search parties in three directions, who were to fire guns at intervals, and to listen for the loud cow-horn, which was to be the signal when she was found or returned. Happily we had scarcely reached the trees when she appeared at the upper end of the clearing. She had lost her direction in a sharp snowstorm, and had finally struck the valley some miles above Lovöen. Here it was narrow and rugged, and there was no appearance of the green fields which she expected to see. At first she thought she had struck the wrong valley, and the farther she followed it the more strange and inhospitable it seemed. She sat down to consider, and at last came to the conclusion that the waterfall she heard below could be none other than one which she had seen some days before, four miles above Lovöen. This determination she fortunately adhered to, and though the intervening ground was very rough, she ultimately came in sight of the homestead. It was a small matter, but the dismay of feeling lost is sometimes no trifle even to a strong man. Fortunately the poor child kept her composure as long as it was necessary.

The topography of the upper plateaux of Norway and Sweden is very puzzling, as every ridge and hollow resembles the next, and the timber impedes a general view. I have known even natives completely at fault, and on one occasion in Jemtland even the *Scormand* of the beat, by mistaking one lake for another, led a member of my party *ten miles wrong*, an error which cost him four hours' walk in the dark, over some of the roughest ground in Europe. I have found that the best way to identify each hillside is to impress upon the memory the pattern made by the lighter foliage of the deciduous trees among the firs, and to find for each some fanciful resemblance, such as a cow's horn, a saucepan, or forked lightning.

In the meanwhile we kept hearing tantalising accounts of further successes of the Swede whom I have already mentioned. News of this kind travels fast in Norway. Once we sent in vain to seek him. A second messenger was more successful, and returned with the mysterious man, whom by this time we held in profound respect. John Wallan is a *Skoemand*, or lumberer, in Jemtland. He has a slim, clean-cut figure, an alert face, and the clear, light blue eyes of a Celt. His words are few and weighty. He also declined to leave his gun at home, but promised not to use it except to prevent the escape of an animal. This was a reasonable condition, as he received thirty *krone* from every man on whose land he killed an elk. Moreover, he said that he must not have more than one Englishman to accompany him at a time, and he evidently considered that we were about as much use in hunting as portmanteaus, and he did not want to have to carry more than one. John was the hero of numerous elk hunts, and could command his own terms. With him were his two dogs, "Peyas" and "Luft." These dogs were past masters in the art of loose hunting, and he had refused five hundred *krone*, or nearly £28, for the former. This may seem an exaggeration, but John had, by his aid, already killed five elk that year, each of which was worth fully £6. He was very particular not to allow his dogs to be handled. I have known him, after some one had stroked them, to take an aromatic wisp of spruce twigs and wipe

JOHN WALLAN WITH PEYAS AND LUFT.

them down, lest the elk should recognise the taint of man when the dog is baying round him.

I met him the next morning at the appointed rendezvous. The dogs were led until likely ground was reached.

Then they ranged about while we walked steadily on, only occasionally catching a glimpse of them. Nothing was seen in the morning, and at eleven we settled in a broken-down hay-hut for the long mid-day halt, made a fire, and tried to dry our wet clothes. It is quite as important for the loose hound hunter to lie by for the mid-day hours as in the more stealthy method of still hunting, because—so they say—if an elk is started from his couch he will not be bayed. In the afternoon we kept along a ridge, while the dogs hunted the birch wood below. Then we heard them find, but indistinctly, and after an exciting five minutes of intent listening, we made a circuit of the wood and found by the tracks that the dogs had run an elk down to the river, which he had crossed. They returned to us, as these dogs would not cross a heavy stream unless encouraged by their master.

Close to the hay-hut, where we had been lying for three hours, strange to say we found again, this time a solitary ox. He also went down to the river, we after him, as hard as we could run. Just before he reached it I caught an inspiriting sight of him, with the dogs at his heels, but too far off for a shot. Across the intervening bog he looked as big and as black as an elephant. As soon as he crossed the river the dogs returned to us, and I thought it was all over, but just then I saw him again beyond the river, crossing another opening three or four hundred yards off. As it seemed to be my last chance I sat down, and aiming well over his shoulder, tried the shot, but the bullet struck under him. Now at any rate he would make tracks, but, on the bare chance, we waded the river, and laid the dogs on again. To my surprise they quickly bayed again, a short distance beyond the spot where I had viewed him, and it would appear that he could not have noticed my shot. We approached at a run, and had got, as I should judge by the sound of the baying, within a hundred yards, when I trod on a stick, which broke with a loud crack. John looked round at me with a blank expression and said, "Now he will spring," and sure enough the sound ceased, for when an elk is going his hardest the dogs pursue in silence. Again we started at our best pace in the direction which they had taken, and in a few minutes a faint and distant bay drew us on again, but the elk knew that the dogs were not alone, and would not be stopped. All this time my companion, who carried no ounce of superfluous flesh, was going well within himself, while I began to labour like a water-logged boat. I shall not soon forget the suffering of the next forty minutes, but I felt it was now or never, and, buoyed up at intervals by the faint sound far ahead, I struggled on, now across open bogs which were soft but not springy, now through masses of tangle and clumps of trees, till my feet were like lead, and I was reduced at last to a walk. Now we find a harder piece of ground, as welcome as water in the desert, and by its help seem to get nearer to the retreating sound. But we are again approaching the river, and I am almost thankful when John says, "He will cross it again, and then it is all up." He does cross it, and the dogs return to us. We throw ourselves down, on our backs, on the bilberries, and gasp, while limbs stiffen rapidly. At last John remarks, "The *Elg* is *krank* too;" and indeed so ponderous a body is not easily conveyed over several miles of such ground. "Is it any good to cross the river again?"

"No, but we will try if you like." I do like, and we wade through once more, but have a difficulty with the dogs, who are as weary as ourselves, and plainly show their disappointment.

Luft climbs on to a rock in mid-stream, and whines pitifully. At last they are over, and we lay them on again. We are reduced to a painful walk, and they pick up a cold scent slowly. Suddenly they shoot ahead, and in two minutes have him again, with a savage chorus, and this time it does not move. He thought to have shaken them off, and stopped almost as soon as he crossed the river. "He has got still now," says John, "and won't start easily, but go softly." We steal up, pushing the fir branches aside. No broken sticks this time; we tread like cats through the interlacing boughs. I see a great gray shoulder and yellow horns. He stands up to the knees in a small tarn, with his head towards the dogs, who are dancing and barking on the bank above him. My arm waves like the arm of a semaphore, and I feel that I could not hit a house across the street. Oh for a rest! But John says, "Shoot through the branches or he will see you." As I fire he crashes out among the dogs, and my heart sinks, for surely I have missed him. But John claps me on the shoulder, and says, "Gud schut." "Do you think he is hit?" "Ja, sikker!" As we run round the lakelet there is a sweet sound of scrimmage beyond, and there lies a *rakker* ox, panting out his life, while the dogs rush in and tear mouthfuls of wiry hair from his back. A five-year-old bull, big enough to satisfy anybody! The shot was a bad one, and would not have served if he had been fresh. Such a run is a severe strain, and I could scarcely have managed the ten miles' tramp home if it had not been for the supreme sense of virtuous toil rewarded.

The next day we rode up—I could scarcely climb into the saddle—to gloat over the prize, photograph him, and bring him down. It took four horses fully loaded to do this, but the ground was unusually boggy. I have generally found sledges a better means of transport when the ground is soft. Great was the rejoicing in Ole's house, on whose " right " the elk had fallen, and his neighbours came in to congratulate him. This is not to be wondered at, for a full-grown elk carries enough meat to supply a family for the whole winter. It is generally minced up and made into sausages, which are hung on the rafters. In Sweden it is salted and smoked.

Two days later my son had another fine run, which was even longer than mine, but had a less fortunate result. I was myself in the woods at no great distance, and by a great piece of luck had heard the baying, and came in for the latter part of the run. The elk was finally coursed out of the woods, and away into the high fjeld, where the dogs bayed him among the rocks—a wild scene. He was galloped to a standstill, and appeared to be " our meat," but just as John and Cyril got within range he slowly rounded a corner. Thinking he would get a standing shot on the other side of it, Cyril reserved his fire ; when the corner was reached the animal had rounded another, and — we never saw him again. Whether, like St. Hubert's stag, he vanished when the fun was over, or had had time to get his wind—the downhill track helping him—I know not ; but the dogs returned almost immediately with a reproachful expression, which plainly said, " Why didn't you shoot?" and the ground being hard we failed to strike the track again. There was wailing and grief that night, but a few days later Cyril got a bull almost without the trouble of a run at all.

This kind of failure annoyed John extremely. It was not so much the loss of his commission as the discouragement of his dogs that he minded. On one occasion, but this was in the following year, we were creeping up in Indian file to a bay by Peyas. Gerald, who was leading, turned round and whispered to me, "A cow and calf." I passed the word on to John, and I never saw so much strong language expressed in silent pantomime. He gave us to understand that our feelings were of no importance at all, but that if Peyas were disappointed he would leave our service and go home. So the poor calf was left motherless; but I ought to qualify that by saying that he was as large as a small horse, and well able to take care of himself. But of all the dogs which I knew it was Skyt who did the cleverest thing. Gerald, who had outrun his Norwegian companion, got up to Skyt's bay in time to fire a snap shot. The result he could not see, but before long the dog again stopped the animal with the usual noisy demonstrations. Presently there was silence, and instead of continuing to bay, as his nature and training would direct, he returned and said, as plainly as dog language could, "It's all right; come along." The dog had found that the shot had taken effect, and, himself unheld, with slow and catlike steps, led Gerald to where the wounded elk was standing.

In very still weather hunting by the ordinary methods is useless. There is then nothing for it but to try driving if any of the ground lends itself to that course of proceeding. I have done it myself, but it is dull work—so dull that one of my companions carried a French novel to relieve the tedium, with the result here depicted. It is only

ERNEST IS STALKED.

fair to say that Ernest, who is smart at a "back-hander," dropped the animal after all. The important point is not to relax attention till the beaters actually appear, as elk under these circumstances are very suspicious, and keep but little ahead of the men. The following letter from one of my Swedish chums, who is experienced at this, as well as all other forms of elk hunting, gives a good idea of the kind of thing :—"C—— and I rowed down Bergsjo in the finest 'elking' weather, *i.e.* with half a gale at our backs, but before reaching our destination it suddenly fell to a calm. We had no alternative but to attempt a drive. There is a certain fjeld there which favoured that method, having a wide lake at its foot, and steep ground above. I sent my two men to the end of this fjeld with orders to return along the wooded slope with such breeze as there was at their backs. C—— and I, after careful search, selected two likely spots as 'passes.' I placed him high up, near to where the forest ceased, as driven elk generally keep as high up as they can without leaving covert, while I took up a post lower down, whence I could command a long bog which crossed the drive. After sitting immovable for an hour and a half we began to hear the men, and shortly afterwards the cracking of a dead stick broke the stillness. I hoped for bear, for it was a likely spot to tempt Bruin. Then a shot from C——'s rifle, followed by the headlong rush of a heavy body through the timber. I waited till the men came up, as I make a rule never to leave my post until the drive is over, as a chance may often present itself at the last moment. Then I joined my companion, and I quickly perceived by the tracks that the animal was hard hit. C—— and the two men with their two dogs hastened to follow on the line, rather too quickly as it turned out. I had handed my rifle to one of them, as my running days are over, and I remained behind with old Don, every hair on whose body stood on end. He would have given his tail to be allowed to go. As I quietly followed, I presently discovered that they had overrun the track of the beast in their haste. The latter had turned short off to the right towards the lake. As I looked in that direction I perceived, about thirty yards off, a grand pair of horns showing above the trunk of a fallen tree. At the same moment the elk must have discovered my presence, or noticed that he was discovered, and sprang to his legs, showing me a broadside of the largest dimensions. Without pausing he plunged down the betangled slope and disappeared. A minute or two later the party of pursuit, having perceived their mistake, returned in hot haste, and I led them on to the true line. Down through trunks, rotting trees, roots and stones they stumbled and ran, for there was no time to lose. If the animal should gain the lake he would certainly cross it. They had scarcely left me when I thought Don might stop him before he took the water, so I let the old dog have his pleasure. Away he went like a streak of lightning, and presently I heard him and the two elk hounds lift up their voices, and a few minutes later a double shot. Scrambling down the encumbered slope I emerged on the shore of the lake. C—— and the two men were sitting on a fallen tree, all three blowing like whales. The elk lay about thirty yards from the shore, submerged, all but one of his sides and part of a horn. On this island the three dogs were standing, and making the hair fly right and left, while now and again one or other got pushed off into the water and scrambled up again. Tiring of this at length they sat down side by side facing me, and occasionally grinning a growl at each other, for the space was too limited for a fight. Nothing would induce the elk hounds to leave their fairly-earned quarry, and Don, usually so tractable, was too jealous to obey my summons."

While in Tydal I was as near making an end as I have ever been. The Norwegian ponies have an exhilarating habit of galloping down the short, steep hills which are so frequent on their roads. At the foot of one of these the road was raised on a river wall, twenty feet high, without any protection at the edge. The pony was going full gallop to gain an impetus for the ascent, and I had a strong pull on his head, when one of the reins—a plain rope in these less-frequented valleys—came away from the bit. In an instant we were off the road, but happily on the bank side; it was the near rein which had given. If it had been the other, we must inevitably have gone over on to the rocks, and no one would ever have known how it had happened.

From Tydal we proceeded to the neighbourhood of Levanger. This expedition proved a complete failure, and I only mention it as a warning to others. My obsequious landlord and his too sumptuous abode inspired me with distrust from the first. His house was splendid, but in the matter of elk ground he had been extremely economical, and the little he had secured for me was divided into two portions, while on the best part of it a gang of woodmen were at work. I don't think he meant to be dishonest, but he had never seen an elk, and apparently thought they lived like rabbits in stone walls or haycocks. The next year I went to Jemtland, in Sweden, and with more experience our bag was a much larger one. Even an elk is, however, easily missed, and as this chapter is a truthful record, I will confine the remainder of it to showing how this may be done.

The first incident of the year was that one of my party stalked and shot a reindeer, as we were hard up for meat. The two Norwegians who were with us were much shocked at this high-handed proceeding, and sat aloof on the top of the hill, as if we had shot Farmer Giles's cow, while we proceeded with the grallock. I sent a message to the Lapps, to whom the animal presumably belonged, and paid them about half as much again as it was worth.

On the opening day of the season I was fortunate enough to kill a bull elk, and the following morning called upon an English gentleman who was fishing a neighbouring river, to leave him a portion of the meat. He asked me to join him in driving a certain large wooded island of which he had the shooting in the middle of the lake of Ann. I declined his invitation, as I had undertaken to cross the lake, a row of about nine miles, and ascertain if there was any good grouse ground on the farther side. Returning in the evening, the course took my boat quite close to the island. As we approached a long tongue of it, which projected towards the mainland, I saw an elk splash through the shallow water towards this promontory. Thinking it was only a cow, I took no steps, but lay to to see it take the water, as its evident intention was to cross to the mainland, and drawing up near the point, we waited. In a few seconds there plunged into the lake, not a cow, but an old bull, with a very fine head. Now, having refused my friend's invitation, I hesitated for a moment or two what I ought to do, but my scruples did not last long, and I told the boatman to bend to his oars. Tump,

A RACE FOR LIFE.

who was my companion for the day, was violently excited, and I had to hold him into the boat with one hand lest he should jump overboard and be drowned by his chain, while with the other I crammed bullet cartridges into my gun. The elk had about two hundred and fifty yards to swim, and I assumed that we should overhaul him with ease. The elk is, however, one of the finest of swimmers, and readily takes to the water, even when not pursued. This one, the moment he realised that it was a race for life, put on a spurt which astonished me. Every stroke drove his great head and shoulders far out of the water, which seemed to hiss past him as he pounded through it like an ocean steamer. By the time he was halfway across I saw that the race was a hopeless one as far as I was concerned, and that it was now or never if I was going to shoot at all. The mark which he offered was so large that I made pretty sure of hitting it at the eighty or ninety yards' distance which he had now put between us. I stood up to shoot, and the shot looked easy, but these light "prams," as they call the lake boats, are far from steady, and at this point we felt the full force of the south wind which blew up a five-mile reach, and drove big waves before it into the narrow sound. The boat rolled and swayed with it, and the muzzle of my rifle dipped and rose like the yard-arm of a ship, now pointing at the sky and now at the water. In vain I tried to steady myself. My first bullet skimmed just over his neck, my second must have been very near, judging by the spasmodic bound he gave, jerking his body half out of the water. Before I could load again he touched *terra firma*, and in a cloud of spray raced ashore. I just got in my cartridges in time to give him a parting double, but I think they were even wilder than the first. We landed, and I laid Tump on. He raced down the island, for it was not the mainland, but was divided from it by another much narrower channel, and stood barking at the other end where the elk had again taken the water. It was pretty clear that I had not hurt him. This was one of those calamities which live by a man all his days, and revisit him in his dreams. Mr. J—— had been lying in wait for this shot all day, and here was I, who had neither toiled nor spun, had dropped in in the very nick of time, got the shot and missed it. I humbled myself before him, and was forgiven.

These large lakes are very convenient as highways for reaching distant parts of the ground, but when the wind is strong it is sometimes impossible for a boat to make way against it. I well remember one wet and stormy day, when for this reason we had to tramp back overland, and when the river was at length reached, wholly failed to make ourselves heard in the farm on the opposite bank. Even rifle shots produced no effect, till we took to shooting *at the house itself*, and a well-planted bullet on the stone chimney brought a frightened face to the door.

A few days after the failure on the lake the agony was still more excruciatingly piled up. Fancy an eager youth panting with a long run. He reaches the edge of a steep bluff and can hear the bay at some distance. But at this moment four other elk cross an opening below, and he proceeds to stalk them. He gets within two hundred yards of the ox, standing by himself, and listening intently to the distant bay of the dog. The youth, fearful of losing the shot if he tries to get nearer, fires and misses. Strange to say the elk *never stirs*! The sportsman thereupon stalks up to within eighty yards and again misses! He then follows the lot which the dog is still baying, reaches them in half an hour, has a steady shot at forty yards at the cow (the ox had left them), and misses! After this it would seem about time to go home. Rowing down one of the lakes they drag the boat across a small portage to another. When they come in sight of it they see a large ox swimming from one promontory to another, and about two hundred yards off. Three shots, each nearer than the other, but none quite near enough! Hoping to get a better chance as the animal lands, Infelix waits, but the elk swims behind a point of rock and lands at his leisure out of sight!

I will draw a veil over the sufferings of the actors in this tragedy, and I think I had better stop there.

HAZEL-GROUSE.

VI

THE FATHER OF ALL THE GOATS

It was not the search for forgotten sites or treasures of marble, a passion which tempts so many learned and enterprising men to visit Asia Minor, but the desire to hunt a rock-haunting ibex, dwelling on certain mountain ranges in that country, which took me there with two companions. Once only during the month which we spent in those regions did we leave this absorbing pursuit to pay a duty visit to the lime-laden waters, pink and white terraces, and earthquake-riven basilicas of the ancient baths of Hierapolis.

The *Capra ægagrus* or *Pasang* is believed by naturalists to have deserved the title with which I have headed this article beyond any other wild type of goat. Mentioned by Homer[1] as being abundant in the Ægæan Islands, in

---

[1] Ὑλήεσσ᾽· ἐν δ᾽ αἶγες ἀπειρέσιαι γεγάασιν
ἄγριαι· οὐ μὲν γὰρ πάτος ἀνθρώπων ἀπερύκει
οὐδέ μιν εἰσοιχνεῦσι κυνηγέται.
                                                 Odyssey 9. 118.

"A woody island, and on it are produced countless wild goats; for no track of man scares them away, nor do hunters come there."

some of which it still exists, its habitat ranges at the present day from the Ægean Sea, through Asia Minor and Persia, into Afghanistan, and therefore in close proximity to the most forward civilisations of ancient times. It is thus not surprising that the various breeds of tame goat, however modified by man, should in many respects "favour," as they say in the eastern counties, this ancestry. The scimitar horn curving over the back, the black shoulder-

And again—

> τόξον ἔϋξοον ἰξάλου αἰγὸς
> ἀγρίου, ὅν ῥά ποτ' αὐτὸς ὑπὸ στέρνοιο τυχήσας
> πέτρης ἐκβαίνοντα δεδεγμένος ἐν προδοκῇσι
> βεβλήκει πρὸς στῆθος . . .
> τοῦ κέρα ἐκ κεφαλῆς ἑκκαιδεκάδωρα πεφύκει.
>
> Iliad 4. 105.

"His polished bow, fashioned of the horns of a lusty wild he-goat, whom once on a time Pandarus himself, having waited ambushed for his coming out from the rocks, hit beneath the breast, and pierced in the chest . . . The horns from off his head had grown sixteen palms long." If the Bard did not exaggerate that must have been a patriarch indeed—48 inches! But Mr. Lydekker, who is an authority on the subject, supports him. He says: "In the male the horns may attain a length of some 48 inches measured along the curve; but a specimen is recorded with a length of 52½ inches."

The following throws some light on the method of hunting:

> Ὦρσαν δὲ νύμφαι κοῦραι Διὸς αἰγιόχοιο
> αἶγας ὀρεσκῴους, ἵνα δειπνήσειαν ἑταῖροι.
> αὐτίκα καμπύλα τόξα καὶ αἰγανέας δολιχαύλους
> εἰλόμεθ' ἐκ νηῶν, διὰ δὲ τρίχα κοσμηθέντες
> βάλλομεν· αἶψα δ' ἔδωκε θεὸς μενοεικέα θήρην.
> νῆες μέν μοι ἕποντο δυώδεκα, ἐς δὲ ἑκάστην
> ἐννέα λάγχανον αἶγες· ἐμοὶ δὲ δέκ' ἔξελον οἶῳ.
>
> Odyssey 9. 154.

"And the nymphs, daughters of Ægis-bearing Zeus, roused the wild goats of the mountains, to furnish dinner for my mates. Straightway we took us from the ships bended bows and long-socketed hunting spears; and, ordered in three companies, we shot, and speedily Heaven gave us game enough to our mind. Twelve ships there were that followed me, and to each there fell by lot nine goats. But for myself alone I chose out ten."

stripe of the old males, the beard, not worn by all species of ibex, are its most distinguishing characteristics. The *bezoar stone*—to which has been long attributed many healing properties, but especially as an antidote to poison—is found in the stomach of this animal.

As an old Turk put it to me, "Why do you come all the way from England to shoot a little goat not worth two medjids?" The truest answer would perhaps be that the old "billy" of the species, who was at that time caged at the Zoo, was a particular friend of mine. His high-bred appearance and pugnacious habits, and the fact that he was occasionally, when in his tantrums, chained up to avoid his damaging attacks on his prison—damaging, that is, to his own handsome head—perhaps first suggested that he was a gentleman of character whose acquaintance it was desirable to make. Be that as it may, a hunting expedition to obtain this goat had long been among my keenly-desired projects.

By dint of pertinacious inquiry from the few travellers who have sought out the haunts of the animal, I had an accurate general knowledge of the ranges where he must be sought. But this second-hand learning would not have sufficed if I had not been assisted on the spot. With such zeal did Her Majesty's vigorous representative at Smyrna second my projects, that one would have thought my success to be of international importance. Unfortunately for the extent of my bag, the limits of my absence from England—a rigid six weeks—precluded me from reaching the best ground, which is the chain of the Taurus forming the rock-bound southern coast of Asia Minor. Nearly a fortnight more of my scanty time would have been consumed in the

THE SALT LAKE FROM MAIMUN DAGH.

to and fro of this journey, and the cholera creeping up that
coast, and the quarantine which might follow in its
track, introduced an element of uncertain delay which I
could not afford to risk. I had, therefore, to aim at the
second best, which I knew to be a certain find. This was
called the "Maimun Dagh" or Monkey Mountain, a small
but isolated range on the Aidin railway, and about two
hundred miles from the coast. I hoped that, once on the
spot, I should be able to hear of alternative ranges inhabited by this goat, but, except to a very limited extent,
this did not prove to be so.

The railway kings at Smyrna can do most things that
they wish, and, thanks to their friendly co-operation, we
reached Chardak, a station close to one end of the mountain, five minutes under the week from London, travelling
viâ Athens; and the return journey by Constantinople was
accomplished almost exactly in the same time. Here we
were at one end of a precipitous range seven or eight miles
in length. These cliffs rose abruptly from the plain to a height
of about fifteen hundred feet, and at their base we pitched our
camp. An angle in the rocks made an excellent fireplace,
and a little cave a convenient cellar where we kept our
supply of water. This had to be brought to us daily from
the nearest village, five miles off, for the mountain was, at
the time of our visit, waterless. In front, a narrow strip
of plain divided us from the basin of a great salt lake ten
miles long and five miles broad; or rather an expanse of
white salt slime, for as we saw it, at the end of a long
drought, only a fraction of its surface was covered with
water, and that, whatever the weather on the mountain,
was nearly always as still as glass, reflecting the white cliffs

of the "Suut Dagh" or Milk Mountain, three leagues away. If there came a shower of rain, which happened later, it lay in a thin sheet of water over the whole area and transformed it for the time into the semblance of a bank-full lake.

In three places at the edge were swamps, where a scanty supply of undrinkable water oozed from the base of the mountain and was trodden into mud. For along this strip of plain was carried not only the newly-opened railway, but an important caravan route, and trains of camels, donkeys, and bullock-carts with solid wooden wheels were continually passing. The harsh "klonk-klonk" of innumerable wild geese, and the plaintive notes of curlew and plover, constantly arose from these swamps, and to them also must have come the ibex for their only drinking place, for the whole face of the mountain was as dry as a captain's biscuit. On one occasion one of our followers saw some drinking there in broad daylight. At sunrise a faint unpleasant odour always came up from these marshes, suggesting a liberal use of quinine; but we were assured that at this elevation—between two thousand and three thousand feet—we need not fear fever. While pitching our camp, we were engaged in clearing the projecting stones from the sites of the tents. One of my followers was busy over a particularly obstinate one with his heavy iron-shod alpenstock, and at length turned up, with much labour, a large living tortoise, which had buried itself there for the winter. It lay on its back, meekly kicking its legs in the air, while the Frenchman blushed up to the roots of his hair with surprise and disgust. Above, on the higher rocks, were a great number of eagles and vultures. On one occasion

I counted nine circling close to me, and high above them a great crane wheeling in similar fashion, with his long legs sticking out behind as the herons at home are wont to carry theirs. The vultures had a curious habit of diving straight into deep fissures in the cliffs and disappearing

THE GRIFFON VULTURE.

with a clumsy plunge of wings. Then they would waddle to the outer edge and stretch out their cadaverous white necks. These holes in the cliffs are very conspicuous landmarks from afar, owing to the profuse way in which the bird whitewashes his doorstep and the wall of rock below. Great numbers of partridges lived on the lower cliffs. During the heat of the day they lay close, and were perfectly silent; but about an hour before sunset they would all wake suddenly into life, as if at a given signal, and begin strutting and talking, so that you might think it was No. 15 Committee-room.

Besides our three selves, my party comprised Celestin, my companion on many such trips, who has appeared before in these pages, and Benjamin—both hailing from the Pyrenees. Our following, as happens on these trips, was rather a large one, and the commissariat required some foresight and generalship, for the country does not produce much that is acceptable to European palates.

Our cook, who was distinguished by the title of *Hadji*, having once visited Mecca, seemed to think that all further effort in life was unnecessary, and that Providence would send whatever it was fated that we should receive; but his manners, I must say, were beautiful, and he had a sweet, responsive smile. Omar, a fine young Turk from the neighbouring village, knew something about hunting, and I got very fond of him, though our communications were confined to dumb-crambo. During the whole trip I only encountered one Turk whose behaviour was rough. Indeed, he was a Yuruk. The genuine Turk has nearly always the manners of a courtier. This exception was Mellut, another hunter of repute from Chardak, whom we employed for certain drives, and whose whole manner expressed the rooted opinion that dogs of Christians were only fit to act as "stops" for the likes of him; but even he softened to the diplomatic flatteries of Findlay, who addressed him constantly as "my pet lamb," "my sucking-dove." My preconceived notions of Christian and Turk received a rude shock. Up here there were scarcely any native Christians, but nearer the coast they abounded. A more villainous-looking lot I never saw, but it was probably only the scum that gathered at the railway stations, and one should not generalise in this way.

But I have still to describe the most important member of my staff. I had heard before my arrival that a "retired brigand" had been secured for our service and protection.

This description was literally true, but we had no reason to regret the selection. We picked up old "Bouba" at a station on our journey inland; and so true to the character was his appearance and dress, including the embroidered and sleeveless cloak that hung down his shoulders, that as the

BOUBA.

train drew along the platform we "spotted" him instantly among the crowd, most of the items of which could have played the stage-villain at a moment's notice. Whatever Bouba's crimes may have been—and they would certainly have filled a book—since his wind got short, and for other reasons, he had become a reformed if not a repentant character. We found him a solid and reliable person, and good company withal. A popular favourite throughout that country, his moral weight would certainly carry him in at the head of the poll if there were a School Board election. I never found out his real name—" Bouba" means father, and is simply a familiar term of affection, much as you say "Grand Old Man." He would sit all day smoking cigarettes in the tent, with a benign smile on his face, but any little emergency galvanised the phlegmatic *cavass* into an energetic leader of men, whose word was law with high and low, and he never failed us. His Martini rifle was rarely laid aside, and he would without doubt have used it in our behalf if necessary. It would have taken him some time to use up all his cartridges, which he carried in an enormous belt right round his rather stout person.

When he got to know us pretty well I drew his story from him one night, with the assistance of the Greek stationmaster. He told it in a matter-of-fact style, without apparent regret, and at the same time without affectation or "side." It was afterwards confirmed by people of authority; besides, I never knew him to tell a lie. Very likely he minimised his little escapades.

"Why did you take to the mountains, Bouba?" He gave a fat chuckle. "It was because of a woman. There was a girl that I was intimate with—I was very fond of her. A man came and took her away. I went after him to his house and struck him." (He did not say what he struck him with, but I believe that, as a matter of fact, he shot him at sight.) "Two days afterwards he happened to die. Then the authorities tried to catch me, but I was always escaping out of the back-door and coming back at night. So when they found they could not catch me they put my father in prison, and then my brother; and I thought I had better go quite away. I was for one year by myself about the mountains, picking up what I could get. I could not at first find any companions that were any good for that sort of work. Then came the time for the conscription. Many ran away to escape being drawn, so I got some good men. There were nine of us, and I was captain, but we had no guns. There was a forest with saw-mills. One of the mill-owners who was enemy to the other told me that this one had many rifles. We went to his house one night and demanded them. He said he had not got any. Then we made him sign a bond to procure them; and as the first mill-owner had told us wrongly, we compelled him to join in the bond—so it was quite fair to both. We got those rifles all right, and cartridges. I was a brigand eight years. I never killed any one for money; but if any one would not stop, or if he was going to give information to the authorities, of course we had to kill him. If one of us were wounded we did our best to carry him off, but if this were impossible"—here he made a significant gesture across his throat. "But we all knew that was necessary. It would never do to leave a wounded man to fall into the hands of the soldiers. He might betray the rest of us. Once a man asked us all to his house to supper. Then he sent to the Governor to say that Bouba's party were there; but we heard a noise and got away. A fortnight afterwards we came back and slit his nose and ears." (This he said in a tone of righteous indignation, as if he would evidently like to do it again.) "We used to stop merchants and camel-drivers, and the villagers gave us what we wanted because they were afraid. If a person had not anything we let him go."

" What was the best catch you ever made ? "

He grinned at this, and after thinking a bit, said : " We once stopped the Imperial Post and got £7000. Then they sent a large number of soldiers after us. There was another band of brigands—eleven of them. We helped one another, but did not generally act together ; but this time we all combined. The soldiers came up, but we were behind rocks. We killed twenty-five of them, and not one of us was touched. We afterwards killed seven more." For having won this victory he evidently considered that he had deserved well of his country. " But," I said, " they surely couldn't have tried very hard to get hold of you ! " " Well, perhaps not always. I used to send money to the big officials, but the sergeants and people like that I did not care for. When we ran short of cartridges for the Martinis I sent £50 to a colonel in the army whom I knew, and he sent me a quantity of army cartridges."

" When the Government found they could not catch us, they offered a free pardon to all who would come in, and I gave myself up and was pardoned. I afterwards helped to hunt down the other brigands. Two of my companions were killed at this time ; others died, and some are still alive. After this another Governor was appointed, and because I would not give him money he put me in prison and charged me with slitting a man's nose and other things. I was in prison thirteen months, while the Governor was trying to get a case against me. He found a person without a nose, but the man would not give evidence against me. He said he did not know how it had been slit, but he supposed he had been born so. This was because I had sent him a large sum." Here the stationmaster put in the following original observation: "In this country the man who is rich is innocent like one pigeon." "At last Mr. P—— got me out. It was all folly, but I should never have gone to the mountains but for that woman." The gentleman mentioned was connected with the Ottoman Railway. Bouba had made himself extremely useful to this Company, and its engineers, in making their extension, owed much to his influence. In fact, he is *caress* to the chief engineer now, and a highly-respected character. No one would hesitate to trust him with a hundred pounds or any other sum, and a more suitable *chaperon* for young ladies could not be found. That is the story as he told it to us, and I have no doubt it is in the main true.

There does not appear to be any brigandage in that part of the country now, though the Agha of the village assured us, with undoubting faith, that there was a brigand about, whom no bullet could penetrate. This story had a foundation in fact, as we afterwards discovered, but it is too commonplace to be worthy of narration.

Given a broken cliff, scarcely any part of which was more than an hour's walk from our camp—for the goats inhabited only the steep side of the mountain—it will be thought that the task of securing an adequate number of specimens was an easy one; but, as my Pyrenean hunter, in whose company I have cut to pieces many pairs of boots, put it, after two or three days' experience, "Le coquin est rusé comme le diable!" The excellent eyes and ears with which the creature is endowed would not, however, have saved him from our scientific approaches if he had not been assisted by surrounding conditions. Not only are these rocks cut up into innumerable clefts and ravines, but they are covered by a thin forest of stone pines, noble trees of a pale green colour, not mean and disbranched like those of Italy, but driving great wedges of root into the rocks, and spreading like Scotch firs into lofty and massive trees of varied outline. Between them a shorter and denser growth of cypress and deciduous barberry, now dying off in scarlet and orange. This covert, though not quite continuous, made hiding for the ibex very easy. Nor was this all. The rock is a kind of pudding-stone, and the round embedded pebbles constantly work out and lie in unstable banks, wherever the angle of solid rock admits of it. The least touch, and down they clatter, starting others. During the first fortnight the drought and heat were excessive. This not only drove the animals to the innermost recesses for coolness, but made the stones more resonant; and the air being dead still, the least noise travelled far. Even the fallen oak-leaves[1] were so crisp and dry that they crackled like parchment. Like all animals that live in good covert, these goats have great confidence in its protection, and we saw them more often near the foot of the cliff, within hearing of the drovers on the highway, than at a higher elevation. The best which I secured I killed within easy shouting distance of the railway.

But this confidence is accompanied by exceeding watchfulness, and their natural alertness is indefinitely increased by the constant harrying of the natives. The

[1] According to Herodotus, "The Phocians were made aware of the approach of the Persians on the mountain-path to Thermopylae by the noise of the oak-leaves as they were trampled by the soldiers in the stillness of dawn."

bands, consisting of from four to ten almost always, according to our observation, posted a sentinel, and more than one promising stalk was spoilt by this inconvenient precaution, the sentinel posted above having been previously invisible to us. On one occasion one of my companions observed a very complete system of reliefs. Each member of the band took its turn on a commanding rock for about ten minutes by the watch, standing immovable while the others fed below. At the end of that time he would go down, and another instantly mounted to the coign of vantage and took his place; but the most remarkable part of it was that the turns seemed to be taken in order of seniority, beginning with the kids, followed by the ewes and young rams — the oldest patriarch, who had by that time finished his meal, being last of all; but he shirked his duties, for he distinctly took a postprandial nap. Another trick of theirs which I twice observed old *solitary* males to be guilty of, was, if they saw, or thought they saw, anything suspicious, to mount a prominent watch-tower, and, after a note or two of alarm and warning—a kind of cough which might spell the letters b-u-r-r-up rapidly repeated—calmly lie down and await events. Woe betide the hunter who, lulled into hope, then attempted a scientific stalk, for his labour would be surely wasted. I remember once to have nearly circumvented a buck chamois who thus flouted me. He saw the tops of our caps against a patch of snow before we saw him, and bounded away, but stood three hundred yards off whistling. Then he lay down, still whistling and watching. The fatal thing would have been to withdraw. It was necessary to give him something to look at. Leaving

THE CAPRA ÆGAGRUS.

my hunter where he was, with instructions to keep his cap gently moving, I drew back with infinite precaution; then, making a detour, got within easy distance of my friend, still lying there and whistling, crept into a beautiful position, and—missed him clean!

But to return to our goats. The only method of hunting them practised by the inhabitants is to drive them to certain posts occupied by the guns; but though we were not above trying this and every method, and did stoop to conquer in this way when we got tired of the other, it is not interesting, and the more crafty individuals, especially the old rams, will not be driven. We preferred stalking, and did so with great perseverance, and, for the reasons given, with singularly little result—at least at first. The best chance was during the two hours following sunrise, and a similar period before sunset. We had therefore to be astir early, and the camp-fire shone red before we returned. The telescopes were in continual use during the day, though, as is the case in all timbered countries, I found a powerful opera-glass often more effective for spying corries where it was all-important not to show over the sky-line. Notwithstanding the facilities for hiding, our industry with the glasses was rewarded by finding the animals almost daily, but the conditions above described generally defeated the stalk. That is to say, when we reached the spot the goats had moved, and even a slight change of position on such ground made picking them up again before we were ourselves spotted by the quarry exceedingly chance work. In the end I thought that what the American *still hunters* call "sitting on a log"—in other words, lying *perdu* in a likely place—probably the most effective means; but for that I had not the patience.

Almost the best chance I had came in my way the first evening. We saw a small herd feeding near the base of the cliff, with some good bucks in it, and got down to the rocks above them in the last twenty minutes of daylight. Arrived within shooting distance, we could see a female and two kids feeding among the trees nearly perpendicularly below us, and were peering down the openings to try and make out the bucks, when one of the kids began to show signs of uneasiness. Perhaps it was the cry of some partridge; more probably the little beast was sharper of eye than I gave him credit for, and the setting sun was shining full upon us. Then they began to move off, and for a moment I saw the bucks, distinguishable by their size and darker colour. I had my bead on one of them, but the shot was long and the light in my eyes. Surely, I said to myself, they won't believe that youngster. Hoping they would stop, and that I should better my position, I withheld my fire. They did stop about three hundred yards off and fed again, but when we arrived near the spot they had disappeared, and, the light fading, we gave them up. That was a fair sample of our experience. I did not get another chance for a week.

Day after day we basked, and sometimes gasped, in the heat, climbed and tumbled on the loose stones or toiled with the glass, the sweet aroma of the pines filling our nostrils. I should be sorry to make the reader as weary as, to tell the honest truth, we became of "Maimun Dagh," and I will confine my narrative to a single day, the most fortunate which I had.

I had heard that some of the railway officials were going to have a drive, so I went up early and posted myself at a high elevation where I could command a good deal of the cliff. There I spied a band of four, comprising two small bucks. They were quite quiet, and lay down in a good place, and I got quickly within fifty yards of one of the bucks. He went off with the rest at the shot, and Celestin, who followed what he thought was the track, could find no trace of blood, and declared that I had missed. As the shot was a perfectly easy one I could not think of any excuse to account for it. In a very depressed condition we climbed up to another high point and stayed there some hours watching. At last we saw two ibex coming away from the drive, and climbed down quickly on the chance of cutting them off; and now a wonderful piece of luck, the only one that fell to my lot on this trip, happened. While sitting and waiting I looked round and found we had returned to almost the identical spot of my first stalk. At that moment I heard stones rolling below, and, looking over the edge, saw my beast of the morning rolling over and over, quite dead. It was scarcely a score of yards from where I had lost sight of him. He appeared to have been dead some time, and it was the most extraordinary chance which led us back to the identical spot at the fortunate moment when his body rolled down, as we should never have seen him except for the movement of the stones attracting our attention.

The beaters now began another drive the reverse way, and across the ground where we were. We lay low and let the men pass us, which of course they did without seeing us, then got on to a prominent rock to see what would happen—in fact, "stayed back for the rabbits." As I expected, the ibex kept coming back. It was curious to see them sneaking out of groves close to which a man had just passed. They knew perfectly well what was up. First came three within shot of me, but they were all small; then a female and a little one; then two goodish bucks with others, very low down. These last we were fortunately able to keep in view, and saw them lie down.

We got down and found a good place for a shot, whence I could see the biggest. It was a longish shot, but I was very steady. However, off he went like lightning, and Celestin again declared I had missed, neither could we find any blood. I could not see how many went away when they crossed the next ridge, but I noticed that they were a long time arriving there, as though something had delayed them. To this circumstance I attached importance, as wild animals always stop and look back if one of their number is missing; so we followed on their line. There was a little hollow behind some rocks below me, which I thought worth climbing down to explore. As I peered into it my beast sprang away through the trees. I could only see a pair of legs, but of course I knew he must be badly wounded. Then we found—where the poor beast had stood and stamped the ground—another sign of a wounded animal. A few yards farther there were spots of blood, and thenceforward we followed the track with extreme care. At last I saw him lying behind a bush. He sprang away again, but that time I was able to give him a disabling shot as he ran.

These ibex are of a light brown colour, the males being rather darker than the females; but the oldest males

A LIKELY SPOT.

undergo a complete change in appearance, becoming light gray with a clearly-defined black shoulder-stripe, which gives them a very smart appearance. It is a sight to stir the heart of a hunter to see such a one sunning himself on some tower of rock, and, by way of morning exercise, bending his head to the ground and driving his sword-like black horns into some bush, of which he " makes hay " in about two minutes. I only once got a chance at one of these grand old " billies," and that I muddled. We had taken refuge from a sharp shower, in a cave, or rather shelf on the cliff, protected by a long overhanging rock. The rain drifted in, and Celestin carried my rifle to one end where it was more sheltered. We made a fire at the other end, and I was sitting over it with my back to the view, when, with a fixed stare, Omar pointed with his finger over my shoulder. There, about a hundred yards off, was a splendid male ibex such as I have described, with black horns which curved back nearly to his tail. There are not more than two or three like that on the mountain. He was quite unsuspicious, and calmly moving down the rocks, on account of the bad weather I suppose. Risking discovery, I crept to the place where my rifle lay. Two trees grew across that end of the opening, and I could not shoot from there. Back I crawled, and sat down for the shot. He was slowly stalking down the rocks, but still within easy range. I levelled my piece, but at that moment a gust of wind blew the flame and smoke across my line of sight, and I could see nothing. The next instant he was round a rock and gone. I nearly turned sick with desperation. Of course we followed and tried to find him again—an all but hopeless task in the complications of this hill. In the course of the search we got wet through, and in trying to dry my coat over the fire Celestin burned the back of it—my best "go-to-meeting" one, as it happened; but I would have given twenty coats to get that beast.

That was not the only piece of bad luck which I had—far from it. Once in a drive I was posted on the edge of a ravine; there were eddies of wind about this ravine, and in the middle of the drive a puff in my back warned me that if I stayed where I was I might spoil sport. I therefore withdrew to a less exposed post a hundred yards behind. I had scarcely settled there, when two capital males came and stood within fifty yards of my first position. It was still a possible shot, but a long one, and intervening trees now made it necessary to shoot quickly or not at all.

The cartridge missed fire. There was no time to change it, as they were just moving, but, hastily cocking the rifle, I tried the same cartridge again. That time it went, but wide of the mark—a miss, but excusable under the circumstances. They went up to Findlay, who got them both, a capital right and left. These were the best two we got, and I fear I was envious.

The Turks are very excitable when they see game, and should never be allowed to remain near you at your post if it can be avoided. One who accompanied a member of my party to his post, and who could not be persuaded to take his departure, rose in his place on seeing ibex approaching, and began frantically gesticulating and pulling at the Effendi's sleeve and pointing out the game which that sportsman had perceived long before. Naturally the goats refused to come any nearer, and, when they turned and fled, this maniac began yelling at the top of his voice.

The ibex were not the only animals that inhabited this mountain. On one occasion a large yellowish creature sprang away and stood gazing at us. If I had not been slow and clumsy, he might have been stopped, but the form was dim among the trees, and hard to identify. Subsequently, Celestin got a glimpse of it through the glass, and pronounced it to be a leopard. I saw it again myself at a long distance, and thought the outline more like that of a hyena; it may have been a lynx. All three of these animals are found in the mountains. A few days later I found some small caves which the tracks showed to be frequented by this big cat, whatever he was. Outside one of these holes was an immense store of bones of camels, bullocks, sheep, dogs, and the shells of tortoises broken open. They must have been dragged a thousand feet up the cliffs, and probably belonged to animals that had died on the caravan route below. According to Pliny, the hyena—which in my belief the animal was—"alone of all beasts will search for men's bodies within their graves and sepulchres, and rake them forth." He has weird tales to tell of the animal—among others that "he will counterfeit man's speech, and coming to the shepherds' cottages will call one of them forth, whose name he hath learned, and when he hath him without, he will worry and tear him in pieces."

Hearing of a distant mountain said to contain ibex, which had the further advantage of being clear of forest in its upper part, and being by this time tired of

"Maimun Dagh," we struck our camp and journeyed thither. At the foot of this range was a charming village, with a copious stream, which sprang full-bodied from the living rock and worked numerous small mills, the splashing of which, and the greenery of the walnut-trees, were refreshing after our arid experiences. Every village has its guest-house, and this one was comfortable, and the Agha or headman hospitable. Indeed, that virtue, according to our experience, is universal among the Turks in the country districts. When any distinguished or very holy persons are received as guests in the villages of the Turkomans, who must not be confounded with the Turks, I was credibly informed that the hospitality of these people extends to lengths which are surprising to our ideas of the exclusiveness of the harem.

The Agha's friends were not less pleased than he to see the foreigners eat. The host likes not only to entertain the stranger, but to show off the latest lion to his friends. These Turks are themselves very abstemious, and our appetites seemed to astonish them. "Heaven be praised! the Effendi wants more meat! What an appetite!" they said. Bouba's customary evening greeting, "May your food sit heavy on you, my lords!" was another sign of this friendly interest, and not the brutal curse which it sounds like.

A word here may not be out of place about the various races which inhabit this land. Turks, Turkomans, Circassians, Yuruks, differ in their customs and modes of life; each race, generally speaking, living in villages apart from the others. The Turks, according to our experience, exhibited a more sincere and dignified, if less ostentatious, hospitality, and a more rigid observance of the Mussulman code of religion, than their neighbours. Of the Circassians not much need be said. They are thinly scattered about this part of the country. Those we saw were a particularly sinister-looking lot, with none of their world-famed beauty. Nevertheless, their daughters are in demand, and, whatever the law, they habitually sell them. Our friend the stationmaster said he had had a commission to buy as many as he could at £15 a head, and within a few days a girl of sixteen had been offered for twenty medjids; £5 does not seem dear, but perhaps she had a temper. Even the Turks accept a very substantial present from their would-be sons-in-law, and the credit of a man with six daughters is always good. The Yuruks, who are the mountaineers and shepherds of this country, are said to steal their wives, but this must be a risky process. They are nomadic, and their black goats' hair tents are conspicuous; but the climate compels them to spend the worst months within four walls. Their flocks are protected by a large breed of white dogs, whose threatening attacks are rather alarming to a stranger; but I always found a stout stick a sufficient passport. They are sturdy folk, but their manners are rough. Thus, on leaving a Yuruk village, Findlay received a somewhat curt demand for his English saddle. As a contrast to this, I may mention the polite request of the Turkish sheriff just mentioned, when we bade him farewell, that a barrel of wine of the country which we were leaving behind should be emptied to the last drop on the ground. The Yuruk Agha would have scorned this self-denial, and would have made it the excuse for a drinking bout. I am afraid the

Yuruks are responsible for the terrible destruction of the forests by fire. This is not accidental, but done of set purpose to improve the grazing. From some of our camps we could, every night, see two or three of these fires raging.

According to our hosts, no stranger had ever hunted on that mountain. They assured us there were plenty of *Kayeek* on it. Some Yuruks whom we met the next morning bringing wood down the mountain said the same, but when I showed them a picture of the ibex, I saw that they looked doubtfully at it. The fact is, the term *Kayeek* is used vaguely, and is generally applied to the largest horned animal in the district. We were assured that there was plenty of water on the mountain, but it took us four hours of stiff walking up a rough path to find the first sign of it. When reached it proved to be a tiny mud pool no bigger than a soup-plate, from which the faintest trickle oozed away, losing itself in slime. Alongside lay a very ancient and disused trough formed of a hollowed trunk, dry and cracked. It was unpromising, but this camp was so beautiful that it was worth an effort to make it habitable. By clearing out the little pool and puddling the trough with mud, we at length got a tiny trickle of clear water, enough for drinking, though not for washing. If we had gone farther we should have found plenty of water, but not so favourable a camp. It was at an elevation of about five thousand feet, and at the upper edge of a gorge or *cañon*, fifteen hundred feet deep. The position overlooked an extensive forest of stone pines, the finest trunks we had yet seen.

Having settled the water, we began collecting wood,

CYRIL ENGINEERS THE WATER-SUPPLY.

and while so engaged, a shout from one of my companions called me to look at a fresh track he had found. There was no mistake about it. It was that of a red deer, but half as large again as any stag's slot which I had ever seen. This was indeed a find upon which we had not reckoned, for few travellers have had the luck even to see the big red stag of Asia Minor.

But duty before pleasure. I had come here for ibex, and must first ascertain if there were any on the mountain. That afternoon was devoted to a very careful search with the telescope of the upper part of the mountain, but we saw nothing, and from this and the complete absence of tracks we soon came to the conclusion that they were a myth. By the time I had satisfied myself on this point there was only an hour of daylight left, but I hurried down to a point which commanded a wide extent of the forest. Here I had scarcely opened my glass before I made out a stag and a hind feeding at the bottom of the valley below us. Celestin was greatly excited, having never seen any game larger than chamois and certain other rock-skippers which he had pursued in my company. Everything seemed to favour the stalk. We got quickly down under the shelter of trees, and had arrived within three hundred yards when the hind started. The fact was, the wind, which had been blowing up the valleys all day, at sunset changed its direction. The stag had not yet caught the taint, and stood a while. I could see that he was large in the body, but the light was too dim to make out his head. I tried a despairing shot, but the distance was too great and I could scarcely see the bead. It was a bad chance and, alas! I never had the luck to get a better. Three times on the way back to camp I heard the roar of a stag, which, when heard on a still evening echoing through the great tree-stems, is a sound calculated to make a man impatient for the next morning. It was the 5th of November, which is rather late for these demonstrations, and, as a matter of fact, I did not hear it again after that night. If they had continued to give out such signals we might have done better.

It had been borne in upon us at mid-day that the arrival of the camels with our equipage that night was problematical, as these splay-footed animals do not travel well on mountain paths, and one of the party was sent back to bring on, by some means or other, something to eat, and, if possible, some coverings. It was long past dark when we heard our messenger shouting, for he had missed the track and got entangled among the trees. Half an hour later he blundered into camp with old Bouba, and a donkey laden with certain necessaries, but we had little to cover our bodies that night, and not over-much to put inside them. Bouba had to squat under the canopy of his cloak, which gave him the well-known bat-like appearance of a tragic desperado, and explained with a grin that he was accustomed, ten years back, to that sort of shelter—that is, before a paternal government interfered with his line of business. We filled our luncheon-bags with pine-shoots for pillows, but as they were gathered in the dark we did not find out, till we were too sleepy to remove them, that most of them had cones attached. Cyril and Findlay tried the same material for their beds, and their dreams were not peaceful. As an old campaigner, I pretended to instruct them in a better dodge, which is to dig and scrape a hollow for the hips. In theory it is admirable, but in practice exasperating.

The next day was a blank, and the following one promised to be another. Cyril and I had long returned to camp. It was pitch dark and raining hard. Bouba was in a state of trepidation that Findlay and Celestin would spend their night in the open, and wanted to start search-parties. A good motherly old brigand was Bouba! In vain I assured him that my Pyrenean could find his way on any mountain in the dark. At last a loud " whoop " proclaimed at once their return and the cause of the delay. When they stumbled into the red glow, drenched with the rain, this was soon explained. Findlay had slain the stag of stags. " Mais que j'avais peur quand je l'ai vu ! " said Celestin. He had made out with a glass from a long distance a single tine of a horn in a thicket of young fir-trees, but for some time was uncertain of its nature. Then the stag removed all doubt by rising and showing himself as he crossed an opening. In time they reached the place, but could see nothing till Celestin suddenly met him face to face in the thicket, and shouted to Findlay, " L'animal ! Le monstre ! Tirez ! tirez ! " but " l'animal " was off, and this was easier said than done. For a moment he showed himself, and Findlay missed him clean. Now what did this polite stag do but cross the stream and calmly mount a knoll, where he stood, fully exposed, as long as you please, at fifty yards. That shot told. The stag went off, but they soon found blood. Then followed a most exciting stern chase for the best part of half a mile, the great beast labouring on through the thicket in spite of his deadly wound, while Findlay struggled after, in vain seeking a chance to plant a second bullet in a mortal place. It is to be feared that some that he attempted would have involved a shilling fine at Bisley. Once he measured his length—which is almost halfway between six and seven feet—in a stream, and hurt himself so severely that I assured him afterwards he would have a stiff knee for life, but would always have the most pleasurable associations with it. His cartridges were nearly exhausted, when a snap shot struck the back of the animal's head, and the huge beast lay conquered. How noble a trophy he had won the following figures will show, at any rate to the initiated. The head carried fourteen points, but one of the "bays" had been broken in fighting. The length of the horn from the "burr" is 43½ inches, span inside the horn 38½ inches. No such stag as this, to the best of my belief, has been seen in Western Europe, at least for many generations. The Castle of Moritzburg, which contains the most remarkable collection of stags' horns in Europe, gathered during several centuries, can perhaps match it with one or two. I do not think the weight could have been much less than 40 stones. This it was impossible to verify, but the foot and shank-bone attached weighs 2½ lbs., which is considerably more than double that of a good Scotch stag. Findlay's initial could have stood for "Fortunatus" on this trip. But, then, the last time we had been together, somewhere in the far north, the luck had been the other way.

The next night an incident occurred which shows how unsophisticated the *feræ naturæ* are in this district. The Yuruk put his head into the tent and said there was a beast prowling about, might he shoot it? Half an hour afterwards he fired at and missed a fox. Undeterred by this, the depredator carried off in the night the whole of the remaining venison in camp. The following day Findlay secured another stag, a much smaller one, the venison of which was placed for security in the centre of the camp. The fox again returned at dusk, and was shot dead by the camp fire, within five yards of us all!

Our host from the village below thought it a necessary act of hospitality to come up and remain at our camp during the whole time of our stay. Notwithstanding the rain, which here came down in torrents for two nights, he sat through it a picture of serene patience. His followers were not so well off, especially his black servant, for there was no room in the tents. Hearing talking in the night, I looked out, and saw this wretched negro sitting in the drenching rain, and carrying on a loud conversation with himself to keep himself warm.

The big stag was our crowning success, and if we could have spared more time we might have repeated it; for, though the forest was fairly dense, they were not so wary as the ibex. At least I thought so then. As Bonba said, "All animals are Sheitan (Satan), but these stags are not quite such Satans as those Satans of goats." The fact was that these same "Satans" were the object of my journey, and whereas up to that time we had done scarcely anything with them, I was very unwilling to return home beaten by a mere goat. We, therefore, perhaps foolishly, left the red deer and sought out the goats again. That my *amour propre* was saved the following total bag will show. Seven ibex, two red stags, one wild boar (a very fine beast killed in a canebrake on the plain). On our return to Smyrna, we found

IN THE BRAKES

our deeds celebrated in the local Greek "Daily," a quotation from which shall conclude this chapter:

Ὀλίγοι βεβαίως γνωρίζουσιν ὅτι εἰς μικρὰν ἀπόστασιν ἀπὸ τῆς σιδηροδρομικῆς γραμμῆς Διὲρ ὑπάρχουσιν ἐν τῷ ἐσωτερικῷ αἴγαγροι καὶ ἔλαφοι, πρῶτοι δὲ νομίζομεν οἱ Ἄγγλοι περιηγηταί, ἐλθόντες ἐπὶ τοῦτο ὑποδεικνύουσι τὴν ὁδὸν εἰς τοὺς ἡμετέρους, τοὺς ἀγαπῶντας τὰ μεγάλα καὶ ἀληθῆ κυνήγια.

Which Cyril thus freely rendered: "There are wild goats and deer up there, and yet you slow-bellied Ephesians let these English Barbarians come here and show you the way to catch them."

JUNK TAKES WELL-EARNED REPOSE.

VII

THE PYRENEAN IBEX

The range of the Pyrenees on its Spanish side slopes rapidly to the lowlands, but its soft limestone has been cut and carved in strange fashion. Some of the trenches thus formed are of extraordinary depth and steepness. I have heard the valley with which I am most familiar, described as being narrower at the top than at the bottom. Certainly for depth and steepness it has no rival with which I am acquainted. To heighten the contrast, the valley widens in one place into a small level and park-like plain of grass, dotted with great spreading beeches whose stems of silvery bark are flecked with velvet patches of dark green moss. Where the soil has gathered, tall spruces contrast nobly with the long front of yellow cliff which towers above. A dense undergrowth of scrubby beech and of box bushes ten feet high, covers the slopes. Unhappily the big beeches are gradually disappearing before man, the great devourer, and noble spars of firs which have been felled, but never removed, cumber the paths of the forest, while even the humble box is cut into lengths to make wooden spoons which are sold for a farthing apiece.

But the feature of the valley is the wonderful wall which encloses it. I know no cliffs so tall and so uncompromisingly sheer as those that hem it in. Some of them overhang so far at the top, that a stone, dropped from the edge, will not touch for a thousand feet. In the early spring they carry a fringe of pendent icicles, sometimes fifty feet long, and these huge spears, loosened by the sun, descend with a prolonged whiz and crash audible for miles. The reason for this overhanging character of the cliffs is, paradoxical as it may seem, the softness of the strata composing them, because, when a stratum of greater density overlies less durable material, the latter gets weathered till the upper shelf projects. Also while some strata are harder than the average, others are so much more friable that even the most perpendicular cliffs are scored *horizontally* by what appear from below to be faint lines, but are really narrow galleries or grooves, along which an active animal, and sometimes a man, may pass in safety. This feature has an important bearing on the particular sport described in this chapter.

Sometimes these galleries extend backwards into the rock, forming considerable caves, of the shape of a half-opened oyster, in the face of the cliff or more often at its base. In summer the Spaniards often select such a one, if it happens to be in an accessible position, and herd a considerable flock under its sheltering roof. Well I remember one which I reached in the company of a lady who is an excellent climber. It was high up on the face of one of the tallest cliffs and looked out from it like a window in a wall. It was approached by a narrow overhung shelf which led across the cliff. We sat at the back in the deepest shadow, cooling ourselves after our climb of four thousand feet. The June sun was busy with the snow overhead, and a continuous shower of drops, intensely illuminated, fell across the open mouth of our refuge. Just outside this luminous curtain, a flight of swifts darted and screamed, but this was only the foreground. We were high enough to dwarf the craggy ridge which forms the southern side of the valley, and the eye swept, as if from a balloon, the many-coloured plains of Aragon, spread below us like a map.

The huge battlement which encompasses the valley sometimes projects into it in towering promontories, like that which forms the background in the illustration, and which is connected with the main mass behind it by a narrow isthmus of rock. Sometimes the wall recedes into deep bays, but always follows the same level lines, and offers the same hopeless front to the climber. Only in one spot for many miles is it sufficiently broken down to afford a difficult access to human feet and hands. In one other place the broken staircase above so nearly approaches that below, that it occurred to me some years ago to see what could be done by artificial means. A certain bold mason was suspended from above and chiselled out holes in the sheer face, into which iron pegs were inserted. This *scala de jerro* is not a nice place for a plainsman, but it affords convenient access to some excellent izzard ground, and saves the shepherds, who summer in the upper regions, many a weary tramp. The first time I came down it my hunter followed me carrying an izzard, which I had just killed. The legs of a dead izzard are always fastened together and suspended across the bearer's forehead, while the body

OUR CAMP.

hangs on his back. Just at the most awkward step, where you have to stretch round an angle to feel for the next peg, he nervously glanced upwards. The next moment I was conscious of a body—whether man or beast I could not for a moment tell, for I was myself clinging like a fly on a pane of glass—whirling past my head into space. It took us more than an hour of careful hunting for traces of blood and hair on the shelves of that cliff, before we refound the izzard, crushed out of all recognition, several hundred feet lower.

Below the loftier cliffs, lesser escarpments follow the same level line, divided from one another by sloping shelves or *corniches*, as they are locally called, which may be followed for long distances without the possibility of ascending or descending from one to another.

All the Pyrenean streams are lovely, owing to the absence of glaciers and the consequent clearness of the water, and, from the lime or other particles held in suspension, the deep pools assume a wonderful opalescent blue. In this valley, the action of the water has polished the limestone into a smooth and creamy white—pearls set in amethysts. From these blue depths, the Spaniards draw, with very primitive rods and flies, trout of no mean size.

In the spring, this particular stream presents a curious daily phenomenon. In the early morning it almost runs dry—its sources of supply frozen hard—but the hot June sun soon wakes it, and the volume increases till it reaches a maximum about 4 P.M., by which time it is a raging torrent of great depth and force, a strange contrast to the cloudless sky. To cross it, one had, at that time, to pass a very nervous bridge. Two fir stems, side by side, had been thrown across a rocky place just below camp, with the thin end of one of them against the base of the other. The effect of this was, that while one foot rested on a rigid foundation, the other danced and swayed uncontrollably, and the white water tearing below did not tend to allay the involuntary trembling of the knees.

On a little platform overlooking the river and the little park of beeches, there is a tolerable hay-loft or barn, the only building of which the valley can boast, and there is room besides to pitch the tents. Of late years the hut has been extended, and divided by two partitions so that it affords very fair quarters.

The slopes of this valley, and of one or two others like it, are the home of the Pyrenean ibex, one of the rarest of animals and most difficult to obtain.[1] Unlike the Alpine ibex, which inhabits open cliffs, the Spanish goat takes full advantage of the covert afforded by the dense scrub. This variation of habit results in a different curvature of the horns, the points of which in the Pyrenean *bouquetin* are bent towards each other over the back—a form designed

---

[1] Other ranges in Central and Southern Spain are inhabited by a variety of the same animal, somewhat smaller as I understand, but otherwise closely allied, if not absolutely identical with *Capra Pyrenaica*. According to Mr. Lydekker who is an authority on the subject, "there is evidence that in Andalusia the species has existed since the Pleistocene epoch, its fossil remains occurring in the caves of Gibraltar in company with those of an extinct rhinoceros and other mammals." The younger Pliny appears to have known the animal. His translator renders him : " There is in Spaine a kind of a musmones, not altogether unlike to sheep, having a shag more like the hair of goats than a fleece with sheepes wooll. The beast hath a most tender head, and therefore in his pasture is forced to feed with his tail to the sun."—Philemon Holland's Translation, A.D. 1601.

for easier passage through the branches. Mr. Barrow, who wrote at the beginning of the century, says that "despair sometimes impels the ibex to face his rash pursuer on the edge of some pathless precipice, and he has been known to throw himself headlong upon the hunter, so that both have rolled over into the abyss beneath, and miserably perished." However that may be, that these animals are difficult to hunt may be gathered from the fact that I paid four distinct visits to the valley, and worked pretty hard each time, before I obtained a single specimen of a male. Owing to the hollows in the rocks, and the vegetation which covers them, it is all but impossible to spy them with the glass, and the only method of hunting that is practised, is to drive them. The guns are posted in an ascending line, each one occupying one of the shelves I have described, at some spot where a tolerably open shot may be obtained. The ibex are fully up to every point of the game, and it is but seldom they can be induced to come forward to the guns, though, generally speaking, several are viewed by the beaters. Though a heavier beast than the chamois, they are better climbers, and will traverse places which I do not think the chamois would face. Their aim seems to be to pass along some tiny shelf where no man can follow, to a hollow or overhanging rock which they know of, and there lie down, wholly invisible from above or below. Dogs are used of a close-tracking habit—the noisier babblers the better—to drive them from these retreats, but it has happened on several occasions in my experience, that the dog has reached a place where he can neither go forward nor back, and has remained there all night, his melancholy howls plainly audible at the camp, two or three thousand feet below. There is nothing to be done in these circumstances but to wait for the morning light, when his master ascends to the spot, or as near to it as he can get, and encourages him by his voice to venture a leap, in which case the dog, who has really as many lives as a cat, generally gets down unharmed, but the eagerness of the chase sometimes leads to sudden death, and I have known them to disappear altogether, leaving their fate a mystery.

The Basque Spaniards wear a kind of cloth sandal, a strip of the material being bound over their feet and round the ankles. This gives them a remarkable clinging power on rocks, and however arduous the beat, and difficult the climbing, they never shirk their task. The frontier Frenchmen affect to despise their neighbours over the border. "Ces maudits Espagnols," are words always on their lips, but this feeling is not justified by any inferiority of race— quite the contrary. These mountaineers are a sturdy and agile people, with an air of antique grace, which would make them very charming fellows indeed if it were not for their abominable language. The village, which is situated a few miles nearer the plain, has its municipal institutions tolerably complete. When strangers are in the valley, a deputation, consisting of the Mayor and his deputy, commonly waits upon them to bid them welcome. Indeed the whole parish council, or whatever they call themselves, seemed to enjoy us as much as if we had been a circus. The right to sport in the valley was claimed by the commune, and on one occasion the Mayor, doubtless egged on by his followers, endeavoured to extort from us more rent than he had himself agreed upon. The task was evidently distasteful to him, but a general election was impending. Old Antonio, who I think was leader of the opposition, in public kept on saying nothing, while he secretly besought us to stand firm. The debate which no doubt followed this incident of foreign policy was probably acrimonious. The *Alcalde* whom I knew best was a very dignified and courteous gentleman indeed; but though Signor Gregorio's manners were distinguished, he was not too proud, on occasion, to earn a few francs a day by acting as beater. To the practical accomplishments of a mountaineer, he added those of a good vocalist and dancer, arts which were brought into requisition whenever we had a success to celebrate. The native costume, consisting of a short jacket and velvet knee-breeches, slashed at the side, together with a long sash wound round the waist, which is frequently made use of to lower an inexperienced traveller down a bad place, enhanced the picturesqueness of these occasions.

I cannot say I am enamoured of ibex driving, and if it were not for the rarity of the trophy, I would never have endured those tortures. Fancy sitting through three sermons on end, of the longest kind, on a stone which gets harder and sharper every minute, under the strictest obligation not to move or go to sleep. If on the shady side of the valley, there is a rasping wind, and probably a snowstorm. On the northern slope *frying* understates the case. The solitude and the strange positions in which you find yourself have a strong effect on the imagination. The faintest sound acquires an exaggerated significance, and sets the heart throbbing painfully. I have often fancied I heard shots which were never fired, and the baying of dogs which proceeded from no canine throats. The one hallucination may have been suggested by a little pebble hopping down from the cliff above, or the rumbling of stones in the torrent below, the sound of which comes up to you at intervals, now faint and now strong, then for a long period altogether inaudible. The baying of the dogs is what you are listening for, so the illusion is natural, but the real thing is unmistakable, and, if you hear it, pull yourself together, for a dun-coloured body may spring across the *couloir* which you are commanding, either above or below you, and won't wait till your hand stops trembling. Much more frequently nothing happens at all, and the tension of your heart-strings is finally put an end to by a sudden and unexpected yell from a beater, which nearly cracks them outright. He appears round a corner of rock and looks round in a bewildered way, for though he knows you are there, he cannot see you till you rise stiffly and stretch the aching joints, with a sense of relief that that penance is over at any rate.

Some interest is afforded by the birds and lesser animals. Flights of thrushes coming from the direction of the drive afford the first indication of the approach of the beaters, though these are still inaudible. As you are stationary, and nearly the colour of the rock, the live things do not see you, and consequently come very close. A squirrel pattering over loose stones is a good imitation of the sound made by the larger animal which you are expecting. They are mostly coal black, with a slight tinge of gray on the tail—a very pretty species. When at last they discover the enemy, they chatter angrily. Dusky jays express their views on things in general in the same way as their blue-winged cousins do with us. The little wall creeper is one of the prettiest birds;—black and gray, with brilliant crimson wings, and beak curved like a curlew's. He flutters about the hot rocks—a close imitation of a butterfly,—and this resemblance is enhanced by his habit of spreading his wings in the sun when he alights. Eagles

THE WALL CREEPER.

are numerous, and the great lämmergeier is not rare. I have known as many as five of the former to come down to the body of an izzard, which had been too much smashed by falling over the cliff to be removed, and commence a furious contest before we had left it for five minutes. There are a few foxes about, and occasionally I have seen pine martens. One of these animals came and sat within thirty yards of me. As the drive was nearly over I put a bullet through him, and he makes a very handsome mount in my hall.

The first time I actually got an ibex it gave me long warning of its approach, as the slope consisted of loose stones, and I could judge by the sound, of the spot about eighty yards below me, where it would cross. I fired the moment it appeared, going at a good pace; the goat turned and sprang downwards out of my sight, but I had seen the hair fly from the shoulder, and knew that ibex was "my meat." The next gun, who was placed a hundred and fifty yards below me, fired almost at the same moment. He shouted—"I have got him!" I replied—"My ibex, I believe"—when the drive was over we both hurried to the spot and met over the body. "It fell to my shot"—"But it was my shot she got; you will find the bullet in the off shoulder which you could not see"—and so it proved.

Like most animals driven in this way, they seem more or less conscious of danger in front, and their aim is always to break back; consequently a drive seldom takes place without the beaters seeing more than the guns. "Walk in line with the beaters" may be said, but the beaters are often not within hearing of one another, and the ground is so complicated and difficult that even a practised mountaineer, unless he were familiar with its intricacies, would be sure to get into trouble. I have however sometimes thought that one might do something by sneaking about early and late among the cliffs, in the company of some native familiar with their feeding grounds, but I have never heard of any one trying this. My first ibex was only a female, and it was long before I got her a mate. My son had another a few days later; after that we left the ladies alone, and of course as they were not wanted,

they often came and confidingly offered themselves to the
sacrifice. At the same spot where I achieved my first
success, I lost one of my best chances at a big male. A
messenger had come breathless from the beaters to say
that *le vieux* had been seen to take to a broken cliff,
where he was believed to be in hiding. The two upper
guns went in haste. In the meanwhile, I climbed up the
scaur from my post below, and awaited them in the basin
at the top of it under the cliff. One of the beaters had
come up and stood by me. Suddenly pointing as I thought
to the cliff, and wildly gesticulating, he shouted. "See the
bouquetin ! the big one ; Madre de Dios ! why don't you
shoot ?—Make haste—he will be gone here, close by.
Oh ! Father of devils ! he is gone, and I could have
touched him with my stick ; he went quite slowly too."
During this excited speech I gazed and wondered, and
gazed again with all my eyes. The cliff was within forty
yards and I seemed to command every inch of the intervening ground. I thought the man insane or joking, but
his frantic gestures seemed genuine. Five seconds later
I caught the flick of a stern as it disappeared in the scrub.
The truth is, there was a slight depression which crossed
the rocky basin within ten yards of us, of which I was
unaware, and while I was scanning the ledges on the cliff,
the ibex, of course the largest ever seen, passed quite close
to me. My companion, who stood a few feet higher than
I, could see the top of his back and horns, hidden from me
by a rocky hummock.

 I always was an unlucky, or else a stupid sportsman, and
such measure of success as I have had, has been attained
by sticking to it till luck changed. In the case of the

Pyrenean ibex, I suffered tribulations indeed, but I will drink the bitter draught over again to the dregs. My brother and I had gone to what we thought were to be our posts, but there was a misunderstanding. When the beaters came up, we were told that we ought to have been at the "cascade" posts much farther on. There was not much daylight left, but, instructing the beaters to come on in an hour and a half, we hurried down into the main valley and up a lateral one, and arrived at our posts very hot and thirsty, just after the time appointed for the drive to begin. Now it is a recognised rule that one should never leave his post during the progress of a drive, but on the day in question, literally the only occasion when I transgressed, my thirst overcame me; the river was scarcely two hundred feet below. I thought nothing could possibly come yet, and climbed down to it. As I was stooping to drink, I saw a hoary old grandfather of goats standing within ten yards of my deserted post. I seized my rifle but the hammer was locked, and before it was ready, the beast had sprung down out of my sight and gone on towards my brother. The next moment his rifle rang out, but ineffectually, for the old billy raced back along the line by which he had come, just showing me the top of his back for a moment. That was an unlucky spot for me. It was just there on another occasion that I was standing by one of the beaters who had come up to me. The drive being over, we were talking together without any attempt at concealment, when I saw a young male ibex standing within a stone's throw, and apparently unconscious of our presence. I made sure of him that time but the cartridge snapped. I had burnt some hundreds of similar ones that year at a target and otherwise, and had had only one other miss-fire.

It will be understood that after this sort of thing I had to go on till something happened, but as I have said, it was not till my fourth visit to the district that I secured a head worth counting. It came in this way. There is, on the southern flank of the valley, a very wide *corniche* with sheer cliffs both above and below it, which are without a break for several miles. It is comparatively free from scrub, and, being very rough and broken, is often resorted to by the bouquetin if the lower woods have been much driven. We had driven it on that occasion without result, but Antonio who had been placed as a stop, had seen two males on a tiny ledge on the face of the upper cliff. This ledge was far above us, and barely traceable from where we stood. He said that one was very old and walked lame. The men had to make a detour of six miles to reach the other extremity, but lest the goats should take it into their heads to shift, we made haste to guard our end. We were assured that this ledge, though nowhere more than two feet wide, was continuous for five miles. Indeed the cliff seemed like a wall, but a man could easily pass along this little shelf, for the whole distance, *provided the rocks were dry*. There were places which the men, bold climbers as they were, would not attempt when the surface was moist. One man would of course have been sufficient, but, lest they should get in our way, we sent them, all but one, to make the long round, and they came along it in Indian file. One experienced old hand we retained to show us the way up to our posts, as the ascent was complicated and difficult. At this point the cliff was some-

what broken down, and there were several possible routes
which the ibex might take. Of these, I was placed in
the most likely post—the highest—on the ledge itself.
My view was bounded by an angle of cliff thirty yards in
front of me, round which the little shelf wound, and which

CYRIL.

hid everything except a portion of the main cliff half a
mile off, and across this the faint line of the ledge was
drawn as with a ruler. We had agreed to watch this point
carefully with a glass, so as to be forewarned of anything
which might approach that way. Cyril, who was posted
a hundred feet below me, took five-minute turns with me
at this task, and we signalled to one another with a silent
motion of the hand. After a couple of hours of this
industrious watch, a slight drizzle came on which for
the time partly obscured the middle distance. When
it had passed, I resumed the watch but could not tell
if, in the meanwhile, anything had passed the point in

question, and was now perhaps approaching just round the corner.

Now Cyril could command more of that part which lay close at hand than I could, and he saw the much-coveted pair of horns approaching, and already within reach of his own rifle. Loyally he let the bearded patriarch come on to me—but imagine his feelings when, glancing up at me, he saw me steadily spying the distant cliff, instead of watching the foreground. Still he was proof against the temptation, so anxious was he that I should secure the first honours. In vain he tried by a faint whistle to attract my attention. The goat passed on out of his sight towards me. Then followed an agonised period of suspense, so prolonged that he thought I must be asleep, till he saw the glass hastily dropped and the rifle seized. Still the shot did not follow, and he supposed I must somehow have let the beast pass me. At last the rifle rang out. He heard the stones clatter as the animal raced back the way he had come. The sound ceased, and the next moment the dead ibex whirled past him through space, twisting as it fell. In reality, though I kept the glass glued to the distant cliff, I had many years before learned the stalker's trick of keeping the left eye open, and I saw the horns of the approaching animal the instant they appeared round the corner. This history might be described as the confessions of a duffer, and it must be admitted that the beast was very near me indeed, before I discovered that, though I was ready, my rifle was still on half-cock. However, "*le boiteux*," for he it was, advanced with a dignified hobble, and when within ten yards of me, he came into full view and instantly received a shot full in the chest.

With that short gallop peculiar to an animal shot in the heart, he turned and fled, but fell and died on the ledge; turned half over, slid a yard or two and shot out of my view. No one uttered a sound for a few minutes, hoping that the second ibex must follow the same way; but whether he had found some means of escape from the trap, which was beyond the power of his less agile companion, or whether he had left it before we closed the door, I do not know. When it was clear that there was nothing more to come, we woke the echoes. The poor old veteran had fallen fully five hundred feet before he struck, and with such force that his body bounded fully as far again down the slope. Of course the horns were broken but were recovered after a short search among the rocks. He was eleven years old by the rings of his horns, and weighed ten stone clean, or about the size of a red hind. His meat was the driest and toughest I ever broke my teeth against. The accident to his fetlock joint had apparently happened many years before. There was a sound of revelry in the hut that night, and the Mayor danced his stateliest measure.

I am tempted to quote a similar incident from a letter written to me by an excellent sportsman who knew the valley many years before I did. He had wounded and lost an old male two days before, and had chanced to spy it where it had taken refuge, high on the face of the northern cliff. He thus describes the attempt to reach it:—
"François and Michel started for the ascent, P—— and I taking up our two old posts below, which we are intimately acquainted with. I did not envy the men. It is about as villainous a bit of climbing as I know, and the height has an effect even on François's head. Michel had to give up the last *mauvais pas* and sit down. François, bootless, went on alone. Vainly he peered into all the various recesses in the face of that gruesome cliff; the bouquetin was not to be found. One chance remained and that was on what we call the back *corniche* of the '*Chateau*.' François disappeared round the corner, on a ledge about a foot wide, at a height of at least a thousand feet above our heads. To our disappointment he reappeared in about half an hour, and began to come down to us. Of course I thought he had not found the bouquetin, but it appeared that he had not only found him but had got close to him, lying in a hole in an awful place, but could not get near enough to dislodge him. After a bit to eat, *pour donner courage*, he and Antonio would go up again another way. Accordingly, when primed, up they went again, and disappeared round the corner. Presently, the most tremendous row proceeded from that uncanny region. Anxiously we kept our eyes on the little ledge leading from the back *corniche*, but the old boy would not leave, down he would not come, but dashed past Antonio on three legs, and

instead of taking the usual, and what we believed to be the only pass, he made straight for the face of the precipice itself, and we saw him appear, like a fly on a window-pane, apparently glued to the smooth rocks, along which he passed at a terrible height to a little ghostly ledge we had not noticed before, high above the *chambre à coucher*. Here he lay down, and from below we could only see his head and neck. François and Antonio managed to get to within one hundred yards of him, but not an inch farther. Seeing that nothing could now be done to get him down, we determined to send a rifle up to François, and make him finish the poor brute. This we did, sending three cartridges. The first two had no effect and it was not to be wondered at, for Antonio had to hold François by the belt when he fired, and all he could see was his head and neck. At the third shot the bouquetin swerved violently, though still untouched, staggered, sent two or three rocks whirling as pioneers, in his endeavour to recover his balance, lost it, and the next moment was flying like a little leaf through the air. It was a sickening sight. So much does the precipice overhang, that he appeared to us to be flying away from its side: six or seven hundred feet he fell before he touched anything, and he only touched twice, each time bounding high into the air, and revolving like a Catherine wheel with the violence of the fall, before he got to the bottom: a fall of at least a thousand or twelve hundred feet. Both horns were smashed off close to his head, but are none the worse themselves, and his skull was smashed into atoms."

A few days after my first success, I had another stroke of good fortune. The posts used for a certain drive being

limited in number, and the ground to be driven being
easier than usual, for once I accompanied the beaters, but
the covert proved so dense and the clambering so continuous, that the chance of getting a shot seemed hopeless. I
locked my rifle, and devoted my whole energies to keeping
my place in the line. Halfway through, I noticed very
fresh sign of ibex, and shouted to that effect to the nearest
beater. Just then "Medore" began whimpering a little,
and slowly picking out the scent *behind* the line, and in
the opposite direction to which it was moving. To quote
a junior member of my family " I *saw* the scent go round
the corner," and then, thinking it a cold one, moved on:
when suddenly the dog opened eagerly, fifty yards behind
me. I heard some heavy animal crashing through the
brush towards me, with a noise like a mad cow in a green-
house, and had just time to unlock and cock the rifle, when
a brown shadowy object passed within four yards of me.
I was at the moment struggling in the midst of a dense
thicket of young beech stems, the branches of which quite
prevented any play or sweep of the barrel; but I fired the
veriest snap shot in the world. By the merest fluke I
happened to cover his shoulder, and in fewer moments
than it takes to write this line, the dog was tearing at the
dead body of another old ram, scarcely inferior to the first.
I must have passed within a few paces of his place of concealment, and as I regarded myself only as a beater,
I was making noise enough to wake the valley. This
incident shows the reliance which these goats place in
mere concealment, and explains how this scarce species
has maintained itself against extinction for so many
ages.

Since the date of this double success of mine several well-appointed parties have visited the district expressly to hunt them, but, if I am correctly informed, their efforts were fruitless except in one case—that of an Englishman who killed a female ibex, while his servant got a young male. The natives of this valley, knowing how small is the chance, scarcely ever attempt to hunt them for themselves.

In the course of one of my visits to the valley, I made a discovery which is worth recording. Masses of a very beautiful white daffodil with drooping flowers were growing on elevated platforms. I remembered to have seen it in collections at home, and, though I could not put a name to it, I recognised it as a scarce species. I dug up a quantity of bulbs with my alpenstock, and when they flowered the following year, it proved to be *Narcissus moschatus*, a daffodil figured by Parkinson, a writer of the time of Queen Elizabeth, and described by him as coming from Spain. It has been in cultivation in this country or in Ireland, probably during the whole of the intervening period, but until I found it, its habitat was not known. A drawing of my flowers appeared in a gardening newspaper, and I was besieged with inquiries as to the locality, but I only imparted the secret to two well-known enthusiasts, who together made a journey to obtain it. Unfortunately, some brigand discovered the native who had been with me when I made the find, and bribed him so heavily that he dug up 10,000 bulbs, and made a small fortune.

When I first knew this district, there were a good many bears about. They appear to have now deserted it, but at that time one heard almost daily of some raid which they had attempted, or perpetrated upon the flocks. The shepherds took great pains to fold their goats in defensible positions, and kept up a frequent fusilade during the night to scare the enemy. Their great sheep-dogs, which are as large as St. Bernards but pure white, with black muzzles,

NARCISSUS MOSCHATUS.

were said to have frequent encounters with the depredators. I have seen dogs who had been badly scratched, and with all of them the effect for the time upon their temper towards casual strangers was very marked, so that it was even dangerous to approach one of these camps alone, and without a stout stick.

The only way to hunt bears in these forests, is to proceed as for the ibex, and to drive them. A favourite beat was in a neighbouring valley, and the post, reputed to be the best, was a little hollow, overgrown with box bushes, situated above one cliff, and below another. From it one looked down into the depths of the valley, and up at gaunt cliffs, but the immediate surroundings were in gloom and overshadowed by masses of box. It was rather an exciting spot, for the visible space was so small that it was obvious, that if a bear came that way he would infallibly be almost on your lap, before he would be seen. I remember the first time I occupied this position expecting this to happen every moment, and indeed the tracks showed that "Nicholas" frequently passed that way. I had sat there for three hours with senses keenly alert, and fancying all the time that I was the first human being who had ever entered that eerie spot, when I spied something white on the ground. It proved to be a fragment of the *Times* newspaper. After this, my sentiments were of a less exalted nature. The nearest approach that we made to seeing Bruin ourselves in that drive, was that, on one occasion, one of the beaters—the most infirm, who for that reason was at the bottom of the line, where the slope was easiest—nearly trod upon a large bear, who sat up and stared at him for some moments, before he quietly strolled off in the opposite direction to that of the hunters in ambush.

I never saw a bear at the post I have described, but once an izzard ran up against me there to its own hurt. This particular wood was a sure find for one or more of these animals, which were always old male *solitaires*. Just by this post, I once found the trunk of a fir-tree, against which a bear had sat up, and rubbed his back,

The hair still clung to the resinous bark to the height of six feet six inches; so that these Pyrenean bears sometimes attain no mean size.

On another occasion my friend the late Sir Victor Brooke killed a large female, as luck would have it, the day before I joined him. He wounded her severely at the first shot, and, following up the bloody track, entered a patch of tall box bushes, so dense that he had to crawl in on hands and knees. The dog, who had been following up the line, joined him, and, moving by his side step by step, showed by his erect hackles and trembling limbs, that the bear was close at hand. This was a very risky proceeding, the more so, as when the shot was fired, she had a cub at her side. But she would not face her determined pursuer, and bolted into the open where Mr. P——, who was stationed on the other side of the river, finished her with a well-directed shot.

Once only had any member of my party a success, with bears, and that was in a drive for ibex. My brother was posted at the foot of a cliff, where it projected in a sharp angular mass. His position was on a favourite track of ibex, but at some height above it, on the face of the cliff, there was another alternative route which had to be guarded. Old Antonio was placed here with orders to turn anything that appeared. I think he must have been asleep: at any rate, he realised so suddenly that some wild beast was within a yard or two of him that, forgetting his instructions, or feeling himself unable to turn it, he fired his rickety old piece which was loaded with buck shot, into the flank of the animal. The bear, for bear it was, turned, and sprang straight over the cliff. Now the remarkable part of it was that my brother never heard this shot. Whether it was that he did not consciously distinguish it from the shots which the beaters fired at intervals, or that he was so intent on the baying of "Tembelle," who was obviously pushing something in his direction, I do not know, but so abrupt is the grooving of this mountain that I have known more than one case of this puzzling phenomenon of smothered shots. The first warning of which he was afterwards conscious was a scrambling sound above, followed by a flying leap of some heavy body, and a crash on the slope of loose stones where he was sitting. He had fired his shot which had finished the business, and the bear lay dead before him before he had fully realised that it was a bear at all. It was a rather small bear, and had probably been considerably disabled by the charge of shot, which accounted for this rude and very clumsy descent. There was more rejoicing among the peasants over the death of this their enemy, than over a dozen ibex; and as the panting beaters gradually assembled, they made the valley ring again with cries of "L'Osso! L'Osso!" We ate a part of this little gentleman, but he was less juicy than a bilberry-fed cousin of his in Norway, into whose steaks I had had the pleasure of sticking a fork some years before.

Once more we thought we were in for a chance. The way to our posts lay through the dense covert near the base of a favourite drive, which we called "The Great Chaos." There, in a muddy place on the narrow track was the imprint of the characteristic plantigrade foot, so fresh that the water was still oozing into it. Without stopping to scrutinise it too closely—what else but a bear could have any business in such a place?—we pressed on with rifles cocked, and hearts in our mouths. Another wet place and more sign! He is evidently just in front of us! A large sunlit patch of wild raspberries showed ahead and—now for the supreme moment—some hidden body was moving about in the tall canes. We stood in a group, with the rifles almost at the shoulder, when—oh! the blank disillusioning—a rippling laugh rang out, and faces appeared, not furry, but raspberry-stained about the mouth, and two strapping sirens stood grinning in the sunlight, and inviting us with a shrill welcome to the feast.

That reminds me of another sell which I experienced, and which might have had unpleasant consequences. My post, at a great height above the valley, commanded a rugged torrent-bed, and the opposite slope of rocks, thinly covered, where the soil admitted of it, with a scanty growth of pines, as favourable a chance for ibex as there is in the valley. The roar and swish of the water, and the wildness of the spot help to keep the nerves on the stretch of keenest expectancy. Piling up a few rocks, you crouch behind them, and try to look as much like one of them as you can. All the possible openings are vigilantly kept under review, and not a movement escapes notice. At last there *is* a movement. Something two hundred yards off is coming through the trees in my direction, with cautious steps, as if aware of danger in front : at first only a brown patch—looks like an izzard—a hundred and fifty yards - too big for anything but an ibex ; a hundred and twenty yards—I bring the sight to bear. Now it is hidden, but it must come into full view between those two trees—here it is, but not just where I expected—the little black head is well defined against the hairy flank I begin to put a slight pressure on the trigger, but something in the clumsiness of the gait arrests me; then the lash of a long tail. Blessings on that tail!—think what a fate it saved me from—if it had not been for that, I should have gone down to my grave as the man who shot the cow! How that cow got there puzzles me to this moment.

Talking of cows, I once found a heifer at a lower level but in a more awkward fix. She had been stretching up after the young leaves, but, slipping, had wedged her head between two beech stems, which sprang V-shaped from one stool. When I discovered her, her head was pointing down the hill, but in her struggles, her body also had worked round the tree and down the slope, till it was a miracle her neck had stood the strain. When we found her, the last flicker of life had nearly gone, and her eyes and nose were already *fly-blown*! Releasing her with some difficulty, we poured the contents of a whisky flask down her throat, and to our astonishment, she presently came to, but with a crook in her neck which she probably has still.[1]

[1] An accident of this kind happened some years ago to a red deer in Windsor Park, and terminated fatally. When discovered the animal was dead.

VIII

BEAR HUNTING

THE Reader may think that the last chapter has been poaching on the domain of this one, but it will be seen that while the headings of my chapters relate to the different wild animals, the chapters themselves refer to distinct localities, and I now pass to a region two thousand miles to the north of my last described ground.

Nearly every Englishman who takes a gun to Norway has a latent expectation of shooting a bear. There is a very old story of one of our countrymen which is calculated to dispel these illusions. It is current in a hundred forms, but the most familiar version is, that after spending twenty years in the search for bears, he finally shot a tame one in the suburbs of Christiania. There are indeed few British sportsmen who ever see one in its native wilds, still less secure it. That supreme good fortune was however mine.

In 1873 I had rented a red-deer shooting on the seaward side of the large island of Hitteren, which lies close to the Norwegian coast, just south of the entrance to the Throndhjem Fjord, that is to say, I had hired the rights of about twenty farmers, each of whom is entitled to kill two deer. I need hardly say that the right to kill, is by no means equivalent to the power to kill. Indeed, I doubt if there were forty deer in all that part of the island. They live in rather dense woods of Scotch fir, dwarfed by the Atlantic gales, and it is not possible to do much without driving, which has few attractions for me. But I may say in passing, that these deer reach heavy weights and carry fine heads, and that the islanders are particularly unsophisticated and hospitable. At the end of three weeks our stalking—if poking about the woods on the chance of a snap shot, at the stern of some animal of indeterminate sex, can be so dignified—had not been particularly successful, and we came to the conclusion that hunting the red deer in this wise was not a noble sport at all. Besides, exciting rumours reached us of bears on the mainland— there are none on the island—and we determined to try pastures new.

Crossing the island, we hired a fishing-boat, and sailed across the sound which separated us from the continent towards the narrow entrance of the Hevne Fjord, then up its quiet reaches till we came to a green patch denoting a habitation of some sort. This fjord is less stern and forbidding in character than most of the show fjords farther south, but to my mind is more varied and lovely.

We landed at the farm to pass the night and make inquiries. From the heights above it, I remember seeing a strange sight. We looked down on the still waters of the fjord, here about two miles wide. Halfway across it there appeared a distinct wave, apparently propelled by the nose or fin of some large submarine creature. It moved on for a full mile towards the shore below us, keeping a straight course; but the leviathan, or whatever it was that caused the commotion, never showed above the surface. We could only divine it to be the *Kraken*, or sea-serpent, which old Bishop Pontopiddan particularly describes as inhabiting these coasts: "the only place in Europe," as he says, "visited by this terrible creature." Among many other veracious facts in its natural history he mentions that its presence is sometimes discovered by the fishermen, who find a shallow in their fishing ground where none should be. Their surmise is confirmed if they encounter great shoals of fish, on the principle that

> "Great fleas have little fleas
> Upon their backs to bite 'em,
> And little fleas have lesser fleas,
> And so *ad infinitum*."

These they haul in at a great rate — I mean the fishes. Only if they find, by the shortening of their lines, that the *kraken* is rising, they flee away. Finally when the animal appears, "its back or upper part seems to be about a mile and a half in circumference (some say more, but I choose the less for greater certainty) and looks, at first like a number of small islands surrounded with something that floats and fluctuates like seaweed." He further quotes Olaus Magnus, a much older writer, to the effect that it leaves the sea "in moonlight nights to devour calves, sheep and swine. It has a mane two feet long. It is covered with scales and has fiery eyes." . . . "It disturbs ships and raises itself up like a mast and sometimes snaps some of the men from the deck." These are what the good Bishop, who governed the diocese of Bergen one hundred and fifty years ago, calls "credible facts which he has gathered from many corroborating accounts;" but he is very shy of "sportsmen's and anglers' histories, which ought not to be admitted as authentic." In the former category he places mermen and maidens which also inhabit these waters. These are said to swear roundly in the Danish language, and when the boatmen "grow apprehensive of some danger and begin to retire, the monster blows up his cheeks and makes a kind of roaring noise, and then dives under the water, so that they see him no more." It is of course the mermen only who behave in this vulgar manner. The mermaidens, according to our right reverend historian, are not guilty of any more forward conduct than "rolling their eyes about strangely"—perhaps he meant winking—"as if it was out of surprise to see what they had not seen before," and of "making lamentable cries."

While I am delving in this mine, I may as well gather from it some particulars of the natural history of the bear, the subject of this chapter. Says the Bishop, " When he goes out in the spring of the year he is found to be fattest. According to the common saying, he has sucked his paws. He sucks them till they make a white froth which makes them sore and tender. He is at this season lame, and hops about for some time, and of this the huntsmen take advantage. His stomach is also sick at this season, and drawn up of his long fasting; and to cure it he looks out for an ant's hillock of which he swallows up the whole. This scours his inside, and cleanses and strengthens his stomach." But according to the Bishop there are times when the bear is much better able to take care of himself, for we are told, " he will fire off a gun when he has taken it from the huntsman." Under these circumstances, the latter "has nothing to defend himself with but his knife. This he takes crossways in his hand, to run down the bear's open throat. If he does not succeed in this his life is lost; the bear flaes his skin, and pulls the hair and flesh over his head and ears, face and all." But he adds "If the hunter conquers, he then flaes the bear." It appears that the bear has a particular dislike to a cow with a bell round her neck. "At this bell he is mightily offended; he tears it off and strikes it so flat with his paw, that it shall never speak or vex him again." When he wants to cross the water, "if he sees a boat by the way, he will go after it if it be only to rest himself; if he gets in he will sit in the stern quite quiet and peaceable: the farmer, however, does not care to let him in if he can play his oars fast enough." However, the bear is sometimes useful. "for," says the Bishop, "I was told that an old grass-bear was many years known to follow the herds like their guard, and stood often tamely by, as the maid was milking, and always drove the wolf away. He did no hurt to any one; only in autumn, when he was almost going to look for his den, he would take a kid or a sheep, as if for summer's wages: but I doubt if there are many of his kind that use that discretion. They say, however, for certain that in his proper jurisdiction or the place where he usually resides, he will take but one piece from a man." The last statement is slightly ambiguous. This human element in the character of the bear is further illustrated by Lloyd, who says, "When he finds a 'gin' set for his destruction he springs it, after putting stumps and roots between the teeth." The same author quotes M. Vergelanit,

"That the bear, when mortally wounded, makes for the lake and there disappears, has long been a general belief among the people of Norway. . . . While the drag net was being used in a forest lake a sunken log was drawn up from the bottom, with the skulls of three, if not four, bears firmly attached to it, the fangs being deeply embedded in the wood itself." According to Turberville " When a bear is hurt sore and escapeth the huntsman, she will open and stretch her wound, yea, sometimes she will draw out her own guts and bowels, to search them whether they be pierced or not : and by that measure many of them die when they might well escape." The same writer gives the following advice to beginners " If two men on foot have boar spears or javelins, or short pitch-forks, would stick well one to another's defence and revenge, they may kil a great bear : for ye beare is of this nature, that at every blowe she wil be revenged on whatsoever come next to hands. So that when ye one hath striken ye beare, she wil runne upon him ; and then if the other strike quickly, she wil returne to him again. So that the one may alwaies help and succour the other."

There were no bears in the neighbourhood of the homestead where we first halted, but there were reports of their presence farther up, and we ultimately ran these rumours to ground at a farm called Klonglevik, many miles up the fjord, where lived the noted *bjorn skuter*, Per Klonglevik, who had killed no less than eleven bears in his time. He supported himself on his little croft, but his passion was to hunt all kinds of fur, and in the spring he migrated to Nordland for seals and otters. Most of the bears he had killed were murdered half asleep in their winter *hies*, indeed it is in that way that nearly all those recorded are obtained.

With what poor appliances this is done the following incident, which was told to me, will show. Ole and Magnus, two mere lads, went up on to the fjeld to shoot ryper about the time of the first snow. Finding the footprints of a bear they tracked him to a hole under the rocks, where it was evident that he had just ensconced himself for the winter. They had nothing but small shot in the gun which they carried, but, cautiously retreating to a safe distance, they made a fire, and, melting some of the shot in an old pipe bowl, produced some rough bullets with which they loaded their piece. Armed with this and a long pole they returned to the attack, and, while one stood over the hole, the other sounded it, and vigorously prodded at the sleeping beauty. Presently there was a bite, and so vigorous a demonstration, that Ole retreated to a safe place, but Magnus stood his ground, and successfully discharged his piece into the head of the beast.

According to Peter the chance of our finding a bear at that time of the year was not very good; but of their presence he quickly offered proof by showing us his stooks which had been pulled about a few nights before, and other and unmistakable traces which the perpetrator of the mischief had left behind.

The next morning we were off early, all four of us following in the wake of old Per. This was not the way to kill bears, as the chances of disturbing a wild animal, carrying ears so well strung as a bear's, is as the square of the number of the party. But this was only a trial trip.

The old man bore an enormous single-barrelled rifle,

weighing 20 lbs. and carrying a 4-oz. bullet. It had been for several generations an heirloom in his family, and he looked doubtfully at our express rifles, the bore of which he kept contemptuously measuring with his little finger.

Bears are passionately fond of all kinds of berries which ripen in this month of September, and they greedily devour bilberries, blueberries, cranberries, raspberries, and *moltebær* or cloudberries. We therefore crept stealthily about, to the various points which commanded the banks and hollows where such berries abounded, and especially the copses where the rowan grew. Many of these trees were found broken and bent down, for the sake of the scarlet clusters which adorn them, for, if there is a dessert which Bruin prefers to all others, it is these. But of the bears themselves we saw none that day, and this was not surprising. Thereafter we never went more than two together. Bears do most of their feeding and travelling—often for long distances—at night, and during daylight are on foot for a short time only, morning and evening. The intervening hours are spent in some secure ambuscade whence they can make a rapid retreat through the thicket if disturbed. For this reason we made two distinct expeditions each day—at the earliest dawn and again about sunset—and devoted the middle of the day to replenishing the larder with ptarmigan or grouse, from some beat which we had thoroughly hunted. On the third day news was brought to us of a large bear having attacked a horse on the other side of the fjord. That "Nicholas" occasionally does this with success has been frequently attested. Old Lloyd describes his method of proceeding, which is "to grasp the neck of the horse with one arm and to arrest its

headlong career by seizing a tree with the other, which
always brings him to the ground with a jerk." I should
think that a horse in good condition would, with his heels
render a good account of a bear which attempted this trick,
and indeed when the latter desires a meat diet he generally
contents himself with mutton. But according to Pontoppidan this is not his method of defence. That author says:
" Horses show a great deal of courage when they fight with
the wolves and bears, which they are oft obliged to do,
particularly the latter, for, when a horse perceives any of
them near, and has a mare with him, he puts the weaker
behind him and attacks his antagonist with his *fore-legs*
which he uses like drumsticks to strike withal, and comes
off usually the conqueror. . . . But sometimes the bear
who has the double strength gets the advantage, and
especially if the horse happens to turn about to kick with
his hind-legs. If he attempts this he is ruined, for the
bear instantly leaps upon him and fixes himself on his
back." Bears must occasionally attack elk, for in the forest
of a friend of mine a cow elk was shot from whose
shoulder a large triangular piece of skin had been torn, and
the wound showed unmistakable signs of a bear's claws.
The state of her udder proved that she had been suckling
a calf, in defending which she had perhaps received her
wound, but which had probably fallen a victim notwithstanding.

Whatever the truth of the particular tale which reached
us may have been, it was sufficiently exciting to induce us
to change our quarters, and we crossed the fjord and went
several miles up a lateral valley. We were early afoot
the next morning but it was not my turn to go with Per.

Leaving what was supposed to be the most likely fjeld to the other party, accompanied by my cousin and a young farmer, I followed the track along the bottom of the valley for some distance, hoping that fortune would send something in our way. The lower slopes were covered with a forest of spruces, but between that and the sky-line there was a considerable belt of rough mountain side, less densely clothed, and which could be fairly well surveyed with the glass. Each slope as it came into view was carefully examined. At length we reached a little knoll, in the middle of the valley, which commanded both sides. Stretching ourselves on the soft carpet of heather, and basking in the sun which was already high, we toyed with our telescopes without much expectation, for it was now nearly bear's bedtime. I was sweeping my glass rather vaguely over the ground above us, when my attention was arrested by the rounded back of some whitish animal, feeding far up the mountain side. "A sheep," I said to myself; but what should a sheep be doing up there and alone too? Besides it was too big for a sheep, and yet it seemed too white for a bear; but at that moment the beast turned broadside and disclosed his proportions. It *was* a bear! How B—— jumped when I told him! But there was no question about it. He was plainly visible to the naked eye—a great walloping whity-brown bear!

And now in a moment we were in a frantic state of excitement. How to get at him? It would take us fully half an hour to climb up through the forest, and during that time the animal would be concealed from us, and might change his position or retire altogether. He was evidently busy feeding, and had now reached a long flat

slope which looked as if it would occupy him some time.
If we went up a little to the left of this we should be
under the wind, and might hope to encounter him, if he
continued his present course. It was everything to cover
the intervening ground in the shortest possible time. The
young peasant did not seem anxious to improve his acquaintance with bears, besides which, like most Norwegians,
he wore very dark and conspicuous clothes. So we left
him behind, with orders to remain where he was, and if
necessary to signal the movements of the bear. My young
companion and I were both in first-rate condition, and we
went up through that wood at a pace which would be hard
to beat. In twenty minutes we must have got up nearly
a thousand feet, and it was now of the greatest consequence
to get a sight of the bear as soon as possible. Fortunately
there was a rocky ridge close to us which rose above the
tops of the trees. This we climbed and eagerly scanned the
prospect. To our great joy we soon again made out our
friend, who was still busy with his breakfast and remained
nearly in the position which he had occupied when we left
the bottom of the valley. Diving once more into the
gully which scored the mountain side, we again rapidly
rose, and in ten minutes more had reached, what I judged
to be, the proper level of the place where he had been last
seen; but now the bear had entirely disappeared. We
cautiously drew along the mountain side towards the spot
where he had been feeding but could make out nothing.

There were several little coppices of dwarf birches near
where he had been; he must be hidden in one of them.
We sat down and got out our glasses, for a more careful
inspection. After a long search I made out a patch of

something which might be bear's fur, and, after keeping it in view some time, it moved, and, soon after, the bear showed himself once more in the open. He was now not more than two hundred yards from us, on a ridge similar to the one where we ourselves lay, and between us there was another and rather lower ridge, divided from us and from him by deep and narrow rocky gullies. While we were considering our next step, he drew towards us and descended into the second ravine and out of our sight. We immediately drew to the edge of the first ravine whence we could command the intervening ridge, which we expected him to cross. Once we heard him crashing through bushes, and then for minutes which seemed ages we neither heard nor saw anything, till I began to fear that he had crossed, some way above or below, and out of our sight; for we could not command more than about a hundred and fifty yards up or down the slope. I was afraid to move on, lest he should come over upon us, while we were struggling among the scrub and rocks of the ravine immediately below us. Anxiously we debated the question and decided to give him only two minutes more before we went to seek him; but before that time had expired we saw the gray top of his head, as he moved straight towards us with that swaying motion peculiar to the animal—his head close to the ground, and now and again sucking up great mouthfuls of berries on either side of him. He was not more than sixty yards off; I got my bead upon him and kept it there as long as he moved forward towards us. At length, some bunch of fruit more tempting than the rest caused him to turn broadside, with his head down the hill, and I let him have it behind the shoulder. It was a

relief when the rifle cracked and the mental strain was over, whether I had missed him or not. But then I knew for certain that I had not missed him. When the smoke cleared — it was before the days of Schultz or E.C.—the bear appeared running straight towards us, quite unaware of the quarter whence he had been stricken, and it almost looked as if he were charging us. Now he reached the opposite edge of the ravine beneath us and began climbing down its face, but lurching so heavily that I could hardly keep myself from shouting, for I saw that he had the lead in a vital spot. Telling my companion to reserve his fire for close quarters, I gave the enemy a second barrel which made him reel again. At the bottom of the ravine he reared up on his hind-legs, clasping a young tree and swaying it to and fro in his struggles with death. Two more shots and then he rolled over. As we ran towards him we danced and yelled and shrieked as if we were demented. But we had sense enough to draw near with some care and from above, as he lay on his side apparently *in articulo mortis*. Tenderly approaching I tried to turn him over with my foot, when he suddenly raised himself on his fore-feet, with a very unpleasant rattle in his throat, and tried to scramble up the hill after us. For this we were prepared and springing back I finished the business with a shot through his forehead. We proceeded to examine our prize. Though I have hitherto spoken of it as a male it proved to be a she-bear four years old, and five feet long from the nose to the tip of the tail. Now that we came to inspect her closely her light colour was even more strange than it appeared on the hill side. Seizing her fore-paws we dragged her down the steep slopes till we were joined by our native and two others from a *sæter* below. They were almost as delighted as we were, for they had suffered much. About the time we got her down into the valley, there was a shout from the top of the ridge above us and there were the other party. They had heard the shots and our shouts which sounded to them like a wail of distress. Old Per had said " Spring vi over fjeldet," and they must have " sprungt " indeed to have accomplished the distance in the time. With their glasses they had made out the body of the bear in the midst of the group, and more answering whoops went up from us to assure them there was no delusion.

A cart was sent for, and the bear was conveyed to the farm with all the pomp and circumstance befitting our important victory. Then we had a grand skinning in the presence of the whole population; I never felt myself so big a man before or since. I was told that I must immediately proceed to the nearest *landsman* or magistrate, and claim the reward, but, as that would involve a two days' journey, and the mutilation of my trophy by the extraction of two of the claws, I preferred to forego the five dollars which I had earned, whereat the natives wondered. On investigation it appeared that my first shot would have sufficed, and after Per had seen the destruction which it wrought, he did not again take the trouble to carry his cannon when he went with us. But though we worked harder than ever, we saw nothing more that year. Then we sailed back to Havnen on the island, and nearly ate a famous old sportsman who was staying there out of house and home, while we waited the coming of the old *Tasso*.

What Norwegian sportsman of the last generation does not remember that old ship? She plied from Hull to Throndhjem, threading the islands for the last quarter of the way, and dropping or picking up her ardent passengers at various outlandish points. How jealously they guarded the secrets of the rivers and fjelds, and yet how friendly they were! If I remember rightly she had been once cut in half and mended again to suit the passenger traffic. In the winter she returned to her vocation of carrying stockfish to the Mediterranean, and you would have known that too without being told. In spite of the tumbling seas on the Dogger, and the fat pork, and greasy stewards, which things were a snare for weak stomachs, those of her patrons who have not gone on a longer voyage must have memories of jovial hours on her salted decks. The last I saw of the old ship was the tips of her masts sticking up in one of the narrow channels between Stavanger and Bergen. Once more and for the last time she broke her back, but it was on a rock and in a snowstorm. She was past patching that time and her old bones were to be put up to auction on a certain day at twelve o'clock. But at ten o'clock she had cheated the hammer by knocking herself down for nothing, and sinking in deep water. However that was years after the date of which I am writing.

The next time I visited my bear-ground, we disembarked at Christiansund, and hired a little steam launch which carried us through the night up the long and narrow strait of the Vinge Fjord, the head of which is divided by a few miles of isthmus from the Hevne Fjord. When the little engine stopped its panting, we breakfasted in the dark, and as soon as the morning broke, landed and were once more greeted by old Peter and his son, and were quickly devouring the news which they had brought about bears in plenty and of portentous size. We soon found that their accounts were not exaggerated as there was much "sign" about. I think it was on the second day after our arrival that we were trying a long hog-backed ridge called the Rod Fjeld, thickly wooded on its sides, but open at the top—a small place, but a favourite resort of bears. Arrived at the top we separated; I went with Per along one flank, Geof with the lad on the other. Halfway along our beat there was a ridge which hid a useful-looking hollow from our view. I suggested that we should make a detour so as to survey this depression before advancing to the windward of it. But Per said it was no good, and I followed, too tamely, at his heels. We now reached an eminence which commanded the ground in front of us, and had scarcely sat down to spy it, when a large she-bear and her half-grown cub galloped out of the hollow which we had thus foolishly missed, and passed scarcely a hundred yards from us; I levelled my piece, but Per arrested me, saying, "Don't shoot; they will stop, they are only going to feed." If that was so, they must have been in a great hurry for their supper. Of course they had smelt us and were bound for the next parish. They never paused till they had put several hundred yards between us, and then dived into thick trees on the other side. We followed, vainly hoping that Per's surmise was correct, and that we might yet find them. We did see something moving in the bushes. As we stealthily crept forward some dimly-seen form was approaching

T

us from the opposite direction; drawing behind a bush I waited with my rifle ready. There was a faint rustle and Geof appeared with his rifle presented at my head. We had been stalking one another.

After this we shifted our ground to Krokstad on a branch of the fjord that runs far up into the mountain, and here, unlike the generally soft tone of this fjord, tall cliffs hang over still and inky waters. This moving about from farm to farm is very pleasant. The quality of the quarters varied, but, though we never knew what we should find, we were always sure of a cordial reception. Here in this darksome corner of the world there was quite a fleet of herring-boats which were busy day and night, and with good results, to judge from the boats, nearly gunwale full of silver treasure, which were being rowed across to the larger smacks, for conveyance to Thromdhjem. These fish are called *fat* herrings and they deserve the title. They were entirely without roe and all the oily juice of their bodies was concentrated in the flesh. I want some scientific man to tell me why they don't make maiden herrings like that on our coasts, and why we are condemned to eat them only when in an interesting condition.

The attractions of this beautiful place were further enhanced by vast flocks of gulls continually in motion, and shoals of porpoises, justly called *cacciatore di mare*, who were also engaged in chasing the herrings. I was told that a whale occasionally follows the shoals into these narrows, and it is recorded that "sometimes he swallows such vast quantities, that his belly will hardly contain them, and is even ready to burst, which causes the whale to set up a hideous roar."

At this place the bears had been committing great ravages, and the evening of our arrival I saw one—very large and nearly black. He was feeding about six hundred yards from me on the top of a cliff. I quickly halved this distance and was just counting on a first-rate chance when he disappeared into the tangle which clothed the face of the cliff and I saw him no more.

We did not however return from that expedition

GEOF.

quite empty-handed. It was at Beerdal that Geof got his bear. When we reached the foot of the mountain the people at the farm told how they had seen a bear only an hour before. We again took opposite flanks of the same ridge, a method which I do not recommend, as one party is very liable to interfere with the other by giving the wind, and from the difficulty of defining the beats beforehand. At four o'clock I heard two shots and then after a pause two more. My companion and I set off running and crossed the intervening crest. Guided by loud talking we quickly found the other party. Geof had seen something through the tree-stems and pulled Per down into the bilberry bushes. From this place of concealment they made out two bears, as usual busy with the fruit. Keeping very flat he crawled forward. Then one of the animals moved towards him and gave him a good chance. He took a steady aim behind the shoulder, and knocked him right over. But, as he was about to fire his second shot at the other bear, the first gathered himself together, rose up, shook himself, and made off. A second shot failed to stop him. Loading as he went Geof ran forward as fast as the roughness of the ground would permit, and actually overtook the bear, or at least got near enough to perceive the wound in its side; but the meeting was so sudden and unexpected to man and beast that, while the latter slid off the edge of the rock like oil, two more bullets went over his back. He was evidently severely wounded but he had now reached the edge of a steep declivity down which he went, sliding, rolling and tumbling, and was instantly lost to view.

Geof was under that common delusion that the lost bear was of very large size. The next hour was therefore almost too exciting to be pleasant. We hunted every cranny of that cliff, never knowing from moment to moment whether the infuriated beast would not spring out upon us. At last darkness drove us down, and in a very depressed condition of mind we rowed away to our night's quarters. But the first streak of dawn found us on the spot again, reinforced by a company of peasants, and we carefully quartered the ground. This measure proved effectual, and in a quarter of an hour one of them had recovered the blood-stained track, and, following it up, had found the bear, quite dead, at the foot of the cliff. The only disenchanting thing about it was that it proved to be a mere hobbledehoy of a bear after all.

I did not have an opportunity of revisiting that country for a good many years, and when I did so, I learned that the bears had left their old haunts, and this information was completely confirmed by a search of all the favourite places. There was no sign of a bear having been there for years. It was difficult to account for this for they had been little hunted. Perhaps it was a bad year for fruit. I daresay they are back there by now, and if any of my readers should be tempted to visit the place, I hope he will let me know the result.

I will conclude this chapter with a story which was told me by an Englishman, long resident in Scandinavia, and for whose veracity I will vouch. It shows that though Bruin almost always runs away, accidents do sometimes happen. Two poachers, Nils and Lars, were out after elk in the winter. The dog in Lars's charge was drawing on something. Nils kept some way to the left on a parallel course. Suddenly Lars saw something gray in a clump of fir-trees and fired. Confident of having held true, he ran forward to ascertain the effect of his shot. Instantly a large bear charged him, and, before his friend could intervene, had so mauled him that he died the same evening. Wild with grief for his friend, Nils started with a dog to avenge his death. The task should be easy, for the bear had gone off leaving bloody tracks in the snow. But Nils never returned. Three days later a search party found him bitten and clawed to death. Strange to say his gun had not been discharged, and still more strange, his dog had also been killed by the bear, who had himself succumbed to his wound, and lay dead a few yards farther. Thus of all those concerned in this tragedy there was no survivor.

IX

A TANTALISING QUEST

The red deer of Asia Minor is by no means widely distributed over the peninsula. The essential conditions of its existence — forest, seclusion, and above all running water—are combined in comparatively few of the elevated ranges of the country. In a former chapter I have recorded a trip which I made for the purpose of hunting the wild goat or ibex of that country, and how, in the course of our search for that animal, we, by chance, discovered a mountain and a forest where the red deer existed in tolerable numbers. Our stay there had been necessarily restricted to a few days, and during that time, my companion secured two stags, one of them being of great size, and carrying a grand head of fourteen points, while neither my son nor I got a chance. Considering the splendid dimensions of these deer, which are, I think, even larger than the Himalayan *Barasingha*, and inferior to no other species of red deer in the world, except the wapiti of America, it was not to be expected that I should sit down patiently under this rebuff. In the autumn of last year, I revisited the same range, in the company of Mr. A. E. Pease, in the confident expectation of securing some trophies. In this, however, for various reasons, we were completely unsuccessful, although, on several occasions we nearly grasped the prize. I appreciated more than

THE BIG HEAD.

ever the ease with which my companion, Findlay, in the previous year, came, saw and conquered, where I, after infinite toils, had twice to retire, confessing myself routed; and, to show that I am not jealous, I here insert a picture of his big head, literally copied from a photograph of it taken immediately after it was brought into camp.

Our failure will not perhaps make our experiences the less interesting to sportsmen. The conditions of this quest were unusually difficult, and the details may perhaps suggest to those who may follow us, the best means of overcoming them; for though this chapter may read like an apology for our defeat, I do not pretend that we did not make mistakes. What Nimrod so inspired as not to do so? I only say that in addition to any errors of judgment we may have made, we had more than our share of bad luck.

The Continental journey, the triple voyage, the glimpses of Corfu, Athens, and Smyrna need not be dwelt upon. Let me begin by describing the ground we designed to hunt. Abruptly, out of the level plain, springs one of the Pisidian ranges, the "White Mountain," so called from its twin peaks of limestone, which rise, to a height of 7000 ft., gaunt and bare by contrast with their lower slopes, the last-named being sombre-hued from the cypress and scrubby oak which, on this side, clothe the base of the range. Its leading feature is a ravine of extraordinary depth dividing these peaks, and literally cleaving the mountain to its roots. The tool which has carved this narrow groove is a little stream which seems quite out of proportion to the work it has accomplished. It pursues its silent way 3000 feet below the double summit, and through depths which never see the sun, while nothing that has not wings can follow its course throughout. It actually disappears from view before it reaches the plain, though an extensive cane brake, a favourite resort of wild boar, marks the place where it oozes forth again. The sheer cliffs which face one another on either side of it, are honeycombed with holes and caverns, and show how the water has gradually melted out a way for itself through the soluble limestone.

A rough pass crosses the mountain at a great height above this ravine, and near the highest point of the path we pitched our first camp. Our pack train, which comprised a varied assortment of horses, camels, and donkeys, had dawdled by the way. This was the more trying to our patience as a thunderstorm was gathering and growling behind us. Just as we reached the camp it burst upon us, and in a few moments the ground was white with large hailstones. Hastily pulling one of our little tents from the back of the animal which carried it, we held it up—there was no time to pitch it—and as many as could gained a partial shelter by crouching inside; but such of our packages as were not waterproof were presently reduced to draggled rags, and our bread to sodden pulp. This dusting was not the pleasantest form of greeting, but it was soon over, and the bushes around were presently arrayed in a strange assortment of garments, British and Oriental, steaming in the setting sun. We had no reason to grumble, for thenceforth for twenty-eight days we enjoyed a heavenly climate, once only similarly broken. Frosts at sunrise, fresh sparkling mornings, then four hours of blazing heat for salamanders who liked it, or, for those who did not, a soft bed of pine-needles in the cool shade among the fir-tree columns, and the sweet resinous smell which the sun distils from them. Then again, the cool shade of the mountain, for the sun dipped early behind the lofty ridges, while, for two hours more, its shafts of light continued to stream through the great gap, painting its white cliffs red; and when, as sometimes happened, the twin peaks were capped with lurid storm clouds, the level rays were deflected downwards, and dispersed in prismatic colours.

From our elevated camp we overlooked the country beyond the White Peaks—a great expanse of lower hills, of rounded form, and generally free from rocks, but covered from top to bottom with a vast pine forest complicated by numerous hollows, pockets, and deep narrow ravines, at the bottom of which trickled tiny streams generally half blocked with fallen stems. Beyond, lay the plain again, dotted with patches of green, indicating villages and water, and beyond that again, range upon range of mountains, most of them of a uniform light gray colour—an important fact from the sportsman's point of view, for it denoted their waterless and treeless condition, and indeed the almost total absence of any kind of life.

The forest consists of pines of the Corsican variety which throws grand trunks, but carries, comparatively, scanty tops. Fires are of constant occurrence, and their track is marked by wide patches of whitened stems. These are terrible places to get through, for the ground is littered with rotting branches, and the admission of light and air induces a tremendous tangle of undergrowth. This forest, like every other in Turkey, is rapidly disappearing. On one occasion, in the course of a two hours' ride into these hills, I counted thirty donkeys, or horses, laden with roughly-hewn beams or firewood, and this process goes on all the year round. The finest trees are cut down to furnish perhaps a single joist, or even left to rot if not precisely to the mind of the woodman.

Such was our hunting ground. We knew there were red deer there, and were eager to begin, but before doing so, let me describe the *personnel* of our party. It must be admitted, that on this occasion, our following was too large, and the consequent increase of luggage was a serious impediment. The supposed difficulties of the country accounted for this. Nevertheless, it was a mistake which I here place on record as a warning to others.

On Celestin, who has appeared before in these pages, I, of course, placed my chief reliance as a stalker. I had also engaged a countryman of his who combined the joint functions of hunter and camp servant. To Achmet, a Yuruk, who summers his goats in these mountains, we looked for local knowledge. He has the reputation of being a great hunter. Careful cross-examination elicited the candid confession that he had only killed three deer in his life, all hinds. Indeed, he admitted that he had found them so difficult to get, that he had given up trying on his own account.[1] Achmet had, however, some knowledge of the haunts and habits of the denizens of the forest, and he kept our spirits up by his sanguine belief in the power and accuracy of our rifles, and our infallibility as hunters. If he heard a stag roar, he danced a triumphal *pas seul*: "Inshallah, we will have his head to-night."

[1] It would appear that others are not more fortunate, for I could hear of no horns in the villages, and very few pairs find their way to Smyrna or Constantinople. This is, perhaps, in part accounted for by the custom, which, I understand, prevails among the villagers, of presenting any shed horns which they may obtain to the mosques.

Bouba, the erst-while brigand, whose early escapades have been described by me in a former chapter, acted as our general adviser and protector. Then there were the interpreter and the cook. The selection of Levantine servants is always a lottery, and in this case we drew a blank as well as a prize. François, a Smyrniote, acted as our interpreter, but was ready to assume at a moment's

JANI.

notice all other functions, such as tailor, washerwoman, kitchen-maid, postman, beater, and even on one occasion, relieved me from much pain by his skill as a chiropodist. In old Jani, whom we hired as cook, we carried dead weight. He had never learnt to build a camp fire, which is rather an essential beginning, and his soul scarcely soared above the mysteries of *pilaji*, that universal Turkish dish consisting of boiled rice and scraps. Of the washing of pots and pans, or indeed of any ablutions at all, he could not see the necessity, because, as he said, "They dirt themselves to-morrow." But besides this he had the most muddled mind I ever encountered. Standing erect, among a chaos of utensils, on his shoulders an old soiled blanket which he wore day and night, he would slowly revolve on his axis with a vacant, searching expression on his face, while he vainly endeavoured to recall where he had last mislaid the handle of the frying-pan, or some equally essential article. Why we kept him on I do not know, except that he could never have found his way back alone, and that we regarded him as a sort of court fool, whom we carried for our amusement. His pigeon English was certainly worth preserving. In reply to a ravenous sportsman as to what he had got for dinner: "I know; chickens. One chicken cooks you : one chicken eats men with pilaff; one chicken soups." "But, Jani, we are getting rather tired of chickens." "Buy sheep upstairs" (on the mountain). "And how far may that be?" "Two o'clock to another small country—half a street." That is obscure, but we, who understood the workings of his mind, knew that he meant, "two hours to the next village—quite a short journey." At last, one day, he disdained even the slight preparation indicated above, and remained rolled up in his old blanket. When roused he excused himself: "Something twist in stomick; he very smart." I gave him a rousing dose of castor oil and essence of ginger, after which, if not very smart, he was rather smarter than before. He had a private remedy of his own which he thus described:—"He makey very hot rocks in fire; one for belly, one for what you call derrière." We discouraged the practice of this drastic cure; which, however comforting, was an inconvenient one for the cook.

Last, but not least, I may mention my dear dog "Smoke," a Norwegian elk-hound, who I hoped would prove useful in the forest. He is a *bind-hund, i.e.* his *métier* is to indicate by his manner the presence of deer, and to lead his master towards them. If it had not been

"SMOKE."

for an untoward mistake, which I will presently narrate, he would have justified his presence, and as it was, he amply repaid the trouble of bringing him by his agreeable company. He is of a sociable disposition and wishes to make friends with every two-footed or four-footed creature he meets. This did not always answer, for a Turk regards all dogs as equally accursed, and the local dogs vehemently resent the intrusion of a stranger of their own kind. He, therefore, soon learned to keep pretty close to heel when we approached a village. In the plains "Smoke's" heavy fur coat was unsuited to the climate, and his drooping spirits were reflected in the attitude of ears and tail. On the hills all this was changed. His eager face was the picture of alertness, and the curl of his grand old tail, like a big steel watch-spring, showed that he respected himself and knew what was expected of him. In a day or two he was familiar with all the signs of game, and the roar of a stag obviously caused the same shiver in the small of his back as it did in mine. When he heard it, he would cock his head on one side, and think how nice a broiled steak would be. Then he would look up at me, and say quite plainly: "If they were only in an open place now, about forty yards off, and feeding." At night he regarded himself as our protector from all kinds of vermin, and lay at our feet until the first signs of dawn appeared, and I told him that I was about to perform my toilet.—a very brief one, by the way, on a frosty morning.

At the first sign of dawn on the morning after our arrival we were ready for the start, but the cold steam caused by the storm of the night before, settled round us in a thick fog. At last the sun dispersed it, and we started in opposite directions. Scarcely five hundred yards from camp Celestin and I found a little opening on a ridge where grass and herbs grew rank and strong—a favourite feeding ground, for it was tracked in every direction. Nor were those proofs wanting which, we are told, the *harbourer* of old was wont to

> "Offer on bended knee
> To the Ladie of high degree."

Close by, too, we found the unmistakable traces of a bear. I may mention here that we constantly met with such signs again, but, as the bears spend their days in some fortress among the rocks of the ravine, and wander only at night, there was not much chance of encountering them in the flesh. At any rate we never did so. They appear to feed on the berries of the juniper, which clothes the higher corries of the mountain. But on this first day what cared we for any game less noble than "a stag of fourteen"?

There were some sheltered hollows just below which looked likely, and, descending to a lower level, we got to the leeward of them and proceeded to quarter the ground with the light breeze in our faces. Now "Smoke" begins to understand. He presses forward a few paces and stands in an attitude as if he were trying to remember something. Perhaps it is the memory of a smell something like that in a far-off land. In a moment he appreciates what he has been brought here for. His ears stiffen up into two black pyramids, and there is an intent look in his eyes as he lifts his nose to the wind, and works it up and down with a tossing motion. Then he pulls on his cord, and, as an old sportsman hath it,

> "When my hound doth strain upon good scent,
> I must confess the same doth me content."

We let him lead, till, in a few minutes, he brings us to some fresh tracks of that morning, a big stag, too, among them. We now took the conduct of affairs into our own hands, and tried to follow the line which the animals had taken, but they had wandered hither and thither, and at last we got confused, and then lost them altogether on some hard ground. Half an hour was spent in making a careful cast below, in what seemed to be their direction, but we failed to recover the line. All this time the dog continued to have the wind, but doubtfully, and as he kept eyeing the ground above him we took the hint and tried up the hill again. Perhaps we had rather relaxed our caution. May be we came too suddenly over the edge of a little gully, filled with a growth of young firs. Something started below us. "*Mais voyez donc. Tirez vite!*" But whatever Celestin saw was invisible to me, and it is no good shooting at a fir clump. We sat down and lunched, and out of our leather cups drank the waters of disappointment. Alas! before we had done, we had to drain them to the dregs. Celestin, meanwhile, consoled himself by apostrophising the stag and his relations. It is his habit to hurl opprobrious epithets at any animal in which he is interested, and the more he respects its intelligence, the stronger the language. Once, when on a visit to me in England, he was taken, among other sights, to see the Law Courts. Much impressed by the judge on the Bench, he felt that he was expected to say something. He summed up his impressions in four words, which, in his mouth, far from indicating any contempt of Court, expressed both reverence and astonishment—"*Mais le vieux cochon!*"

I may mention that Celestin, as is natural for a chamois hunter, has little faith in the dog. He places his chief reliance on the telescope. In my judgment, in a forest such as we were hunting in, it is almost useless. It is true that there are vistas and narrow openings which may be surveyed, and where deer may be occasionally spied, but they do not amount to a tenth of the surface. Assuming that deer have been "spotted" from some elevated position, it is a work of time to reach the place, and, in the meanwhile, it is practically certain that they will have moved, if only a little; and, without a knowledge of their exact position, there is every probability of "jumping" them. I do not discard the glass, but, in spite of our failure to score, I believe in the dog's nose by preference. On the other hand, one must admit, that unless perfectly trained, his impatience may get the better of his discretion at a critical moment, and the chance may be spoiled by an uncontrollable whimper.

But let us go down and find the tracks of the deer that we have disturbed, and see if they will read us any useful lessons. In the course of the investigation the special difficulties which attend this kind of hunting will appear. We soon found them, and also the couches in which the deer were lying when we came over the ridge. Sit down in this bed which a stag has just vacated when he was jumped by us. From behind he was protected by the wind. He was himself in deep shade, and in front of him a thin screen of seedling trees just hid the whole of his body, while his horns harmonised perfectly with the dead snags of a fallen branch. But that did not prevent his having a full view of the opposite ridge. True, it is timbered as heavily as on this side, but he would not fail to see us cross one of the little openings.

Let us follow the page of his story as printed by himself. He probably lay low till we were hidden, then sprang, not with the fore and aft motion of a tame animal, but with a single bound as if he had been ejected by steel springs, and came down with all four feet close together, and driven deeply into the pine needles. He must have stood like that, rigid, for an instant, then took two long swift strides. That was perhaps the moment in which Celestin got a glimpse of him, but if I had seen him I could not have got a shot, for he stopped again almost instantly behind a big pine stem; again five or six strides and he stopped behind an impenetrable screen of young fir-trees. Now his retreat was assured, and he took it leisurely. Dropping his tell-tale head, he softly pushed his way through the close-ranked stems. Apparently, he soon forgot his fright and began feeding about. Probably he only took us for woodcutters, some of whom he sees and hears every day. The deer are unmolested by them, and are consequently little alarmed at their approach, but they are continually moved by them, and become "skulkers," a habit which makes them more difficult for the hunter to come at. Here, our friend stopped and viciously punished a young tree, reducing it to matchwood and twisted fibre, no doubt saying to himself, that that was what he would like to do to the beastly two-legged creatures who had disturbed his siesta.

In this kind of hunting there is first of all the difficulty, which is common to all woodland stalking, of locating the game before approaching it. In Scotland the deer-stalker is practically certain to see the deer before he can be seen. Not only that, but he spends an hour in arranging the exact course of his stalk, and before he starts he traces his approach from ridge to hollow, from hollow to peat-hag, even to the very rock from which he intends to shoot. In a forest like this, on the other hand, he cannot see a hundred yards in any direction, and there is every probability of getting within earshot of the deer before it is possible to see them. They have, therefore, every advantage over the man, and the chances are greatly in favour of their either seeing or smelling him first. In most cases they take their leave without his ever becoming aware of their proximity, unless he should presently come across tracks, very deep at the toe, and with the dirt scattered around—a sure and certain sign that those who made them departed in fear. Unless this is the case, deer are never in a hurry. Even when in motion, their gait is a saunter, which, for strategic purposes of defence, is almost as good as standing still. When lying it is needless to observe that a favourable position is always chosen. Then, unless a man has been brought up to hunting in woods, he is almost sure to forget his legs. The branches hide his view and it does not occur to him that the eyes of a deer are at a level to see under them. After all he is no wiser than the ostrich. Again, as a set-off to all his other advantages as a predatory animal, man is a most conspicuous object. A post six feet high catches the eye on any kind of ground. In deer-stalking in open country where he can discover the game from a distance, he counteracts this disability by making to himself four legs, wherewith to make his final approach.

He is also, for his weight, the most noisy of animals. He makes more fuss with his two legs than anything else endowed with four, and that brings me to the greatest difficulty we had to encounter—the abnormal stillness of the air. In Scandinavia, where elk are hunted in forest nearly, but not quite, as dense, it is considered hopeless to go out on a still day. Here we heard scarcely a whisper in the trees the whole time. But in another sense these woods are unusually "noisy," from sticks and stones, and crisp dry leaves which strew the ground. If you imitate the deer and lie low, you may hear every leaf that falls within thirty yards, and a tom-tit alighting on a twig makes quite a commotion. You realise how difficult it would be for a man to approach within shooting distance without detection, unless he should come up behind a ridge. "Smoke" repeatedly showed that he could hear an approaching footstep long before I could, and a deer's sense of hearing is doubtless fully as acute as a dog's.

It must not be supposed that the deer are as plentiful here as in a Scotch forest; there are comparatively few. Tracks there are in plenty, but it does not do to get much excited over tracks. One deer makes a good many in the course of a night. I attach more importance to the frequency of "beds" and to trees which have been punished by the horns of stags. Both birds and beasts of prey doubtless take toll of the fawns. There is a large black eagle whose table-like nests built on the flat tops of fir-trees, were very conspicuous from above. Then there is a smaller kind, of a lighter colour, which builds in great numbers in the cliffs. There are also many small beasts of prey. I secured a curious little polecat, but that was on the plains. His body is mottled yellow and brown like a tabby cat. He has a well-defined white band across his forehead, and his furry ears, which he carries upright like those of a marmoset monkey, are also white. I learn from Sir W. H. Flower that it is the "marbled polecat." I saw him curled up in the grass and for a moment thought he was a kitten, for it was close to a village, and I called off my dog who was making for him. This woke the creature, and, when he started to run, his arched back and furry tail indicated the weasel tribe. We all started in pursuit and one of the Turks ran him down just as he reached his hole. The curious part of it was that the natives who were with me declared they had never seen one like it before.

One word as to the ancient records of *Cervus elaphus*, as an inhabitant of the Levant. I have made many inquiries for carved representations of red deer among those who are familiar with the remains scattered about Asia Minor; but, though graven images of the wild goat are known, I have not been able to hear of anything like a stag. Perhaps the horns puzzled the artists. That red deer existed in those regions long ago cannot be doubted. Herodotus mentions "gigantic bulls whose horns were carried into Greece." Aristotle describes the *Cervus elaphus* as found at Arginusae, on the Stag Mountain. Some authors of ancient Greece give a curious derivation of the name—ἐλᾶν ὄφεις, the "serpent chaser"—though modern scholars might hesitate to accept it. The implied tradition is frequently met with. Turberville quotes from Isidore: "The Harte is right contrairie to the serpente, and when he is olde, decrepyte, and sicke, hee goeth to the dennes and caves of serpentes, and with his nostrils he puffeth and forceth his breath into their holes in such sorte, that by virtue and force thereof he constreyneth the serpentes to come forth, and killeth them with his foote, and afterwards eateth and devoureth them. Afterward he goeth to drink, and so the venyme spreadeth through all the veynes of his body; and when he feeleth the venyme work he runneth to chase and heat himself, in such sorte that nothing remayneth in his belly, coming forth by all the conduits and pores that nature hath made in him, and by this means he reneweth his force and healeth himself, casting his haire." That deer do pursue and kill snakes there is confirmation from modern observers.

Pliny's statement of the swimming powers of these animals is perhaps the most remarkable part of his account of them. He says: "They pass the seas, swimming by flocks and whole herds, in a long row, each one resting his head upon the buttocks of his fellow next before him. And this they do in course, so as the foremost retireth behind to the hindmost by turns, one after another, and this is ordinarily observed by those sailors that pass from Cilicia to Cyprus; and yet in their swimming they descry no land by the eye, but only by their smelling have an aim thereat."

We soon realised the difficulties of our quest, but we persevered, hoping to fluke something. If the sport is a tantalising one, the excitement is pretty constant. As I have no triumph to record, I must describe one or two occasions when I only just missed securing it. After a long day, spent in futile search for a stag which Alfred had mortally wounded and lost the night before, we returned to camp by separate routes. We knew there were deer in the valley which I intended to try, for as we had gone up that way in the morning, and were approaching a little opening, we were brought up standing by the smell of deer, pungent and unmistakable—a rampant smell, which caused me instantly to cock my rifle. They were gone—how long since, it was impossible to say,—for in that still air, and on the dewy grass, the scent might hang for some time. On many subsequent occasions my nostrils were assailed in the same way, and a very tantalising thing it was. I have heard of people who believe themselves to be surrounded by spirits. Here the invisible essence filled the air and made one feel just like that. I was confident that the deer had remained on that side of the valley, for the opposite side had been occupied during the day by a noisy company of woodcutters.

We had not traversed half our appointed beat, before what light air there was shifted to our backs, and to avoid disturbing the ground, we pursued our way homewards along the torrent bed at the bottom. "Smoke" suddenly paused and made that wavy motion of his nose as if he were drinking and swallowing the air, while he looked steadfastly up the steep slope to the left. He was not very sure, for he could not get the wind direct. We had just passed one of the steep gullies that run straight up and down these slopes. They always contain rank herbage and are favourite feeding places, so that I felt sure that the deer, if deer there were, were somewhere in it. We mounted the slope, not following the course of the gully, but making little loops and returning to it at a higher and a higher point. Still, the dog was doubtful, as was shown by his gazing, first in one direction, then in another. My companion, who is without experience, but fond of making suggestions, said: "*On dirait qu'il doit être libre.*" I do not know if I made any answer to this wild proposal, totally foreign to the principles of a *bind-hound*. If I did I suppose I was misunderstood. Intent on the ground before me, I did not observe what B—— was doing. The next moment, to my horror, the dog trotted past me freed from his cord. I turned and asked B—— what he had done, whereupon he began calling him back; but it was too late. At that moment "Smoke" shot ahead like an arrow, and ten seconds later was heard barking furiously at the heels of a deer, which rushed with tremendous clatter up the slope. I sat down hoping to see under the branches. One vision of brown hide I had—too brief to shoot. Achmet said: "*Boyouour*," ("horns") and with a pantomimic action of his arms indicated a pair of antlers. He was probably right, for it was a solitary deer, but I could not see them. Now this insane act of B——'s was a great misfortune, for it not only lost me a first-rate chance,—I must in two minutes have looked down on the stag's broad back as he was busy feeding in the bottom of the gully,—but it was certain to ruin the steadiness of the dog. Sore in spirit I stumbled campwards. "Smoke," meanwhile, was waking the echoes. When he picked up my track and rejoined me, three-quarters of an hour later, I had to give him a thrashing, for his good, but it was sadly against the grain, for his fault was no fault of his.

Now we had agreed to move our camp that day from its elevated position to a little meadow which we knew of by the side of the main stream. This reached, we found, to our disgust, no signs of our people, and it was now nearly pitch dark. I thought something had prevented the removal, and that we must climb a thousand feet higher to the old camp. We expended nearly a box of matches in examining the horse tracks by the stream. I thought they were all old. Achmet declared them to be fresh. At last he seized me vehemently by the lappets of my coat and then began fiercely pulling off his clothes. It looked as if he wanted to fight me, but I correctly interpreted the action to mean that he would pledge his old coat that his view was correct. I let him have his way, and we stumbled over fallen stems and along the stony bed of the stream, and at last began to see the red reflection of a fire on the pine trees. Just then two shots were fired as a signal, and we were soon at home. This was a pretty camp, and as sheltered as the other was exposed. The little stream ran past the door of our tent. Its deeper pools were full of small trout of a very light colour. They were singularly fearless, and I daresay would be easy to catch, but we did not try.

Two of the animals of our pack train had come to grief on the way down, and rolled forty metres down the slope. The accident had no worse result than this:—Alfred's favourite tin of flea powder was smashed and all his possessions were permeated with its contents. In the morning every fly in the tent clung to the roof a shrivelled corpse, and the ultimate consequence was still more serious, for when the bag was opened the insidious dust gave him such an attack of asthma that he did not completely recover from its effects for three weeks.

We had timed our visit to make the most of the season of "love and war," hoping that the "belling" or "roaring" of the stags would help us. It has always seemed to me that the latter term is a misnomer as a description of the sound, which is more like the exaggerated yawn of a big lusty man. It did not prove to be such an assistance as I expected. Comparatively few of the stags seemed to roar at all, at least during daylight. One reason of this may have been that there was at this time a good moon, and when this is the case deer do most of their feeding at night and lie very quiet during the day. Then a roaring stag is generally a travelling stag, and, therefore, a difficult beast to come at. I heard the first on September 28, in the big ravine far below our first camp. A few hours later he was heard and seen by one of our party, miles away, and the next day he was far in another direction. I had no doubt of his identity. He was in the first access of passion, alone, but seeking the hinds. Of course I hoped to become better acquainted with the voice of this charmer.

An extensive hill rises about a thousand feet above our second camp. It is a favourite resort of deer, but much of it is covered with a growth of young firs twelve or fourteen feet high, which are even more difficult to traverse and to see through than the bare stems of older trees. We soon found an opening where deer had fed that morning, and where their fragrance still hung in the air. The tracks tending in the same direction as the dog indicated, we allowed him to lead us. Over ridge and dale he took us. There was clearly something in front, but he hesitated a good deal as if something puzzled him. At last he showed signs of great impatience when we reached the edge of a basin, full from side to side of young fir-trees. As it was a hopeless place to get a shot in, I sent Celestin round to drive it towards me, but when he rejoined me it was to tell me that the dog still hankered after something beyond. To cut a long story short, he led us, at length, into the middle of a fine sounder of hogs. "Smoke" must not be blamed for this. He had never smelt wild boar before, and he had no reason to think that pork would be less acceptable than venison. The family party were all so busily engaged in turning up the ground with their long black snouts that I might have taken my time and picked out any one, but I was so disgusted at this descent to the ridiculous, that I fired wildly at a sleek young porker and missed him clean. I think that, at this time of the year, these pigs come up from the marshes on the plain for a kind of mushroom,—coarse but edible—which grows in quantities in the black pine *humus*.

On a subsequent occasion I was more fortunate. I jumped a big solitary boar from a mass of fallen timber and scrub. Springing to a more open place, I waited for the chance. Then Celestin silently indicated that he saw him. I softly crept back to his side and made out a large black *something* which seemed to be standing and listening. There was a slight motion, and I instantly pulled the trigger, but as I did so, the stem of a tree mixed itself up with the dim outline. However, a careful examination of the trunk failed to reveal a bullet mark. So we laid "Smoke" on. At first he showed some signs of trepidation, but presently taking to it more kindly, led us on the track till we found a large patch of blood, and, a few yards farther, the boar himself, leaning against a tree and quite dead.

But to return to the day in question. We were now opposite to a long wild corrie where I felt sure there would be deer, and though it involved a stiff descent and reascent, we determined to try. We had not gone far before "Smoke" again winded something, and when he had led us some way his opinion was confirmed by the faint sound of a stag's challenge far up the glen. I believe him to have been the Don Juan I have already mentioned. He had found his wives but was roaring lustily for more. I judged from the intermittent and gasping sound, that he had rivals and was busy defending his rights. I afterwards found, near his track, part of a brow antler broken off— a significant trophy of battle,—but I had not the luck to see an encounter. On subsequent days we came across the tracks of many solitary stags—large animals too. They were not roaring, and I infer from this that they had been defeated and were not in the humour to assert themselves.

We now got to a higher level to approach more rapidly. Each time we surmounted a ridge and looked into the corrie below it, we had to wait for another signal to assure ourselves that the stag was beyond the next shoulder, for this sound is not one which is easy to locate. After passing successively five or six ridges and corries, we made sure that the sound proceeded from just beyond a steep rise which faced us. What with the labour of climbing it and the excitement of the moment, by the time we had reached the top my heart felt like bursting its bounds. We knew that we must be close to our quarry, and "Smoke" amply confirmed this, for the previous misteaching now showed itself. He was pulling furiously on his cord, so that Celestin had all he could do to hold him, and I was trembling lest he should make some more audible demonstration. No doubt I ought to have retired for some distance, and waited for the next challenge. It is so easy to be wise after the event. What I did was to push forward as softly as I could through the intervening clump of young firs, but all the time my steps were hurried by the sound of the struggle behind me, and that which I dreaded occurred. I have no doubt that the stag heard it too. As I gently pushed aside the last branches I saw a great pair of brow antlers pointing skywards, the crowns of the same thrown well back behind two attentive ears, and a keen nose pointing in my direction. A very quick shot might have got his rifle off, but that I am not, and before I could bring mine to my shoulder, the stag whipped round and was hidden by a bush. At the same moment several white sterns flashed away. I ran as hard as I could to the edge of the next hollow. The deer were crashing through it, invisible to me. In a moment they appeared, and there stood my stag in all his glory, not more than a hundred yards away, but in a dim light. Why do I say my stag? the stag that ought to have been mine. Oh! what a head he had! But how long would he stay so? A single stride would hide him again. I dared not sit or lie down for a steady shot. I must take him just so, as I stood, panting. I did all I knew to pull myself together for that shot, but, as the hammer fell, some restless overtaxed organ refused to be quiet. My left hand dropped, ever so little, and the bullet—well! I suppose it grazed him, for he sprang in the air as if he were struck, but I never found any other sign that that was so. In the meanwhile, "Smoke's" struggles were so violent that he actually broke away out of his collar and had another little course on his own account, and my feelings towards the biped who had caused the trouble were not friendly. Then came the weary tramp home, and just

LOVE AND WAR.

as we were trying to forget our misfortunes in the evening pipe—there was the stag again, or one with a voice just like his, right above the camp, on the very hill where we had toiled so hard in the morning—Maa-a-a-augh, like an old cat on the housetop.

After this I saw only one other first-rate stag. We were attempting a drive. He passed me high up on the face of the opposite hill at a distance, as I should judge, of 250 yards. I refrained from shooting, hoping he might come near me. I have never ceased to regret it. Yet if I had fired I should have almost certainly missed him at that distance, and then I should always have blamed myself for not waiting. I afterwards followed the tracks of this animal. He was close in front of the men when I saw him. Yet he had only walked about a hundred yards farther, as if he were strolling down Bond Street, and had then lain down to watch, although their shouts were ringing in his ears.

The ground was not generally favourable for driving. There was, however, one drive, that of the big ravine below the first camp, from which I hoped something. There were generally deer in it, and it was closed by a line of cliffs on either side, which completely barred the way down the valley, so that if the beaters drove towards it, the deer must either break back through the line, or escape by a steep *couloir* which led to a pass. I made a great circuit and descending this *couloir* placed myself scientifically, so that nothing could pass unseen. I had sat for two hours when a party of jays began to talk at the bottom of the ravine. I have often observed that it is the habit of these birds to do this when any large

x

animal is moving below them.[1] In America, squirrels act in the same way, and are often a useful guide to the whereabouts of game. As the shouts of the men were not yet audible I was sure that there were deer on the move. The chattering company gradually ascended the hill towards me, till they stopped a little below, and just beyond a ridge, after which they gradually dispersed. I drew my inferences that something had come up to that point and stopped there. The men had had orders to bring the valley down, and then to swing up the side of the hill towards my post. To my disgust, when they had accomplished the first part of their task, they omitted the second. I stayed where I was for another hour, vainly hoping that they would carry out their orders. Then with my glass I made out one of the Turks far below me, busily engaged knocking crab-apples off the trees. It was useless staying where I was, so I steered straight for the place where I had last heard the jays and there found the fresh bed of a stag, and tracks showing that he had vacated it in haste, probably when he heard me descending the stony *couloir*. A Turk often begins a job well but seldom completes it.

All these days my companion, whose superior energy deserved and obtained more exciting adventures than my

---

[1] Since writing the above I find that old Turberville made much the same observation more than three hundred years ago. He writes, "you shal see by experience y^t if there be any pyes, or jayes, or such byrdes, which chatter at them [the deer] and discover them, they will streight way return unto their thicket to hyde themselves for the shame and feare that they have;" and again "Furdermore if in casting aboute the covert, he heare either pyes, jayes, or such byrdes wondering, . . . that is a token that the harte is yet on foote."

own, was even more tortured than I with the pains of Tantalus. I will resign some pages to his parallel experiences. He writes:—

"We had not been out of camp an hour when B—— cleverly found with his glass a large hind lying in the thicket of young pines on the opposite side of the valley we were in. After a patient search with the telescope, I made out two more, resting, and whisking their ears in a patch of thick scrub. At this time of year it was highly improbable that they would be unaccompanied by a male admirer, so we made for the ridge above them hoping to improve our acquaintance with the herd. Softly we crept down to within three hundred yards of where we had marked them, and waited and watched, but only to discover ultimately that they had moved on. No doubt, in spite of our care our movements had been heard, for there were tracks of a big stag and three hinds, with slips and slides on the wet ground, such as deer make when moving faster than their wonted pace. We followed their track for a while, in the hope of seeing them again, under the delusion that they were simple, unsophisticated beasts for whom the smell of man, or the sound of his steps, could have few terrors, but in vain, and towards afternoon we tried fresh ground. Once while crossing a little gully B—— who was five yards in front of me stopped and spread out his hand behind him, a signal that he saw something; I came quickly to his side, just in time to see a great stag disappearing through thick trees over the ridge thirty yards in front of me. Before my rifle could be brought to shoulder, he was out of sight, though in a most ungallant manner he had left his lady and her child behind him, at our mercy. The hind and calf stood 'at gaze,' with great wondering eyes. The calf, which was quite as big as a Scotch hind, would have been a welcome addition to our larder, but I had no intention of disturbing the valley on the first day with the report of a ·500 rifle, save for a master stag. I returned to the tents full of sanguine expectation.

"The following morning I set out with Achmet and Celestin. The Turk took me from 5.30 a.m. till 10 o'clock on the track of a big stag, down the long slope of the gorge below our encampment, up the opposite mountain, over rocks and through dense forest, till with the heat, already great, and the long climb, I should have called for 'time' had I not been excited by the slot of the stag which was, to my imagination, as big as that of a shorthorn bull.

"At last Achmet stopped, sat down and said, with a little chuck of his chin, '*yok! yok!*' (no good) a conclusion to which I had come some time before. For an hour we carried on a conversation *à l'Enfant Prodigue*, assisted by my limited Turkish vocabulary, while the Turk smoked cigarettes made from my tobacco, and then we resumed the chase and all but secured a prize.—'All buts' seemed to be my fate in the Ak Dagh.

"About mid-day we were clambering over some hot glaring white rocks as softly as we could, to the edge of a patch of wood that filled a deep ravine. On reaching the first clump of trees Achmet seemed to know instinctively that there was game in front, he bent forward over a rock, pulled aside a big branch of a fir tree and stood like a pointer. By the movement of his fingers I saw he wanted me to draw up; I did so inch by inch and distinguished, fifty or sixty yards below me, in the trees the white patch that marks the stern of a deer. Save the haunches and a bit of the belly I could see nothing, but he was evidently aware of our presence, and began to move, I lifted my rifle and hastily took a sight forward of his haunch Bang, and down he crashed. Sure of my stag, I sprang down the rocks, but to my disgust he was up again and smashing through the trees out of my sight. We followed fast in the hope of keeping him in view, but did not see him again till he emerged on open ground half a mile off. There he stood with head lowered and open mouth. We lay down well hidden to watch him. With my glass, the dark red patch, too far back in his ribs, where I had hit him, was plainly visible, and when he lay down I thought the end was only a question of minutes, but he rose again and slowly made his way up the side of the ravine, halting every hundred yards. As soon as he disappeared over the sky-line, in spite of the great heat I ran like a lamplighter over the sharp rocks, but when I reached the spot where he had vanished from my view I saw no stag but an endless sea of ravines, valleys and gullies, one beyond another, covered with stunted pines. Following the blood-stains we found a place where he had been down, and then we waited a while, but not for long. Through the blazing heat of mid-day and far into the afternoon we searched one piece of covert and ravine after another. Celestin kept on saying: '*Mais, c'est sûr qu'il est mort.*' Of this I was equally sure, but I realised as the day wore on that the odds were heavily against our finding him in such ground, and we were reminded by the red glow on the cliffs that we must get back before light failed us. The next day was spent in a further and fruitless search in which all joined.

"On the last day of September, I started in the dark, and, winding upward through the forest, reached the highest ridge of the mountain in time to see all the glories of an eastern sunrise amongst its white crags and black pines. We had hardly begun the descent on the farther side when a solitary hind trotted out into full view and, after returning our gaze for some moments, trotted away, having once more reminded us how easy it was to be amongst the deer without knowing it.

"Soon afterwards the distant bellow of a stag reached us, and we made for the corrie whence the sound came; he repeated his challenge, and at length we got so near that my heart jumped every time he lifted up his voice. We lay down and presently saw a hind's head appear on the sky-line above us. She apparently approved of the prospect and came out. Then another followed, and another, and lastly a pair of great antlers like a withered tree showed above the ridge. We crawled down into a gully and laid our plan for a stalk. The ground for once was nearly free from trees, but covered with masses of rock, and cairns of loose stones, intersected with little ravines. Achmet conducted me rapidly and skilfully across the open, displaying the dash that is sometimes essential to success when deer are on the move, or in a wooded country where they may at any moment disappear from view. When under the cover of rocks, he would run as nimbly and silently as a cat, his feet being shod with goat skin, while he turned to me every minute, patting the sole of one of his feet as a sign to me to make less noise. We quickly arrived within a hundred yards of the stag, and there below me I could see the crowns of his horns, with four or five 'croches' 'on top' of each, showing over a long ledge of rock, as he followed the hinds. We moved on, parallel with him, in the hope he would come up into view, but he disappeared down a gully, and Achmet started on another run to cut him off at the next ravine. I reached the edge of a cliff, and looking over, saw seven hinds quickly passing us, thirty yards below, but the stag was not at first to be seen. When he did come into sight he was moving slowly through thick trees sixty yards beneath me. How often have I wished for the return of that moment and with what remorse I have thought over the mess I made of this golden opportunity.

"I can see it all now, the great beast passing between two trees, his nose near the ground, scenting the hinds' tracks, his massive branched horns lying back over his withers and his shaggy neck outstretched, while I crouched on the edge of the cliff, panting with the run and the suspense of such a moment, the stag so near that I gloated over the triumph of which I felt assured. Alas for my blunder! Was it buck fever or over-confidence? I think it must have been due to the very size of the animal— such a broadside of brown! I fired quickly before his shoulder was quite covered by the trunk of the next tree, he fell on his knees to the shot, but before the echo of the valley had answered the crack of the rifle he was plunging down the precipitous mountain-side bringing with him an avalanche of stones. Once he reappeared four hundred yards off, slowly mounting the opposite side of the corrie. In despair, from the recollection of my previous experience, I fired again, and yet again with my last sight up. A puff of dust under his hind-foot marked the first bullet, he winced to the next, but I saw no sign of his being struck, and he broke into a trot and in another minute was over the sky-line out of sight. I confess those last shots were the height of folly, for had I refrained he might have lain down in view. Achmet, who had beaten his breast with disgust at my first shot, was now full of astonishment at seeing my bullets strike so hard right across the valley, the range of his own mediæval weapon being about forty yards with Turkish powder. After we had searched the ground to recover my empty brass cartridge cases, which were treasures in his eyes, we started on a long and weary, but, alas! useless search for the stag.

"Some days later I nearly attained success, but not quite, with the biggest stag I had seen. Benjamen and I had heard him roaring about noon, and had got within 400 yards of the group of pines whence the sound reached us, when a hind emerged and lay down in view of us. We followed her example, and were stretched there on our faces for two hours in a roasting Asiatic sun, nor could we move a hand without her turning her head and ears towards us. It was an intense relief when, at length, she got up to feed and quietly bedded down out of our sight. We then took off our boots, clambered down the rocks to the trees, and as the bellowing grew louder and louder I assured myself that we were fast approaching the monster whose sixteen points I had counted hours before. Cautiously we worked our way, close together, through the trees. Benjamen in the act of drawing aside a thick branch to allow of our stepping over a fallen giant of the forest, discovered to my gaze three great hinds within twenty-five yards of us. There they were, all eyes and ears, and it did not need Benjamen's muttered "*Sacré*" to tell me the game was up. Off they went, and I had just time to think of our camp larder, long without anything more substantial than chickens and eggs, and to fire at the sleekest of the disappearing trio. Leaving the dead hind, I ran on to see if I could make out the stag, but only heard the distant clattering of the stones on the slope above me.

Long before we reached familiar ground, night fell and with it a drenching thunder shower. What a journey we had! Benjamen, who had been lame with sciatica all day, was now completely overcome. For several hours we struggled and stumbled through wet tangled undergrowth, tumbling into water-courses, climbing in and out of ravines in pitch darkness. In spite of my companion's light-headed exclamations that we were lost and that he would never see his home again, I felt sure of the direction of the camp, and alternately pulling and abusing him and sometimes coaxing him, we at length reached a ridge whence we saw the welcome light of the camp fire. Benjamen did not throw off the effects of this day, and we had to invalid the poor fellow home.

"To complete my tale of misfortunes I must mention one other occasion when Achmet led me in thickest forest almost too cleverly up to a stag, for he brought me within twelve yards of a great pair of antlers which were sticking up over the edge of a thickly-wooded ridge as if planted there. The animal appeared to be listening, every inch of him save his horns covered by the rising ground. We waited till the last point drew slowly out of sight, and then I ran to the ridge, but all was still. The animal, probably with an inkling of danger, had dropped his head and crept away like a snake in the grass. Achmet's belief in the penetration of my weapon was such that I could not convince him that it was useless for me to try and shoot him in the head through the top of the ridge. Such was my share in the tantalising disappointments of our quest, but I felt that, in spite of my two bad shots, had we had the slightest turn of luck, we should have secured grand heads of what must, I think, be the most beautiful deer in the world."

Disheartened by our failures, we felt that we must try some range where the forest was less dense, and the conditions more favourable to success. Such a one we believed we knew of in the Emir Dagh. Bouba had visited it in the early spring. He had seen deer there, and, as a proof, had brought back some horns. It took us four days to reach it, for our pack train contained some sorry animals. Alfred, who knows a good horse when he sees it, was mounted on one which had seen twenty-three summers, each of which had left its scars on its knees or elsewhere. Then there were all the other delays which arise in a country where procrastination is the rule of life. The Turks have a saying which aptly expresses their attitude towards any one in a hurry. "Let us put it under the cushion of the divan," equivalent to the Parliamentary expression—"that it do lie on the table."

Our way lay along a chain of elevated plains, flanked by barren mountains, and separated from one another by low rocky passes. It followed, for the most part, one of the ancient trade routes to Konia. Camels pass all day in long strings, grunting under their loads, as they have done for fifty centuries, and the solid wooden wheels of the arabas, as if they, too, were alive and suffering, still creak and groan along the plains at two kilometres an hour, as they did in the time of Abraham. There is little to vary the monotony of these plains. The great heat seems to drive all kinds of life into shelter. Even the

ALFRED'S MOUNT.

villagers have circular underground chambers to which they retire. Only the children seem indifferent to the heat. They roll their little brown bodies in the dirt all day, and amuse themselves by hurling sharp sticks at the dung-heap to see which can drive their tiny spear the deepest. But towards evening birds and beasts begin to appear. The Great Bustard is common on these plains, but is difficult to see except when feeding, about sunset. This they do in a line like tame geese on a common; yet they are by no means unwary. On the approach of danger, first one and then another stretches out his great wings, showing an expanse of white; then after a pause they start running and flapping till they get enough way on to begin their heavy flight. This is so slow that they are sometimes coursed and pulled down by

THE GREAT BUSTARD.

greyhounds. Sand-grouse shoot by with the arrowy flight of blue rock-pigeons. A curious phenomenon of the plains was a *dust-spout*, if I may coin the word, caused, no doubt, by one of those whirlwinds which sometimes occur in abnormally still weather. It may have been twenty miles off, or farther, and was mushroom-shaped like the column of smoke in a conventional eruption of Vesuvius, but much more airy and transparent than that, and it appeared to be stationary.

To save the time occupied by pitching and striking camp, morning and evening, we resorted to the village "odas" or guest-houses. This institution is universal, and is one example of the hospitable instincts of the Turk. All comers are entitled to use them gratis, and to receive such coarse food as may be going. Some are passable enough; to enter others requires the strongest nerves. Vermin abound. All the best kinds of fleas, ticks, *et hoc*

ONE TOUCH OF NATURE.

genus omne in Asia get imported there on camel-back, and have combined to produce breeds of extraordinary intelligence. They all seem to know by inherited instinct the way to that part of your person which cannot conveniently be reached without the assistance of a friend. Those which omit this precaution get killed off, and thus the race is improved. Add to this the pungent odour of the stables, which are generally under the same roof, and of burnt camels' dung, which is the only fuel in these villages of the plain, and it will be seen that a man must harden his heart to enjoy himself. Your welcome is, however, nearly always cordial. When you are established the villagers troop in, to the number of a dozen or more, and seat themselves without restraint. Their manners are courteous, but they show their friendly feelings towards strangers, chiefly, by telling pleasant lies. As one is truly a guest of the village, it is impossible to resent this very natural attention.

Travelling in the interior, is, at the present time, perfectly safe, and there are no thieves because there is nothing to steal. Scarcely any of these small cultivators carry guns. I had a revolver somewhere in my luggage, but I was far too much afraid of it to load it. Such organised brigandage as there is, takes place within reach of big cities like Constantinople, Salonika, and Smyrna, where the scum of the Levant congregates, and where information of possible good hauls may be obtained. Osman was the last professional gentleman who exploited the country near the latter city. To save further trouble the authorities enrolled him and his whole band as gendarmes, but the proverbial rule did not work well in this case. They began, like the law officers of the crown, to combine a little private practice with their official duties. Summoned to Smyrna to account for this, they came to the Konak, but with revolvers concealed in their belts. When their arguments failed to convince, they used more forcible ones and shot two or three policemen and spectators in the court-house itself. But somebody had taken a mean advantage of them by placing soldiers with loaded rifles in the gallery, who presently made mincemeat of them. At the end of two minutes there was nobody left to be hanged.

In the larger towns, of which we passed two or three, travellers put up at khans. These consist of a courtyard, round the interior of which runs a verandah or balcony, into which the guest-chambers, which are bare of all furniture,

THE CARAVAN BARBER.

open. The traveller is expected to provide his own food, no easy matter if he has arrived late, for the Turk is not accustomed to eat or transact business after sundown.

The most striking place which we passed was Afioum Kara-Hissar, but that was on the return journey. The town lies round the base of *the black rock* which gives it its name, a cone which rises abruptly in the proportions of a small Matterhorn, to a height of 700 feet. As we approached it by the light of a golden sunset, an air of mystery was imparted by a low-lying cloud of smoke which hid the town, and floated away in the shape of a gigantic ostrich feather. The only substantial things visible were the frowning black pyramid and innumerable white minarets which projected through the blue haze, while their bases were shrouded by it. Othman, founder of the Ottoman race, arose like a meteor from somewhere within sight of this slender tower of rock—fit type of his dynasty— ever threatening to fall, but saved by the inertness of its mass, it lasts on through the ages.

Two long days in the saddle took us within sight of the desired haven. Eagerly we scanned, through our glasses, the distant outline of the range, to try to make out the character of the ground. The fourth morning found us at its base. The rest of the day was spent in stumbling up a dry water-course at the bottom of a narrow gorge. This natural staircase was the only access for horses to the upper part of the mountain. At length, we emerged upon a broken plateau, and, after winding about for some time among rocky eminences, began to skirt along the northern slopes near to the highest summit, and overlooking the great salt desert which lies in the middle of Asia Minor. The sun was near its setting, but we could not see any dead wood about—a prime necessity of a hasty camp,—nor any water. Notwithstanding this, our spirits rose, for the ground looked attractive. The slopes were scored by numerous deep ravines, and hollows covered with patches of oak, while on the ridges were wide stretches of the finest mountain pasture—first-rate stalking ground. Delusive hope! The next minute my heart sank for I saw a large flock of sheep. I knew very well what that meant. We had come all that way for nothing. Presently, we saw another and another. The mountain was covered with them. A capital place for deer, doubtless, but much later in the year when the flocks go down. But our immediate concern was to find wood and water. At last we had to stop, for it got too dark to go on. Fortunately, we discovered a heap of chips on a little plateau where we could pitch a tent, and immediately called a halt, and bundled the packs on the ground, while we sent off two men to seek for water in the valley. In an hour they returned, with enough for drinking, and we made ourselves comfortable.

In the morning, inquiry of the shepherds confirmed our impression as to the deer. They were no doubt somewhere on the range, for we, subsequently, saw some horns in one of the villages, but it is very extensive, and the valleys were too deep to get our pack train along it, parallel with its axis. There seemed to be no other course but to go down on the northern side, and up again at some other point. A distant part of the mountain was pointed out to us where there were "*sugeun chok*" (plenty of stags). It looked quite close, but it took us a day and a half to reach. There was said to be a Yuruk who knew it well, and was a mighty hunter, and we went out of our way to find his village. He was engaged in thrashing, and his wife, a regular termagant, declared in most forcible language that he should not go hunting. "Why, you idle vagabond, you never catch anything when you do go. Look at these poor dear little children, and attend to your harvest." That is what she seemed to be saying. Then she seized his gun from him and threw

y

it back into his tent. This is what they call the subjection of women in Turkey. At last, the sight of silver appeased her, and he was allowed to come, *but she kept his gun*. When we reached the fresh hunting-ground, it was only to repeat the same disheartening experience. Here, too, were flocks of sheep, and this, apparently, our Yuruk expected, for having got his dollar, he deserted in the evening. We hunted the surrounding ground diligently for two days. A few stale tracks only were found, and they were made by "travellers." We could hear no roaring. Perhaps we ought to have made another attempt, but at the time it seemed to us the most sensible course to return whence we had come.

This chapter is already unduly long, and I must draw a veil over our further labours. When the month which we had allowed ourselves in the country had expired, we were still without any of the royal antlers which we had dreamed of. It was very bitter. Shall we admit defeat, or try again?

ARABAS.

X

REINDEER STALKING

Salmon and reindeer were the object of my first trip to Norway—now a good many years ago. At the farmhouse of Hoass in Sundal, we hoped to be in time for the end of the salmon fishing, but the season had been an early one, and the salmon were all red and sleepy at the bottom of the pools. I could not beguile a single one; not that that is a fact of any significance, for I never was a fortunate fisherman. I habitually console myself by the profound belief that the salmon fisher owes his occasional successes to circumstances over which he has no control whatever. To me the strange thing is that the most exciting part of the capture, and that which demands the most skill and agility, I mean gaffing the fish, is generally left to the ghillie.

On the occasion in question I take credit to myself for early realising the hopelessness of the attempt. On the second day I determined to take a preliminary canter on the neighbouring fjeld, while my more persistent companion remained flogging away at the still more obstinate salmon. I did not expect a very tangible result from the experiment, because the Sundal valley is rather populous for Norway, and the hunting expeditions of these people are sufficient to scare most of the reindeer to less accessible places, even though, as far as I could learn, but few were brought to bag. More could not be expected with the native pop-gun, which at the time of which I am writing was generally the handiwork of the local blacksmith. Go back three or four hundred years, and it requires an effort of the imagination to estimate the craft and patience which it must have taken to secure so wild an animal. That the pursuit was attempted I once found presumptive proof, for I picked up an iron arrow-head among the bare stones near the top of one of the highest peaks in those parts. It could hardly have been used for any other purpose. I had little expectation of success on this first trip. Nevertheless, I hoped to gather some hints, and experience that would be useful for a more extended sojourn on the fjeld, which we proposed to make in a few days.

I was accompanied by an excellent stalker, a farmer from a neighbouring valley, named Tostin, of whose reputation I had heard from a friend, who, fortunately for us, was free from the jealousy with which one Englishman in Norway generally regards another if he happens to be on the look-out for sport, and also by his dog "Barfod," a splendid specimen of the Finnish or Esquimaux breed, to which all the dogs in Northern Europe approximate. It is characterised by short upright ears, an alert expression and a tail that curls like the horn of an old Highland ram. The vital parts are protected from the cold by a dense ruff of hair. The tail also carries a splendid brush and this is not for ornament alone, for when the dog sleeps you notice that he uses it for a respirator. "Barfod" was the size of a collie, but coal black all over, except for one white foot which gave him his name. His fine fur seemed to be the object of his especial pride, and three or four times a day, he cleaned himself in the snow, scattering it about, and rubbing his back on it till his coat shone again. The expression of "Barfod's" face showed that he was as honest as the day, and as shrewd as a Scotchman, and, besides all these qualities, he possessed a far-reaching power of smell, by the help of which he would not only indicate the presence of deer at a distance of three or four miles, if the breeze and the nature of the ground were favourable, but his master could tell from his manner whether it was the deer themselves that he winded, or only their tracks. Moreover, he was as mute as an undertaker when the case required it, but when the occasion was past, as garrulous and as cheery as a fox-hunter after a good run, provided the stalk had been successful. Besides "Barfod" I hired two inferior beings who professed to have local knowledge, but who I should judge had never been on the fjeld before.

At daybreak next morning, we ascended a small lateral valley, and after passing a group of *sæters*—as the Norwegians call their summer châlets—where I proposed to pass the night, struck up a steep ascent, and in half an hour came out on the edge of the dreary fjeld. This consists of a vast plateau of heather and rock, cut through at rare intervals, by the deep trench of a cultivated valley—low ridge and shallow valley alternating for forty miles, with here and there a small half-formed glacier, or little lake, still nearly choked with the winter snow. In places, the ridges rise more steeply, with some pretence at jagged edges and cliffs, but I suppose the level is nowhere less than three thousand, or more than six thousand feet, and for the most part the outlines are round and tame. In the sheltered places a few patches of grass are found, and cows are brought up for a few weeks in the year, and tended by a solitary girl.

The high fjeld is singularly barren of life and the reindeer and ptarmigan have it almost to themselves. The chief exception to this rule is the little lemming, clad, like the Pope's Guard, in livery of yellow and black. These miniature blunt-headed marmots—they are only about four or five inches long, including their stumpy tails—as though conscious of the reproductiveness of their race, are ready to sacrifice their tiny individual lives with wanton courage. As you walk the moor, a chirp *crescendo*, full of anger and defiance, attracts your attention. Looking about, you will perceive this tiny David, bolt upright, and challenging Goliath. Very likely he will be standing by his hole, but he will scorn to fly from dog or man. I have known them thus on a high road to contest the way with an advancing cart, until the wheel crushed the fearless little soul. They vary enormously in numbers in different seasons, and their sudden appearance in hordes accounts for the superstitions anent them, to which old writers have given currency: *e.g.* of their fall from the clouds which Olaus Magnus accounts for, in that " like frogs and other small creatures they may in their embryos be attracted to the clouds, and, being then come to maturity, may drop from them."

Their inordinate increase in certain years, and the

consequent dearth of food, doubtless accounts for their strange migrations in countless hordes. An old hunter once told me that, in a bad lemming year, owing to the complete destruction of all edible herbage on the mountains, the reindeer are constrained to pursue and eat the lemmings themselves, and this statement is confirmed by many observers. Under these circumstances, they move off across country in compact bodies. No obstacle deters them. The migrating army leaves a wasted track behind it. Multitudes perish by the way, either devoured by the birds and beasts of prey which hang on their flank, or by drowning in sea and river. Some say that they return, or a remnant of them, in due time to the high fjelds whence they came.

In hunting reindeer Norwegians rely almost entirely upon their dogs for finding the deer, as such a thing as a telescope was, a quarter of a century ago, unknown in the remote districts. There is some sense in this, for there are innumerable hollows on the plateau which cannot be spied. These are often full of snow, and reindeer are fond of lying on the snow. The hunters' method is to keep a steady course, hour after hour, across the wind, in the hope that sooner or later the dog will catch the scent of a herd, in which case he will indicate it by his manner. At the same time I should by no means advise any sportsman to discard the use of the glass.

Tostin, like most Norwegians, was somewhat lazy, and made frequent halts of long duration, but perhaps he had reason in that too, for the waiting game often pays in hunting. In the course of one of these halts I was idly examining a distant snowy ridge, when a small speck appeared on the sky-line, followed by another and another, till there were seven of them. That was my first sight of wild reindeer. I was eager to start in pursuit, but Tostin declared that these deer were too distant to reach that day, so we proceeded in the same way as before, alternately walking and smoking pipes on rocks, the while taking no particular observation, but leaving everything to the dog. I had no great expectations, and therefore was not disappointed that, for a long time, nothing came of it.

We were sitting down for the twentieth time to shelter ourselves from a passing shower, " Barfod" was lying in his favourite position with his head between his paws watching his master's face, when suddenly he jumped up, ran a few steps towards the wind, sat down on his haunches, and eagerly snuffed the air, his hair on end, and his whole body trembling with excitement. There was evidently something up, and Tostin assured me that it certainly meant deer. I lowered my voice, fancying that the dog would not show so much excitement unless the herd were close at hand, but this was a very needless precaution. " Barfod" was called in and tied to a cord, which his master held in a tight grasp. He paused once or twice turning his head about. Then, as though he had made up his mind about the right direction, he bounded on, tugging at the string. We followed as fast as we could walk, along an almost level snow gully. Several ridges were topped without seeing anything, till at last I began to get very much blown, and to think the dog was humbugging us, for it was difficult to believe that he had winded anything at such a distance. After running and walking for three-quarters of an hour, and covering, I should suppose, fully

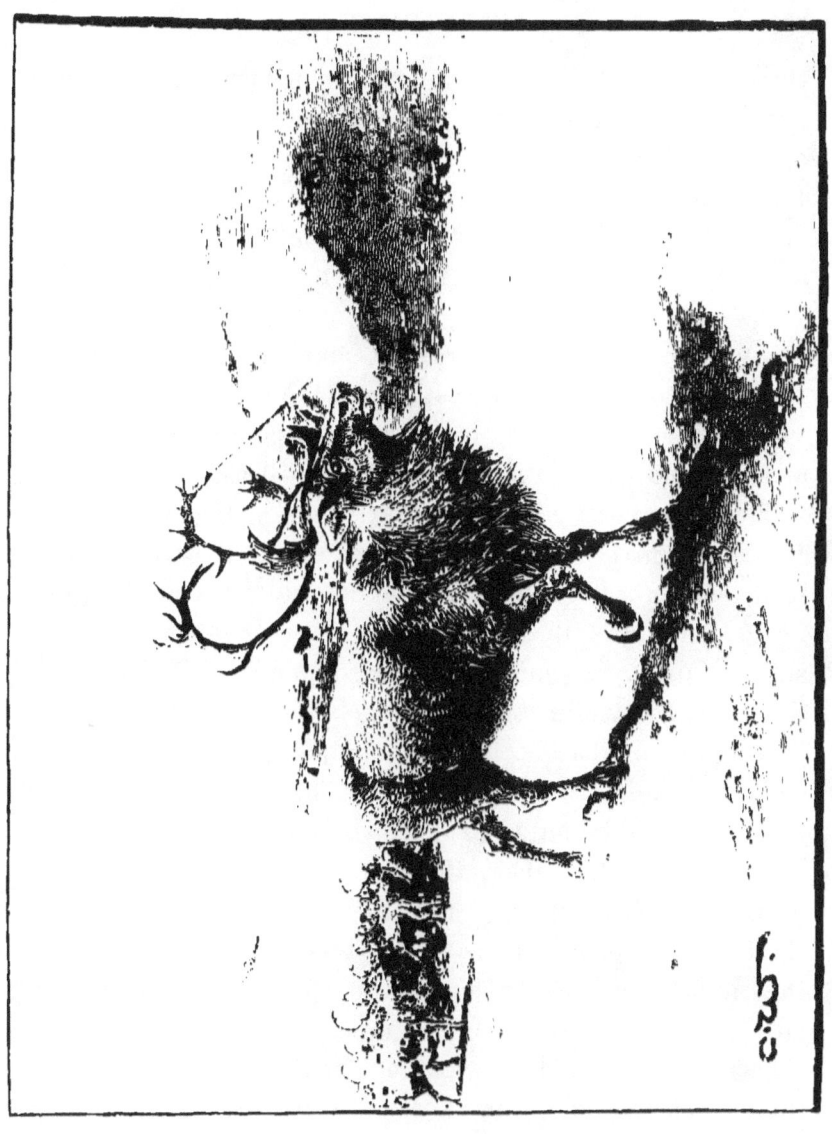

THE REINDEER.

three miles, as the crow flies, from the spot where the dog first detected them, Tostin, who was now some way ahead of me, suddenly crouched down, and got behind a rock. I followed his example, and creeping up to him, took one look. There they were sure enough—eight or nine deer, slowly feeding away from us about three hundred yards off.

A ridge of rock favoured us, and we worked up to them behind it. At last Tostin said, "Now look over and you will see the buck." I did so, and there he was plain enough, but too far for a fair shot, at least I had not sufficient confidence in myself to try him at that distance. It was my first chance at reindeer, and I determined to make sure of a bag, which indeed the state of our larder made highly desirable. A pretty good hind stood broadside on, about one hundred yards off, and I felt that she was to be the victim. As the smoke cleared off she lay kicking on her back. I shall not apologise for this ungallant action. In Norway the pot is the first consideration. Besides I wanted to shoot a reindeer anyhow.

Unlike the red deer, the hinds carry horns of their own. They are said to carry them some months after the bucks have shed theirs, and at this time, as I am told, they inflict condign punishment on their lord. He is a faithless brute and doubtless deserves it. For every chance you get at a buck you get ten at hinds. I do not think that five per cent of the deer we saw in Norway were bucks. The reason of this is perhaps, that their skins are thicker, and they can withstand the attack of the mosquitoes. Therefore while the hinds are driven to take refuge in high ground, the bucks can afford to remain in the valleys where the food is richer and the vegetation sufficient to hide them.

We returned to the *sæters*, and selecting the neatest hut, I marched in and took possession to the considerable astonishment of the fair-haired young daughter of Vikings whose domain it was, as I was totally unable at that time to explain to her in her own language how much gratified she ought to be at my intrusion. But she made a virtue of necessity and retired to the domain of another sister of the craft, presently returning to bring me the one luxury common to all in Norway—a cup of coffee from berries roasted at the moment, ground between two stones, and served with candied sugar.

The next day I took another long stretch over the fjeld, but saw nothing, and returned the third morning to Hoass, where I was welcomed for my meat if not for myself. But the flesh pots were not enough to keep us in Sundal, for the salmon still preferred the grovelling worm to the painted fly, and we made preparations for spending the rest of our time on the fjeld.

We drove down the valley to the head of the fjord, and boated as far as the mouth of another valley, the Oxendal, which extends some miles up into the fjeld. Here, on the shore of the fjord, there was a post station where every traveller must enter his name. The book included the records of thirty years, but the entire list hardly covered a page, and contained only one English name. We were compelled to spend three nights at a farmhouse at the head of that valley, as the weather was too bad to go up to the fjeld, and I fancy that not even a solitary traveller had ever penetrated there.

Three generations, besides several poor relations, herded together, without a sign that they had ever had any communication with the outer world. Indeed, in these remoter valleys they seem almost independent of all produce save their own. Oatmeal and milk summed up the total of their bodily needs. They seemed to have nothing on earth to do but to cook and eat heavy messes of porridge. It must be frightfully unsatisfying to judge by the frequency with which they recur to it. So entirely did they live on spoon meat that there was not a fork in the house. This indifference to good food must I think be, in part, due to sheer laziness. To eat flesh you must, at least, first catch your beast. The Norwegian therefore contents himself with oatmeal which needs only to be warmed and stirred. Perhaps for the same reason, and on account of emigration, labour is dear in Norway where everything else is cheap. To hire a man for a day costs as much as a sheep. However, every man is "jack of all trades," and every household is self-supporting. To them the Englishman who is unable to cobble his own boots is a subject of melancholy interest, that one should be sunk so low. I once sent a small cask of beer to Norway, which the voyage had put into such a forward condition that I had a difficulty in drawing it. They thought a brewer who did not know how to tap his own beer an extraordinary phenomenon!

During visits made to Norway in more recent years I was struck by the advance made by the Bönder, or farmer-peasant class, in their standard of comfort. Owing to improved communications many articles of food formerly unknown to them, and especially good white flour which they cannot produce themselves, penetrate to the secluded valleys.

In the midst of all the squalor there was one feature which was then common to most farms away from the high roads, but would perhaps be rarely observed now, owing to the pertinacious researches of collectors. The only investment that they seemed to know for their savings was in silver plate. This house was particularly rich; I made a bid for a massive old tankard of quaint device to the old miser of a grandfather, and he would have sold it directly if it hadn't been for his relations. He did run out with it on the morning of our departure when he thought no one was looking. He came out wearing only his shirt, which seemed to have been in use as long as the tankard, and the idea that he and ancestors such as he, had been using the latter for all sort of purposes for many generations, was too much for me and I rejected it. He did however sell me a silver belt, which, as I afterwards heard, did not belong to him.

The first night that we were here a bear climbed into a neighbouring fold and killed three sheep. The people were in great excitement and a deputation waited upon us to beg us to try to kill him. They proceeded to drive some miles of the scrub on the side of the valley. The bear could not escape uphill by reason of a steep scarp of rock which extended along the sides of the hill, and there was a gully which could only be crossed at one point. The beast had been constantly seen crossing at this place, and there we were posted behind an ambuscade of bushes. I thought then that it was a grand chance, and that "Nicholas" ought certainly to come to be killed, but he failed to show himself. Subsequent experience has led me to the conclusion that a bear seldom spends two nights running in the same bed, or even in the same valley, especially when his conscience is burdened with a crime like the above, and also that he is as a rule far too cunning to be driven to guns. If the peasants see a bear twice in the year they think he is always thereabouts, and they are very ready to turn out for a drive, both because they enjoy the lark themselves, and because they like to keep the Englishmen in the place.

On the third morning the weather cleared and we were able to go up to the fjeld. We sent our luggage on a pony to a certain *sater*, and soon reached a high point whence we could survey a large area. We were not long in finding a herd of deer disporting themselves in the middle of a snow-field, but while we were discussing how best to get at them, they suddenly galloped off and we saw them no more. I believe they winded the pony who was in the valley. Before long we made out three more a great way off. We had to go over some rough ground and so lost sight of them, but about mid-day we found them again. They were half a mile off, in the middle of a little plain at the bottom of a valley, so that we were fully exposed to view if we moved towards them, but by moving in line on hands and knees, and stopping when they looked up, we got, after an hour's crawling, to a big rock within four hundred yards of them, behind which we could again stand upright. Beyond that, there was not a stick or stone to cover us, and there we had to wait, hoping that the deer would shift to better ground, or that something would turn up, but for many hours they refused to move. We began to be anxious, as we were far from our night's quarters. For part of the time they lay, apparently fast asleep, but we could not presume upon that. I never yet could determine to my own satisfaction whether deer close their eyes when they sleep. If we are to believe our old friend Pontoppidan it would not much matter in the case of the reindeer, as, according to him, they have a hole in their eyelids, for use in a snowstorm.

It was nearly six o'clock before they rose and fed towards more uneven ground. We crawled fifty yards nearer, and waited again. Farther than that we dared not go, until, one by one, they disappeared behind a shelf of rock. We jumped up, and ran down the hill as hard as we could, and got within range before they reappeared. Kenny had the first shot, which was successful in bringing up one deer, and I managed to knock over a second. The stalk had lasted from first to last seven hours; it was a six miles' walk over heather and bog to the *sæter*, and it was quite dark long before we reached it. We didn't expect grand things at Holbue, as the tiny settlement was called, but were rather aghast when we found how very limited were both board and lodging. We tried several *sæters* afterwards, but a description of this one will suffice for all, though I confess that it was not one of the best specimens of its class. There was a little den about ten feet by six, built of rough stones the chinks of which were stuffed with moss, and about a third of this space was taken up by the shelf on which the girl slept, and the fireplace and copper for cheese-making. The two men who had brought our luggage and the *sæter pige* seemed to fill the available standing room, and I am convinced that, with the whole of our party inside, the door could not have been shut. An inner chamber about the same size was filled with utensils and the produce of the season. I believe that eventually our men slept in this place, on the top of the cheeses. When we afterwards visited another *sæter* we took the hint from them, for this inner room is always kept clean. The floor makes a capital bed when well covered a foot deep with reindeer moss and heather, and Kenny and I just filled it from wall to wall. I would only warn others from my own painful experience, that a column of milk-pails eight feet high in the neighbourhood of one's head is not a very stable piece of furniture.

On arriving at Holbue, we turned out some of the men, that we might make our way to the fire with our frying-pan, a fortunate purchase from Sundal, without which we should have been badly off indeed. I had besides one of those neat little copper toys called, I think, a Russian Stove. The spirit lamp vaporises some more spirit which is contained in an inner vessel, and which rushes out through a narrow orifice as a long tongue of superheated flame. This plays on the copper lid of the thing and would doubtless cook a lark or piece of bacon in a few minutes, if the handle did not get so hot that it was invariably upset on the floor. Besides the spirits of wine always gets among the venison in some mysterious way. This is tantalising to such appetites as we had developed, but, on the other hand, the ambitious little roar which the baby furnace makes while it does all this, is distinctly comforting. Our frying-pan was a much more substantial piece of furniture, fifteen inches in diameter. It was filled every morning with collops cut fresh from the carcase of a reindeer, which lay ready to hand on the roof of the *sæter*, and with plenty of butter, this made an excellent fry. It was our mainstay for breakfast and dinner and also cold for luncheon, and it is the best tribute I can pay to reindeer venison, to say that we only got a little tired of it at the end of a fortnight. Kenny generally had the advantage when it was set between us. He always got to the middle of the pan first, and encroached upon my side of it.

KENNY.

Fortunately I found in the intricacies of my apparatus a wonderful knife and fork in a small compass. From that time, I had the better of him, not only could I eat much faster, but I could detect and pick out all the tender bits. Such is the power of intellect when opposed to brute force. We felt the want of bread very much. The native article, *fladbröd*, is loathed by most English stomachs after a few days. The meal is made from badly-ripened oats.

The cake is fired for about 45 seconds on an iron plate. It is of the texture of brown paper and is like that to eat, with the addition of a certain flabbiness due to the moisture which it quickly absorbs. We were also rather hard up for something to drink. We had one bottle of brandy which was reserved for cold days on the high ground; also half a pound of tea, which we managed to spread over the whole time in infinitesimal doses. Towards the end it did get very weak, but by boiling it at the end of dinner in a venisony pot, we infused a little spurious colour.

The grand difficulty is the fire, if, as in this case, the *säter* is too far from the valley to bring up wood, for then, the only fuel is dwarf creeping plants, hardly thicker than a pencil, and full of moisture. But a great deal may be done by keeping up a great blaze for a little time, so as to warm the hearthstone which gives out its heat slowly. Then if a fresh heap of sticks is laid ready, after a time they become sufficiently dry to make another blaze.

But to return to that night at Holbue. After supper, we inquired for our bedroom, and were vaguely directed to a big hollow rock that lay somewhere near. We sallied forth in quest of it, and found a good many rocks about the height of one's shins, with sharp edges, and well concealed, but the night was too dark to find the particular one that we wanted.

There was however an old *säter* close by, which had been long deserted, and here we deposited ourselves and luggage. The cows had adopted it for their own, so we enjoyed a rich carpet, but we rigged up a shelf with an old door, and I slept as well as I could, with the consciousness that I was contracting a severe cold, for all the moss had rotted away from between the stones, and the wind blew against us freely. This was partially remedied the next day with fresh moss, but even then, I could see to write by the daylight that came through the holes, so that windows were not missed. The door was guiltless of any fastening, and, in a high wind, could only be made secure by a pole jammed against it by somebody else on the outside, which was awkward if you wanted to get out in a hurry.

The right of pasturage on the fjeld is not I believe, as in Switzerland, common to all the inhabitants of a valley, but is—unless the law has been altered—the property of individuals, who have obtained a prospective right by long usage. Perhaps this is because it was not worth quarrelling about. They do however convert it into good milk, cream and cheese—the kind generally made, and which is called *mys-ost* (whey cheese), being of a dark brown colour. The whole establishment is managed by one strong-minded female who leads a solitary life, except when her supplies are brought once a week. She has to milk the cows, make two or three different kinds of cheese, and keep all the utensils clean, so her time does not hang heavy on her hands, and I came across none who did not seem to like it.

The second day we were again successful. We had had a fruitless grind over an extensive snow-field and were coming home, when the infallible " Barfod " again told us of the presence of deer, and led us up to them—a herd of ten. It was my turn to have first shot, I made a very bad one and hit the deer too far back, but retrieved my honour, by knocking him over with the second barrel. As we walked home. I heard behind, and quite close to us, a kind of croak, which is the sound the deer make when they are startled. This deer must have followed us, having probably seen something moving in the valley and mistaken us for his relations. He was wildly alarmed when he found out the *gaucherie* of which he had been guilty, and went off like the wind, so that our rifles could not be got out of their cases before he was out of range.

The next day was a blank, and the next after that I was obliged to stay in the *sæter* and nurse myself, for the cold I had contracted the first night had become serious, and I dared not face the biting wind on the high ground, till it got better. I improved my knowledge of the language, by consulting the *sæter* woman about the economy of cheese-making, but most of that weary day was spent within the four walls of our windowless hut. There was a small quantity of rice among our stores, and I taught myself how to make a rice pudding, by an exhaustive series of experiments carried out upon infinitesimal portions of rice. I extemporised a Turkish bath, by raking out the fire, and sitting in the fireplace, while I exhausted our literature by the light that came down the chimney. I dumped the holes in the wall, which occupied more of the time than anything else. Tailoring, cobbling, wood-carving were successively tried by the meagre light—anything to pass the time—but the bitterest pill of all was, when after fourteen long hours, Kenny came back, for I heard that I had missed the most interesting and successful stalk of our trip.

One of the men, whom we had sent into the valley two days before, had told us, on his return, that he had seen the tracks of four large deer which he believed to be bucks (they turned out afterwards to be very old hinds) which had gone up into a small valley, from which there was no exit, but that by which they had entered. On the following day we had looked for ourselves, but could not see any signs of their having come out. On the morning in question, when the party were opposite the valley, the dog winded them, apparently not far off. He quickly brought them into sight of the deer. They were about two hundred yards off, but it was dangerous to try to get nearer. Instead of lying down as might have been expected, for it was now ten o'clock, they kept feeding on right up the hill, and Tostin remarked with a grin, that, if they went on, they would get into a place where they could only come back the same way, and that would be in the face of the hunters. They were now on a steep slope, forming the base of a broadish ridge, which led up to the top of the mountain, and this is flanked by steep precipices on each side. The deer fed upwards without pausing, the hunters following as closely as they dared. This went on till they got fairly upon the ridge. Not being able to see them, they took the top of the mountain before them like a turnip field, the two men on either side, Kenny in the middle but a little behind. They had not gone far, before he saw the deer some distance off, apparently nearly as far as they could get. Up to this time Tostin had thought that they could only escape by coming straight back in their faces. He now fancied that they might possibly know of a passage over the top of the mountain, and accordingly changed his mode of attack. He would go on, and, by climbing along the face of the cliff, get beyond them. Kenny was to stay with the other man, and so get the deer between them. As soon as they attempted to turn back they were to show themselves, and keep them on the ridge as long as possible. The plan succeeded perfectly. Tostin had my breechloader, at that time quite a novelty, and, with the unaccustomed facility, he was rather reckless of his bullets, which began to sing past his companions' ears. The poor brutes were quite pounded, and did not know which way to go. Before they could get past Kenny, three of them lay dead on the ridge. The fourth made a bolt to get back, but he cut her off, and put a bullet into her as she passed within thirty yards, which quickly brought her to a standstill. He had them all four lying dead within two hundred yards of each other. It was not till then that he found that they were all hinds. This was rather a damper, but at least the meat was very welcome in the households to which it found its way.

The next day we went down into Eikisdal to spend Sunday at Tostin's farm in the hope that my ailments would yield to a warmer climate. This valley forms a very deep trench. There were no preliminary slopes, but, after walking for several miles over fjeld more or less level, we came suddenly to what seemed the edge of an enormous rent in the hills. In front of us, the cliffs were broken at one point by a gap which admitted of a steep zigzag path being carried down its side, through a tangled copse of creeping birch. At first, clouds filled the valley and prevented our seeing to the bottom, but as we got below these, we saw the inky surface of a lake extending for several miles. It fills the valley from side to side, and washes the base of the precipices. On the opposite side, black sheer cliffs extended as far as we could see, and over these a splendid waterfall made one leap from the sky-line to the level of the lake. Tostin assured us that he once wounded a deer which got into this stream and was carried over the fall never to be seen again. It was, in fact, no mean river.

It is this peculiar conformation, of valleys of extraordinary abruptness, and separated from one another by a wide extent of plateau, which makes the Norwegian high fjeld so different from mountains of the normal type. The Norwegian fjelds are not the place to go to for scenery. Unless a man is attracted by mere barrenness and a sense of space he will be disappointed. It is featureless to a greater degree than any hill country which I know. Of colour too there is none except melancholy hues. A proof of this is found in the birds and beasts, which generally match the ground they live on. They are all dull-coloured, though I will not deny that the white-winged willow-grouse is a pretty bird.

But this remark does not apply to the scenery of the fjords, some of which are of an exquisite softness, and others, which are walled in by lofty sides, falling sheer into the water, of surpassing sternness. There is nothing like them anywhere else. On the other hand, the climate is the reverse of bracing. It has far too much of the vapour of the Gulf Stream in it for my taste.

It took us nearly two hours of bone-shaking descent to reach the shore of the lake. Here was a little green patch and a farmhouse, the only possible settlement for man or beast on the edge of the lake, and seeming to guard the gates of the happy hunting ground above.

We rowed to the head of the lake, and Tostin's farm was close by, in the middle of a fertile little plain, or rather a plain which would be fertile, if a little more sunshine could reach the bottom of the valley. Tostin was a prosperous man, his fields carry good crops and many beasts. His range of farm buildings was extensive. The house itself was one of the best I came across. Inside there were large well-furnished rooms, pictures on the walls, and newspapers lying about, beds clean and comfortable, but alas! the table carried nothing but a snow-white tablecloth and silver spoons, whose brightness mocked our empty stomachs. There was nothing in the house to eat but oatcake, coffee, and milk products. However, it was some change to have the venison we had brought with us cooked by other hands than our own, and to miss the familiar flavour of our fry-pan.

Tostin's pay for one day would have covered our bill for board and lodging for two nights at a roadside station, but it was not sufficient to tempt him away from home when we returned to the fjeld. He rejoined us later on, but, for the time, he found pottering over his unripe oats, and eating gruel, more interesting. Certainly, the corn hadn't the slightest tinge of yellow upon it, but he said it never did get riper in that valley. So for the time we had to content ourselves with a young and inexperienced hunter. Up to this time we had shot eight deer in six days, but Kenny's great *coup* had exhausted all our luck. Thenceforth, we had nothing but failures. For eight days we failed to bag a single deer, though we saw them nearly every day. We moved from *sæter* to *sæter*, but nothing reversed the tide of misfortune. On one occasion, we spied deer on the top of a ridge which there were only two ways of reaching. We stationed ourselves by one of these ways, and sent a man up the other to drive the deer towards us, but contrary to all reason, they doubled back past the driver and went down by the way he had come up. Another time, we wounded one out of a herd, which fell over a precipice where it was not possible to recover him; at least so Tostin said. Twice the wind chopped round to our backs just as we were approaching deer. Once a thick fog came on when the dog was leading us up to deer, and they saw us before we saw them. Once only I made a downright miss, and as it is usual to attribute that sort of misfortune to some extraneous cause, I will say that I shot over his back owing to a stiff neck.

At last our time was up, and we had to get across to the Romsdal valley, and take to our *karjoles* again. Our last quarters on the fjeld were at a pleasant place by the banks of a grand trout stream, which afforded a welcome change in our larder.

The last day came, we had twenty miles to walk to the valley. We were very anxious to score a final success, and to improve our chances we separated and took different ways, Kenny taking Tostin, and I an old hunter from Aursuen, named Bjornen, or the Bear, which appropriately described him. Kenny saw nothing all day. Luck still seemed against us for the wind shifted to our backs as soon as we had started, making it very unlikely that the dog would get the wind of deer, and highly probable that they would get ours, and this in fact was the very thing that happened. About five miles on the way, we saw a herd of eleven deer in front of us, galloping off as hard as they could, having taken the alarm before we saw them. They were led by the finest buck I saw all the time we were out, and I could have cried when I saw them going. We sat down and watched them go. They settled down into a long swinging trot till they disappeared over a ridge about two miles off. It was likely to be the last chance, and it was worth making a special effort to come at them; so we made a circuit of some miles to be sure of getting to leeward of them, and then quartered the ground up the wind, in a series of long swinging zigzags. This was a protracted business, for the dog, who was a very inferior specimen to "Barfod," seemed to have some family cares on her mind, and took no interest in the proceedings. Thus, we had to trust entirely to our own senses. After some hours of this search I began to despair, but at length Bjornen. who was in front, stooped stealthily, after peering over a ridge, and there, as good luck would have it, were the missing herd.

They had recovered from their fright and were lying down by a little lake basking in the sun. We left the dog in charge of Bjornen's son, and got up within fair distance, sheltered by a rock. Here I left Bjornen, and dragging myself by my elbows through the grass for another thirty yards, reached another rock just big enough to hide me, and lay quite flat. Resting on my elbows, I could look over and survey them. The whole herd, except their leader, lay exposed to view on a little knoll. He was couched on the farther side of it, and I could only see his horns, and occasionally his head and part of a great shaggy neck, when he lazily raised his nose to snuff the breeze.

Any one of the others could be covered by the bead as they lay, but I had to wait till the master stag gave me a fair chance by rising. The fawns, of which there were two or three, were as impatient as I, and several times got up and tried to rouse their dams, but I had to wait more than two hours for my opportunity.

Now perhaps some may think that lying on your elbows in the sun is an agreeable way for a lazy man to pass his time. So it is for a few minutes. Try it for an hour, and you will alter your opinion. Unless your muscles are made of steel they will refuse any longer to carry the weight. Your head will be suffered to sink on your hands and your thoughts will wander anywhere until you presently forget where you are. That at least was what happened to me. How long I had been dozing I do not know, but something roused me with a start, and in a moment I realised that I had all but lost my chance.

The herd had risen, and were trotting down the other side of the knoll, all but the big buck, who fortunately still remained for his final stretch. As he turned to follow, he gave me a fair broadside for one moment, and I fired. They all went off in a mob together. For a moment I thought I must have missed him, from the way he raced after them, but something spasmodic in his gallop made me hope. They disappeared behind a ridge, and I anxiously watched for them to top the next hill. When they came in sight, the buck was not with them, and for a certainty there was ample cause for his lingering. In a minute he appeared, struggling gallantly with his fate, but the hill was too much for him, and he came down on his knees. As I got up to him, he made a vain effort to regain his legs, but in doing so, he rolled over and died. My bullet had been well placed for it had cut the heart and passed through his body. I found it under the skin on the opposite side. Yet he had run two hundred yards before he fell. He was a grand stag in the body, and his horns though small in proportion, had sixteen points. We secured the meat from marauders under a heap of big stones, to be fetched subsequently, but, as we were determined to have something to show, we cut off the head and a haunch as trophies. Bjornen carried the haunch, and I hope he liked it, for I found the head quite as much as I could manage for a rough walk of fifteen miles, but I would rather have sat on the horns all the way home than left them behind. We found Kenny at Læsjevœrk in the Romsdal, and the next morning took to the road again, and in five days were in England.

Nowadays, I believe that one has to pay a heavy license, amounting to £11, for the privilege of shooting reindeer, or any other wild bird or beast on "public" lands. This restriction is aimed at foreigners and especially Englishmen, but if further protection is needed for the reindeer, it is a pity that the existing laws are not enforced against the natives, who, with all their excellent qualities, are the worst poachers and pot hunters in the world. Though I have only once been out reindeer hunting since the experiences here described, it ranks high in my estimation of wild sports.

XI

THE IZZARD

The Izzard, as the chamois of the Pyrenees is locally called, is practically identical with its cousin of the Alps. It is a proof of the persistency of the race that, notwithstanding the enormous geological period which must have elapsed since the two branches of the family were separated by the Rhone and the Plains of Languedoc, they have diverged so slightly. The facial marks of the Pyrenean animal are rather darker than those of its congener, and in all its parts it is perhaps somewhat smaller, especially in the horns which are more slender, but this is only part of a general law under which certain animals, such as the chamois and the red deer, show a more vigorous development as you travel eastward to a wider continent. There is fully as much difference in this respect between the chamois of Transylvania and that of the Alps, as between the latter and the izzard.

The Pyrenean peasants, whether on the French or Spanish side, rank, with one or two notable exceptions, far below those of the Alps, both in enthusiasm for the "chasse," and in the science of hunting; and some of their methods would be despised as unworthy, in regions where the honourable rules of the chase are as much regarded as they are with us. A *gemsen-jäger* prides himself on his fine rifle-shooting, and practises the art every Sunday in friendly rivalry with his neighbours, but the *chasseur d'izzards* will tell you that there is a better chance of killing two at a shot if you use a charge of buck-shot, and that the herds are tamer in the spring when the kids are running at the sides of their dams.

My first introduction to the izzard was, in fact, in the month of March. I paid a brief visit to the charming village of Gavarnie without any idea of hunting at that time. There is a finely-engineered road to it, one of Napoleon III.'s extravagances, but more excusable than some of his follies, for it was constructed to please his wife. This, and the miracles of Lourdes have had a vulgarising effect on Gavarnie since I first knew it, and at the present time the hunter who regards his bag, will do wisely to seek more unsophisticated quarters. But this remark requires explanation. It is about twenty-five years since a lady in gauze wings appeared to a shepherdess at that hamlet. The miracle was endorsed by the Pope and all his cardinals, and has brought much pelf to the coffers of the church, as well as to the ecstatic damsel's cousins and aunts, who advertise themselves as such over the doors of the wine-shops. The *pèlerins* flock in thousands from every part of Catholic Europe, and great numbers of them find their way up, twenty-eight miles farther, to Gavarnie. This has not improved its moral atmosphere, but it is still delightful quarters, and the eternal features are always there.

The chief of these is the *Cirque* of that ilk, a wonderful amphitheatre of black cliffs, surmounted by snow-fields and the airy-looking crests of the range. At the time of my first visit the famous waterfall, of no great volume, but said to be fourteen hundred feet in height, which falls over this cliff, was frozen to its walls like a white curtain, while great shoots of snow, that had poured from above, lay in dirty white slopes at the bottom of the abyss.

Across one of these, as we entered the *Cirque* we saw some black dots moving, and immediately had our glasses on three izzards. This had a very exhilarating effect on our spirits, and I allowed myself to be persuaded to attempt a stalk on the following day, though Gavarnie was shrouded in snow, and I was sceptical as to the possibility of getting about in the higher corries. Having no weapon, I borrowed a 10-bore gun which carried a ponderous spherical bullet. Two of my daughters accompanied me, and I did not look upon the expedition in a very serious spirit. It snowed so heavily in the morning that we did not leave the inn till mid-day; but, after an easy ascent of two hours, a point was reached which overlooked the Val d'Especière, and we almost immediately spied a solitary buck izzard disporting himself on the rocks. I was half inclined to think that he was a tame one put there for the delectation of travellers, but I swallowed my scruples and seriously entered upon the stalk, while the ladies watched from below. My hunter and I toiled upwards for an hour through powdery snow, ever increasing in depth till we got well above the cliff where we had seen the buck, but he was nowhere visible and it was clear that he was reclining in some hidden corner; so there we had to wait for an hour, sitting in a biting wind, with snow well above the knee, till he chose to appear. This at last he did, feeding below us and we quickly got on better terms, as it was easy to approach silently through the floury snow. I never felt much more hopeless of doing any good, for my fingers were almost without feeling, and the flakes, which now fell again, piled themselves on the rib of my gun faster than I could shake them off. However, I had got to let off that gun at that izzard, and I was quite relieved when I had pulled the trigger and got it over. The poor little rock jumper raced, with a frantic scamper, down the snow slope, but almost instantly rolled over with a hole right through him which might have been made by a crowbar. My *bourgeois* weapon had carried true.

The ground which the Pyrenean chamois frequents is certainly steeper and the climbing more difficult, at least on the Spanish side, than I have found it in the Alps when similarly engaged. There are also long lines of cliffs which cannot be negotiated except at certain points, few and far between, and which therefore involve long detours. These cliffs are often more than sheer; they overhang at the top, or, as one of my party, somewhat given to exaggeration, described them—"they are not so steep after all, only that the slope is inside out." A dead or wounded izzard sometimes falls over them, and gets smashed out of all recognition. Gerald had to make a circuit of three hours to reach one which had thus escaped him, and found it already annexed by birds of prey; a circumstance which mattered the less, as there would have been nothing fit to carry home in any case.

I will not weary the reader with anything like a connected account of my izzard hunts of which I have enjoyed many since that, or I should run the risk of repeating much of what I have said in the chapter on chamois, but a few selections from my notes will serve to give some idea of the sport.

I think the following was one of the most varied and interesting, as well as successful days that I ever had. Our party of three left our headquarters at 4 A.M., and, appointing a rendezvous at the little hamlet of Bouchero, invaded Spain by three different routes, while our luggage followed a fourth—the ordinary mule path. My course lay through the "Brèche," the curious square niche in the crest of the ridge which is visible for so many leagues, both on the French and Spanish side. To reach it one marches straight at the wall of the Cirque, whence, to the uninitiated, there seems no exit; but across the right-hand part of the cliff there is a narrow diagonal ledge which is almost invisible from below, but up which there is in reality a famous natural staircase, very steep, but perfectly easy. After three hours of steady clambering, and when we had got nearly within sight of the Brèche, four izzards appeared coming from it across the snow-field. For a long time we watched them, till they lay down, and we began the stalk. We had to move among some rocks which were in their view, and I think they may have seen something. At any rate they showed signs of uneasiness, and after a time crossed the valley in which we were, to an isolated peak or buttress, called the Sarradets, which projects from the main chain above the Cirque, and went out of our sight

2 A

round the corner. We now took up their tracks in the

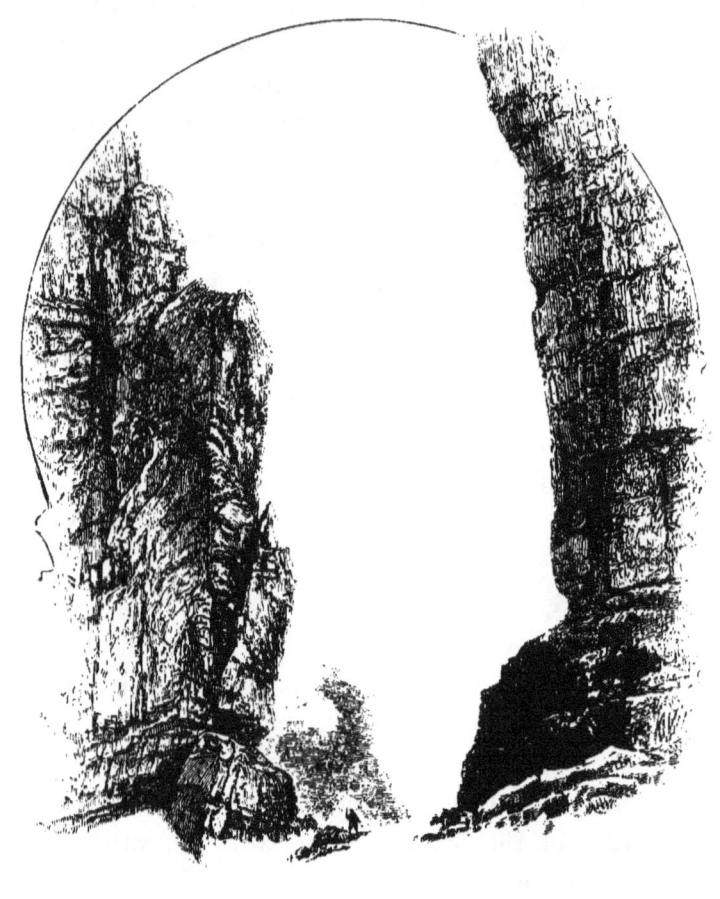

THE BRÈCHE.

snow, but the farther we followed them round the peak, the more the wind was at our backs. I was just making the remark that, for this reason, it was useless to proceed, when Celestin, who was in front, ducked his head. I scrambled forward in time to see two of the animals dashing away, now behind big rocks, and then again appearing for an instant. The shot was a snappy one and as I expected, the bullet tinkled on a rock.

Another cartridge was rammed in and I waited during that absorbing moment of expectation, when you can hear the bounce of the hoofs and the rolling stones. Presently the biggest stood upon the ridge beyond, his outline cut out sharply against the sky. I was ready for him and felt sure of him as I pulled the trigger, but at that moment a little yearling fellow dashed in front of him and got the bullet. It was unfortunate, but he had given me a very pretty stalk at the cost of a four hours' digression. We then tramped on to the Brêche which we reached at mid-day.

This remarkable cleft has been often described. The flanking cliffs are quite sheer, and it is so square cut that it looks as if it had been sawn out. Owing to the narrowness of the range, one has the sensation there of dominating the world, more than on any other spot which I know. It is a favourite camping place for hunters, but is too high except during the most settled weather in the summer. A small cave has been hewn out of the perpendicular face of the rock and is closed by an iron door, but it is too dark and damp for my taste, and I prefer the shelving hollow under an overhanging rock on the Spanish side. One's couch there, is, to say the least, a knubbly one, and the situation is perhaps as airy as any in Europe; but with a little contriving one can make oneself at home there, and the view from the parlour window, especially when the columns of cloud boil upwards from the hot caldron of Spain, is of extraordinary interest and charm, though these vapours are always regarded with suspicion, for they are the most frequent marplots to the sport. On the present occasion we had no intention of remaining, for many hours of the roughest rock tramping lay between us and our night's lodging.

From the Brêche you look out to the south over a wild waste of rocks and snow, below which a tremendous range of cliffs walls in Spain. Out of this tableland, if I may call it so by contrast with the precipices, though it is in reality broken up by many deep ravines, rise several isolated peaks. High up on the face of one of these, the Pic Royo, we made out a lot of izzards. They appeared to be quite unapproachable, as they commanded the whole of the comparatively level ground between us. However, under cover of some big rocks we approached to within about six hundred yards, hoping that they would come down on to better stalking ground. In this we were disappointed and we could not afford to wait. Beyond there was no covert whatever to conceal us. We were now on a ridge of rocks, coloured red and ochre, which were precisely matched by a suit of Harris tweed which I happened to be wearing. Feeling sure that it would puzzle the izzards, I determined to try how near I could get by boldly walking forward, although I had no expectation of getting within shooting distance. Leaving Celestin behind, I proceeded to advance towards them in a stooping position, and hanging my arms so as to look as much like a four-footed animal as I could. The moment I left the big rock they saw me, and all stood up, staring intently in my direction.

I kept steadily on till I had diminished the distance by one half, the izzards all the while continuing to stand at gaze, but quite unable, owing to the curious harmony of my clothes with my surroundings, to distinguish friend or foe. When I got within what I judged to be three hundred yards, the red rocks came to a sudden end, and were succeeded by blue shale. It was clear that, with a different background, I must be instantly identified. Now it so happened that, a few days before, I had been shooting a rifle-match at a target, and knew exactly what my ·400 Henry could do at this very distance, although it has only one fixed sight. Besides, the izzards offered an unusually clear mark, standing, as they were, rigid as carved stones against the white slopes of the peak; and, as it was hopeless to get any nearer, I thought I would try the shot; but I was considerably surprised when the smoke cleared, and revealed the one I had selected lying stone dead. It was a sight to see the rest of the herd scatter with tremendous leaps, and, accompanied by the bounding stones which they disturbed and a cloud of dust, bound and slide down the cliff *towards* me, for apparently they could not believe that the shot could have proceeded from the dim and distant object which they had been watching. That was I think the longest successful shot I ever made which was not an absolute fluke.

Celestin had now a very heavy burden, but I was destined to add to his load. After another two hours' clambering, and just before we began the steepest part of the descent, we saw another band at no great distance, but also apparently in an unstalkable place. My untiring companion proposed that I should get as near them as I

THE HERD CLATTERED DOWN THE CLIFF.

could, while he made a circuit and moved them. This scheme we carried out, but they did not take the expected direction. I ran along behind a ridge to cut them off, but I could not get within two hundred yards of them. They had seen me, but thought they were far enough to be safe, and bunched up. The distance was really too far for anything like a safe shot, and I had no business to try it, but, encouraged by my previous skill or good luck, I selected a nice buck and fired. They rushed off helter-skelter and I supposed I had missed, as, perhaps I deserved to do; but ten minutes later, when I reached a spot which faced the slope where they had been, I turned my glass on to it while waiting for Celestin to come up, and there lay the body of the buck where it had fallen, stone dead to the shot, behind the rock on which it had been standing, and which had completely concealed its body from the firing point. Celestin somehow managed to pile all three animals on to his back, and for a short distance, but with labouring steps, carried them so, till we reached a shepherd's refuge and there left them. We had still fully three thousand feet of descent and the way was rough, but it was lightened by a glorious moon, whose beams streamed through the great pines and by an exhilarating sense of success. It was 9.30 before I rejoined my companions.

I think this was without exception the best day's sport I ever had; nor was that all, for Gerald and Geof had each secured a good buck. Gerald's beast had given trouble of rather an unusual kind. It had been killed at the top of a cliff, down which it had rolled for a long distance till out of their sight. The hunter went down to fetch it, and did not reappear for an hour, when he returned without the buck. He had followed it by the bloody trail which its body had made as it slid downwards, until the cliff got too steep for him. From this point he could see to the base of it, and the small snow-field which sloped away from it, but nothing of the buck. To reach the bottom they had to make a detour of two hours; but when this was accomplished, there were still no signs of the dead izzard. At last they came to the conclusion that he must have fallen behind the snow, which had melted away from the rock, leaving a cleft, into which they could neither see nor descend; but there remained one more chance of reaching it. By great good luck the stream which fell down the rock had worn a way for itself under the snow. Proceeding to the foot of the slope they cautiously crawled, on all fours, up the tunnel, and, after a difficult piece of underground clambering, found their quarry and brought it once more into the daylight.

So far as numbers were concerned, I once had a still better day than the above. On the plateau above mentioned there are several curious deep crater-like hollows which ought to be lakes, but that the water, which flows into them, escapes through subterranean passages in the soft limestone. I found a herd of izzards in the bottom of the largest of these, which is about half a mile in diameter, and perhaps 500 ft. deep. I killed one at the first shot, and as there was no escape for them except by mounting the steep slope opposite to me, they kept stopping and giving me a second, third and fourth chance, so that I had three lying dead before they got out of range. I had killed another in the morning, so there was meat in camp that night. I was certainly in excellent form that year, but lest I should seem to boast, I may mention that a few days afterwards, I had three chances, each one simpler than the other, and missed them all!

If a person is willing to face doubtful weather, he may often have the finest sport late in the year, when the bucks are on the move. They are then sometimes seduced within range by their own headlong passions. It is a case of mistaken identity. My friend Sam furnishes me with the following note of such an experience:

"The autumnal equinox is not always favourable for stalking; but if its customary storms are suspended, the patient sportsman may sally out with an assured prospect of sport. If he should be favoured with still bright frosty weather, and fresh white snow, upon which tracks can be picked up at any distance, the cream of the season lies before him. For about this date a new element enters into the game. Even the most churlish old *solitaires* seek to 'join the ladies.' The weighty old gray-face now sallies forth in quest of the fair; and his weakness may sometimes lead him into embarrassing situations. It may seem unfeeling to take advantage of his rash indiscretions—but that these occasions may be profitably turned to account the following will show.

"It was the last week in October—stormy weather had kept us prisoners for several days, when the change came, and we determined to give it one more day before starting homewards. My companion and I had started before dawn, and the morning had broken upon a perfect day. We proceeded up a valley at the head of which we had previously seen a herd. Sure enough they were there, or thereabouts, but the stalk failed, and they went away—uphill as though to cross into another valley. We watched them top the ridge, going very slowly in the deep snow, and made sure they would stop, a little way over on the other side. We were just about to make after them, when we spied, very high up on the opposite side of our valley, two splendid bucks. One was a lord among izzards. His head was good, but what especially distinguished him was his size and colour. His haunches and shoulders were so grizzled as to be almost white, while his barrel was black like a bear, and the long bristles stood up—a wiry fringe along his back. There was only one way up, and the wind was puffing this way and that, in an aggravating manner.

"But it was my last day, so we hardened our hearts and determined to try it. Sometimes we were on good ground, sometimes on bad,—and the wind all over the place. I had not much faith in it. Suddenly, however, the buck we were in search of rose, and disappeared over some rocks. We could not tell whether he had got our wind or had merely risen to feed; but we feared the worst and hurried on to see. Sure enough they had gone. We were just beginning to sigh over our ill fortune when my hunter touched me and pointed. Crossing a wide corrie there he was—the big fellow—standing on a peak of black rock, staring hard in our direction and giving vent to a succession of surprised whistles. '*Sapristi*'— '*Ah! le grand coquin. Regardez-le! il n'est pas sûr—il nous croit d'être femelles, vous et moi par exemple! Tenez vous tranquil—ne bougez pas—Il va nous faire une petite visite!*' And behold! one loud whistle and with every hair on his back erect, he wheeled about and started in our direction with the air of sudden impulse which comes over a man when he catches sight of his lady-love, for whom he has been waiting impatiently at the trysting-place. How he did gallop on the rocks and scramble through the soft snow, sometimes up to his neck! Soon a buttress of rock hid him from our sight. We jumped up and ran for a rock which commanded the spot where he should reappear. Minutes seemed hours, till we heard the slight rattle of falling stones. Presently his head appeared and then his body came in sight. He was looking about eagerly for his *inamorata* but he was not received with the caress which he expected. Bang— a puff of smoke—a moment of suspense and then the prolonged sliding sound of izzard, snow and small stones, combining to make a miniature avalanche into the bottom of the corrie below. '*L'animal! il s'est joliment trompé cette fois là!*'"

One of the most curious shots I ever made was on the "Blue Cliff," so called from the slaty shale of which it was composed, or, as some said, from its effect on the nerves of any novice who attempted to climb it. Certainly it was all but impossible to get a stalk on it, partly owing to its steepness and the crumbly nature of the rock, but still more to the concave shape of the corrie. From its upper edge we spied two chamois lying together on a patch of snow, but too far off for a fair shot, and there was no prospect of getting any nearer unless they moved. We lay flat on our stomachs and watched them till we got too cold to remain any longer, and it was necessary to try the shot, or set down a blank day. My companion put the distance at three hundred metres. That was, I think, an exaggeration, and there was nothing to boast of in the fact that it was my turn to have a stroke of luck, and that I succeeded in hitting the one I aimed at. He rose, stumbled a few steps, then lay down, and I had no difficulty in ultimately recovering him, though I had to shoot him again. But in the meanwhile the strange part of it was that his companion, who lay within two yards of him, *never moved to the shot*, though the echoes of it reverberated round him like thunder. Loading again I aimed at this sleeping beauty, but failed to find the mark a second time. This bullet must have splashed the snow all over him and he fled like the wind, but even now he did not know whence the sound came, and galloped straight towards us round the face of the cliff. I thought I was sure of him too, but he followed a little cornice below me, and the overhanging cliff hid him from view, so that I never saw him again. I have no doubt that the indifference of this izzard to the sound was due to his mistaking it for falling rocks. There had been a heavy fall of snow, which was melting very rapidly at the time, causing big stones to crash downwards every few minutes.

I do not wish it to be thought that there was anything extraordinary in the long and fortunate shots which I have recorded. Every sportsman can recall plenty such, and there is no particular credit to be attached to them. Some would say the contrary. But I have selected such instances for description because, however much they may have been due to chance, the triumph at the time was sweet, and made the impression of those days more vivid than others.

There was a very old buck which inhabited the Escusan, a broken ridge above Bouchero. We constantly went in pursuit of him, but he as often eluded us, as he had done in the case of many other sportsmen, native and foreign. I had been first told of his existence by Sir Victor Brooke who had known him for four or five years before I did, and he was quite a veteran when he was first observed. He had been christened by that sportsman "the Old Soldier," for he had only three legs and a short stump, as if he had just come out of Noah's Ark, the rest of that limb having been left behind in a previous encounter; but he knew very well how to make the best use of this limited number, and there was no fathoming his craft. His horns were unusually long, and the hooks had been partly worn or broken away. No wonder if the natives regarded him with semi-superstitious awe, for he had been repeatedly shot at, and seemed to bear a charmed life. It would fill this volume if I detailed all the attempts we made to secure this child of the mist, and the shifts and expedients he used, to make himself invisible at critical moments, but I will borrow from Gerald's notes the account of the last serious attempt that we made to secure his venerable head. That was three years after I had made his acquaintance, and he can scarcely have been less than twelve years old when I first espied him.

"We went up the Escusan where we spied seven izzards under the big cliff. We ought to have got up to them if Genté had not made a mistake about the wind, which cost us this chance. But we were on the look-out for the 'Old Soldier' and cared very little for this, or for another lot which we found soon after. Long we sought him in vain, and, at length, climbed to a spot which commanded the other face of the ridge. Thence we made out a *solitaire* who looked like the 'Soldier,' but as he was a long way off, and lying down, we could not identify him in the usual way. Now an unfortunate thing happened. We accidentally startled a small band which had not previously been seen by us, and I rashly took a long shot at them, doing no good, and of course disturbing the *solitaire*. Immediately we turned our glasses towards him. It *was* the three-legged one himself. He had three others with him, a very good buck, a doe and a kid. We watched them till they lay down on the long slope of snow and loose stones under the cliffs which overlook the pass. This is very bad stalking ground from the smoothness of the slope and the noise made in walking on the shoots of stones. The two bucks lay down together at the bottom of the snow slope, near to which there is a pile of rocks which have fallen from above, and slid down the snow. The approach might have been managed very well if it had not been for the doe and kid, which lay down in a commanding position, and one in which they must get the wind of any one coming up behind the stony hummock. The weather looked so uncertain that something had to be dared. If we waited till they fed in the evening, the gathering clouds would probably interfere, so I had to take the risk of their being put away by the doe when she got my wind. By descending to the path which crosses the pass, and remounting, I soon approached the position I desired, but, as I expected, started the doe in doing so. Fortunately the bucks did not, at first, see her go. Now by rapid crawling I got up under shelter of the pile of stones from which the bucks were not more than a hundred yards distant, and I began to hope that the chance was within my grasp. Alas! when I looked over it appeared that, though the companion buck offered an easy shot,—and a very fine one he was too—the 'Old Soldier' had so placed himself that only his horns could be seen. I might have killed the other with ease, but waited, hoping that the object of my desire would stand and show himself. I thought he would do this as soon as either of them caught sight of the doe, who was slowly travelling along the rocks above, but instead of that, when the old fellow at last rose, he perversely moved off under cover of the stones, and I could not catch sight of him until he had reached too long a range and was going hard. A running shot at a chamois at any distance is a doubtful business. At a hundred and fifty yards the chance is remote indeed, and he would not halt till he had trebled that interval. I gave him one more parting message at that long range, and knocked the snow all over him, but that was all."

That was the last shot any of us ever had at him, but it was not quite the last I saw of him. We were due on a certain day at Gavarnie, homeward bound, and determined to have one more try for the Old Monarch whose territory lay on the way. The day was unfortunately again cloudy, so that it seemed hopeless to do anything, but now and again the clouds lifted for a few minutes at a time, and each of these brief opportunities was busily used with the telescopes. Suddenly through such a rift, I saw the "Old Soldier" about a quarter of a mile off like the spectre of the Brocken. I could not be mistaken in his identity for I could plainly see the stump of his missing leg, but the curtain came down again before anything could be done. We moved on however through the mist. As if by magic it suddenly lifted. Again I caught a glimpse of a buck just about where the "Soldier" had been, but he saw me as quickly as I saw him, and was over the edge before I could draw a bead. I ran forward, peered over, and could hear him rattling below. As he reached the bottom he stood a moment and gave me a fair view with a good background of snow. I saw the hair fly to the bullet. The buck stumbled, recovered himself, ran a few yards, and fell over dead. The invulnerable lay stricken at last, and the stalwart who had defied us so long was, as I supposed, overthrown; but before descending to possess myself of him I took a look at him through my glass. *Lo and behold he had got four legs*, and, though the biggest izzard I ever shot—he weighed 60 lbs.—he was, comparatively, a young buck. Now whether the "Old Soldier" renewed his youth like Faust, in the person of this vigorous young buck, or whether he went up to the happy hunting grounds as one of the cloud forms which floated around us, according to my information, from that day he was *never seen again by living man*.

Before I conclude this chapter it may be worth while to give a hint to future sportsmen. In the transit across France, cartridges, and the means of passing them through the *douanes*, are always an anxiety. I once had a bad quarter of an hour at Paris. When I went to seek my luggage the usual long bench was searched in vain. At length I discovered it, set by itself in a corner, like a bad boy. The moment I claimed it I was myself claimed by a haughty official and told to consider myself under arrest. He taxed me with carrying dangerous explosives, and described my bag as no better than an infernal machine. Then waxing more voluble he described, with tremendous action, how it had spit fire and bullets; "*Pum! pum! partout.*" Meekly I followed my captor to the condemned cell as I supposed, and in my presence the accused bag was examined. Fortunately I was able to show that all my cartridges were still intact, but I could not deny the palpable evidences of fire. Ultimately to my surprise I got off with a reprimand, and it was not until some days later that I discovered that my whole stock of cigar-lights was missing!

XII

PEAKS AND PASSES

ALPINE ascents have been done to death, and perhaps this chapter will be generally skipped by readers who may have struggled so far in my book. Yet I cannot deprive myself of the pleasure of recalling just one or two laborious but delightful days of struggle, which I spent in the company of friends, no less enthusiastic than myself, and in the capture—not of wild beasts—but of virgin peaks and passes.

There was a wonderful freemasonry among the worshippers at those shrines, and it would be impossible to exaggerate the devotion and enthusiasm of the votaries during the "sixties." It was the decade following on the formation of the Alpine Club. Within that period, nearly every peak and passage of any importance was discussed at home, minutely examined on the spot, attacked, and finally conquered. At that time I was one of the worst victims of this summer madness, and spent hours (ah, how delightfully!) at the little Club room in eager controversies with others like-minded with myself, while I wasted my substance on every kind of printed or graphic publication which offered a foretaste, or a retrospect, of my chosen insanity. Then the gatherings at Zermatt and other favourite centres! There were giants in those days, at least, we thought so then, men with limbs, long and sinewy, and with heads to devise, and to command. On the lips of these masters of the craft outsiders like myself hung with reverence. The professionals too, the Andereggs, the Crozs, Bennen, and a few others in the first rank, whose native skill and agility had conquered so many difficulties, and whom we counted rather as intimates than as servants.

I do not pretend that my own triumphs were anything remarkable, and I should find it hard to select any of them which would rank as first-rate achievements. The two expeditions which I have recalled in this chapter were undertaken within a few days of each other in August 1865. Owing to the detestable weather, they were the only attempts which we were able to pull off successfully in that season. For this reason, and on account of their intrinsic difficulty, they left a particularly vivid impression on my mind.

Messrs. Grove, Macdonald, and I had been for many days unwilling prisoners at Chamouni, and were so weary of promenading on the level that a treadmill would have been welcome as a variety. Sodden and despairing, as we were, the slightest sign of an improvement in the weather was seized upon as a chance of release from the hot steam of the valley.

By dint of persistent shaking, the glass had at length been induced to declare that a change for the better was imminent, and there were certainly some rags of blue visible. Without an hour's delay, we seized the occasion, drove off down the valley, and a few hours later found ourselves at the little Pavillon de Belle Vue, on the Col de Voza, which ridge divides the northern from the western face of the great *massif* of Mont Blanc. That mountain has been almost vulgarised by two generations of the showman's business, but I have often thought that, of all the ranges which I know, it is the most impressive. The pure and stately dome of the monarch contrasts so gloriously with the graceful spires of the attendant *aiguilles*, which rank themselves around their lord. Of these, the Aiguille de Bionnassay, which is the most conspicuous and seductive of the group, of those that are visible from the approach to Chamouni from the west, was, at the time of which I write, nearly if not quite, the highest Alpine peak which remained unscaled. Our intention was to endeavour to ascend the peak by its north-western face, and if successful, follow the long curved *arête* which connects it with the Dôme du Gouter. We expected difficulties which would only yield to a determined attack; but we had tested one another's powers, and I had the utmost confidence in my companions, than whom it would have been difficult to find any more averse to turning their backs on an incomplete undertaking. Our guides, Cachat and Payot, though not in the first rank, were, like most Chamouni men, excellent icemen.

With an hour or two of daylight to spare, we proceeded to examine the face of the peak which we hoped to subdue, and which now came in sight. A well-regulated mountain ought to consist of rocks and snow in reasonable proportions, so that if the conditions of the one are unfavourable, resort may be had to the other medium. In this case, there was no such option. The entire face which was turned towards us consisted of ice and snow, some of it in smooth slopes at the highest angle consistent with stability; and again, where the rocks beneath were too steep to hold a continuous bed, there were cliffs of ice of that pearly blue which denotes recent fracture, and below these, the slopes of older and dirtier snow were scored with long white lines by the frequent avalanches. It was clear that to avoid their dangerous track, we should be driven to ascend some rather puzzling places.

We each of us rose from the usual discussion which takes place on these occasions, with the firm conviction that he alone held the correct clue to the labyrinth, but by mutual consent, we left the guides to decide, and, by way of practising our muscles for the gymnastics before us, played a match of cricket on the skittle-ground, using a young fir-tree and a skittle ball, until a gigantic leg hit of Macdonald's which he landed somewhere in the direction of the Glacier des Bossons, and which he refused to field himself, stopped all further play.

Presently, our men approached us, but their faces did not express confidence. They thought there would be much step-cutting, which was indeed obvious, and that the summit could hardly be reached under twelve hours with favourable weather; an estimate, by the way, which proved inadequate. Of the difficulties which we might encounter beyond it, we had no means of judging.

With this prospect, we determined to walk through the greater part of the night, so as to reserve the full complement of daylight hours for the unknown trials of the route. It is not easy to sup at six, and eat again—I was going to say breakfast—with an appetite at 11 P.M., still more difficult to sleep through the intervening hours. Thus it was not a very hilarious party that started soon after midnight on a very dark night; nor were our spirits stimulated by the weather. The clouds looked oily, and the watery moonlight behind them showed that they were streaming overhead at a great rate, straight from the torrid plains of Lombardy. Such a southerly wind, as all mountaineers know, was certain to give us trouble.

In bad weather mountaineering is uncertain and often risky, so that ascents which in clear weather are comparatively simple, become, under other conditions, most formidable. On the other hand, the mountain gloom, the sudden lifting of the curtain, the visions of fairy light seen through the rifts, the mysterious depths half revealed, make it far more interesting.

At first, the route lay over grassy alps, and we had only to steer towards the frowning masses dimly seen in front. I always found that in these ghostly walks before cock-crow, the time passed quickly enough, provided that the pace were not forced; and in what seemed a short space of time, we were skirting the base of the Aiguille du Gouter. We had engaged a hanger-on of the little inn, whose local knowledge was supposed to be equal to keeping us in the little goat-track which leads towards the Glacier de Bionnassay; but when we got among the rocks, either the darkness was too much for him, or he passed beyond his ken, so that we presently found ourselves plunging and stumbling over hidden obstacles. He hopelessly lost his way, and we our tempers. So we sent him back to his natural function—cleaning boots. But now we rounded an angle, and the dim outline of the Glacier appeared like some large, white, flat fish. The scarcely perceptible increase of light was sufficient to indicate our general route, and by sunrise we had crossed the glacier, and reached the base of the great frozen pyramid, with which we were to try conclusions.

Under such circumstances, it is generally the best policy to attain, at once, to one of the great ridges which lead up to the peak to be climbed, and to follow its crest as nearly as possible; for this reason, that the angle of a pyramid must necessarily be less steep than either of its faces, and also because, from such a position, you can better survey the slopes on either side, and take advantage of any favourable combination which may present itself. In our case the only ridge available was that to our right, forming the western barrier of the glacier. It was of a formidable character, but I am inclined to think that on a closer acquaintance, a way could have been found among its rocky obstacles, which would have occupied less time than the one we adopted. On the other hand, we might have been stopped altogether, and, provided our patience and step-cutting force held out, the ice-route was the more certain. Our men too, as Chamouni guides always do, preferred the glacier, by which I do not mean, in this case, the ordinary ice-stream, but a broken cliff of exceptional height and steepness, from which detached masses were continually plunging downwards.

For a long distance, our route lay up a slope entirely composed of avalanche *débris*. One moment we rested on a solid boulder of ice, half concealed, the next, without any warning, we plunged up to our middles into snow, rendered viscid by the warm moist weather. Under, and among the leaning cliffs we cut our tortuous way upwards, with a sense of relief as each source of danger was passed. At length, we had subdued them all, and there lay between us and the ridge, nothing but a slope of hard ice of great steepness and unknown length. It was only a question of the sturdiness of our men, when we should succeed in surmounting it. In turn they took the lead and wielded the axe.

Hour after hour, with a muscular vigour, only to be found in countries where every peasant is a woodman, the ringing strokes succeeded one another monotonously, and the fragments of ice hissed past the string of patient followers. In cutting up an ice-slope of this length, it is necessary to economise time and labour as much as possible, and the steps are hacked out as far apart as is consistent with safety. This necessitates a cramped position for each member of the party, for one leg is always doubled up sharply, with the knee nearly at the level of the stomach, while the other remains stretched at its full length. The best way to pass the tedious hours, and to prevent the imagination dwelling too fixedly on the obvious possibilities of the situation, is to work away with the axe, and improve the steps which the pioneer has begun. To most Englishmen rocks seem more comfortable. It is the pitiless ice with its exquisite lines, curving over to the unknown, which daunts the nerves. At least that is my experience, and I do not think it is possible for the most practised mountaineer to find himself on such a slope without some tremors. The rope gives confidence, and at that time I used to maintain that it gave security also. But I fear it must be admitted, that experience has proved that, on a slope of such steepness, the mistake of one may involve the destruction of all.

At length, the moment of relief arrived, when the face of ice to which we had been clinging, began to assume a less acute angle to our bodies, and in a few minutes, we were able to stand upright with a tolerable sense of support. Snow could lie, and in the softer material we quickly trod out the remaining steps necessary to land us on the ridge.

Though the narrow edge on which we now stood still ran upwards, and curved out of sight to an unknown distance, there appeared no obstacle likely to stop us. We had been going for twelve hours, almost without a halt, and for seven hours the ice-wall had held us in its toils, but now, for the moment, the tension was at an end, and with a sense of assured victory, we threw ourselves on our backs in the snow, to enjoy the delicious luxury of a stretch, and to recover somewhat from the exhausting labour. We opened our *rücksacks* and fed, but the sense that we were bound to win had a still more restorative effect.

But one thing was clear: that we had occupied far too much time over the preliminary struggle. In describing it, perhaps I have made the same mistake, and I must hurry over the remainder of our ascent, as in fact we did on that day.

To my mind, the last two hours of a narrow *arête*, leading to a virgin peak, offers the most exhilarating exercise which falls to the lot of man, descended from a monkey. The difficulties encountered are generally of small account, compared with those already overcome, and the sense of overlooking both sides is only comparable to the exaltation of the skater when he first succeeds in balancing himself on the outside edge. In this case, we had quite enough excitement to keep our powers on the stretch, for now a fresh trouble met us.

A heavy thunderstorm had for some time been cracking and growling below us. We stood as it were, on an island with a curdling sea of thunder-cloud at our feet, not inky as such a one appears from below, but brilliantly illuminated from above. This light was so strong that it subdued the flashes of lightning, and we could only see those that were near us and on the edge of the cloud. They appeared from our position to take a horizontal course. Some of them were instantly succeeded by rending explosions which seemed to send a vibration through the mountain itself, as the shock of a broadside wave shudders through an ocean liner. It was still more trying to the nerves when our axe-heads began to hum audibly with the stream of electricity passing through them into space, and the loose hair under our caps became distinctly sensitive to the same mysterious influence. Such an experience has occurred to most Alpine climbers, and to myself on more than one occasion, but never under such startling circumstances.

Quite suddenly, the storm rose and enveloped us, and the air became thick with a *tourmente* of snow, driven before such a wind as is only felt on the loftier ridges. It seemed like some live and angry beast, which strove to comb us off the crest. Lest I should seem to exaggerate in this, I may remind the reader that we were within a mile of the Bosse du Dromadaire, where some years afterwards such a fate is believed to have overtaken a party of seven. We literally crept along the snowy neck, often stopping to cling with hands and feet, until some blast of surpassing fury had spent itself, and sometimes even astride of the thin knife-edge. In fact, in this ignominious position, we finally arrived at the top, half choked and wholly dazed by the whirling mist of snow-dust.

The summit of the Bionnassay is not a needle, as the name implies but a scimitar-shaped ridge. We were uncertain which point in this ridge was the actual summit; but a partial clearance, which occurred a few minutes later removed all doubt that we had passed it, when the delicate white blade—for such it looked like—fell away in front, and then dived downwards to describe the great catenary curve, nearly two miles long, by which our peak is connected with the Dôme. It was by this highway that we had hoped to escape, and we had expected the ridge to be comparatively level, as indeed from below it appears to be. Perhaps, we were confused by the blizzard, or our nerves may have been shaken by the strain of fifteen hours' continuous toil. Certain it is, that the moment the nature of the ridge was revealed to us, our guides recoiled from it, and we had no more stomach for it than they. One of my companions, who knows most of the nastiest places between the Dauphiné and the "Frosty Caucasus," afterwards described it in the *Alpine Journal* as "the most terrific thing he had ever seen in the Alps." And so it was to us, for, although if we had had a reserve of force and ample time, we might have effected the passage in safety, it was now nearly four o'clock in the

THE AIGUILLE DE BIONNASSAY.

afternoon. It was manifest, that a ridge so long and forbidding could not be passed in the daylight that remained, while, to be overtaken by nightfall in that situation, and in such a wind, would be to be caught in a trap from which there was no escape. On the other hand, to return by the way we had mounted was out of the question. To descend the ice-wall by the staircase we had constructed, would be, now that the steps were hidden under snow, to court disaster.

But *aut viam inveniam, aut faciam.* There was no alternative but to find, or make, a way down the cliff on our right. It was impossible to see from above what this might lead us into, or how long it would take. But we had a tolerable confidence in being able to extricate ourselves by one or other of the *couloirs* with which it was scored. It was not extraordinarily steep, but the rocks were slippery with fresh snow, and intensely rotten. However, with caution it could be done. There was always some solid point or shelf on which one or more of the links of our human chain could steady themselves, while the others tenderly let themselves down the ticklish places. The pioneer had a bad time of it, for he could not be sure of the stability of anything, till he tried it with his weight, and he repeatedly lost his footing, and started with great suddenness down the slope, to be pulled up again by the rope, which we kept as taut as possible. In the course of one of these involuntary *glissades* he tore the seat of his trousers completely out. More than once, we came upon unexpected *faults* in the cliff, which compelled us to retrace our steps and traverse its face in search of practicable ways. We were troubled by quantities of falling rocks and stones, loosened by the wind and the melting snow, which shot over our heads every few minutes, or struck the rocks near us, glancing into space with a highly suggestive whiz. But we had chosen our route on a careful estimate of the balance of risk, and as we could not avoid these missiles, we grew callous to them.

My recollection of the next four hours is dim. I only know that when at length darkness overtook us, we were still entangled on this grim face, and high enough to look over the Col de Miage. We had had no temptation to dawdle, so that if in that time we had only made fifteen hundred feet of perpendicular descent, it was because the place was undeniably treacherous and nasty. The spot we had reached was about two-thirds of the way down the black face immediately below the summit. The positions of Mont Blanc and the Dôme are dimly seen to right and left of it respectively.

When light at length failed us, we had perforce to stop. A shelf was found, if that can be so described, which was not flat, but tipped at an angle that necessitated great caution throughout the night. Our clothes were soaked with perspiration and the fine penetrating snow. Any garment which we took off froze in a few minutes to the rigidity of a board. Such meat as we had left was also frozen; but we had little inclination for food, for our drink was exhausted. A stream which we could hear somewhere below us, but could not reach, made this more tantalising. This sound gradually died out, as its sources were dammed by the frost. Fortunately for us it was, relatively, a warm night, that is to say, it would, with a clear sky, have been much colder, but the wind had moderated, and, as it blew from the south, a canopy of cloud arrested the radiation from our bodies. There was not much to fear from the cannonade of stones, for that quickly stopped after sundown. I had some reason to dread getting frost-bitten,[1] but though our sufferings were great from the cold, no result of that kind followed. Alternately we crouched with our knees up to our chins, or stamped away the stiffness. With grim buffoonery we warded off any tendency to a dangerous drowsiness. At least we had the sense of victory to warm us, and Macdonald's spirits which were in inverse proportion to the depression of others—were contagious. Alas! that his cheery voice has long been still!

The weary night passed at last. As soon as the light permitted, we continued—though rather stiffly and with a certain trembling of the knees—our downward progress to the Miage Glacier; and before mid-day, reached the bathing establishment of St. Gervais. One of us had to hold his two hands in a mysterious manner to the seat of his trousers; the rest were stained and dishevelled, and to

[1] A season or two before this, I had been severely frost-bitten on Monte Rosa, without being conscious, at the time, of any unusual inconvenience. The night was intensely cold, but whether my foot lost its vitality during the ascent, or on the top where I went to sleep for an hour in the sunshine, I do not know. Although conscious of something wrong with my foot, it was not till I reached the little tarn by the Riffel Horn, that I realised the cause. There I stripped for a bathe, and, when I tried to put on my boots again, it was impossible to do so, for the toes of one foot had suddenly swollen to a portentous size. It was not without difficulty that I hopped down to the Riffel-berg Inn, and thence rode to Zermatt to consult the village practitioner. He told me that I ought at once to have returned to the glacier and immersed the frozen part in an ice-pool until it was frozen again. As it was too late for that remedy, he applied hot glue, but the toes were so badly injured, as to disable me for some weeks, and I fancy I had a narrow escape of losing them altogether.

run the gauntlet of a double row of smartly-dressed, supercilious *baigneuses*, was a more terrific experience to modest men, than any we had encountered.[1]

After the expedition above described, we were again imprisoned at Chamouni for ten days by stress of weather, bargaining for artificial agates, eating heavy dinners, racing to the Montanvert against time; and feeding our imaginations on all sorts of ambitious schemes against neighbouring

MAC.

passes and peaks, the broad bases of which were all that we were permitted to see. At length, we became almost callous to misfortune. We gave up even our daily constitutional in the rain, and sought refuge from our despair in gambling and tobacco.

During part of this time, we were enlivened by a strike of our guides—a strike, not for a rise of wages, but against the employment of non-union men. We had one day found young Taugwald from Zermatt, outside the hotel, and looking out for a return job. As he was a strong lad, we engaged him as our porter. He was one of the

[1] This was the scene of the tragedy of last July, when nearly the whole series of buildings was swept away in five minutes by a flood which came down the gorge almost without warning.

survivors of the terrible catastrophe on the Matterhorn, which had happened a few weeks before, and of which all men's minds were full.

Just then Jean Baptiste Croz had returned from Zermatt looking ill and crazed at the loss of his brother. His grief found vent in half-formed accusations against the men who had been with him at the time of his death. The wild tale found ready credence among the suspicious Frenchmen, who are always jealous of the German guides. The next morning our men came to us, and deliberately accused Taugwald of having cut the rope on the occasion referred to, at the same time demanding his dismissal. They reckoned that we could not do without them, and indeed we should have preferred to retain them, but we could not desert Taugwald in such a strait. They were rather astonished when we paid them off, but our prompt action did more than anything else to dispel the cruel rumour, at least in Chamouni. Cachat eventually begged to be taken on again, and we allowed him to rejoin, but in a subordinate position.

In the meanwhile, the resources of civilisation were not exhausted. We posted off Taugwald to Zermatt. He accomplished his mission in extraordinarily quick time, and returned with a tower of strength in the person of Jakob Anderegg. Jakob was a rougher man than his better-known relative Melchior, and with less experience than he, but he was a splendid specimen of humanity, with more dash and determination than any Swiss I ever knew. He arrived just in time for another partial clearance of the weather.

At midnight on August 6, we fled from the seductions

of Capua, and took the path to the Pierre Pointue, which is on the route for the ascent to Mont Blanc, with a vague idea of forcing our way somewhere, over the highest part of the chain, and descending on the Italian side to Courmayeur. As we walked, our plan took shape, and ultimately we determined to go over the Dôme du Gouter and descend by the southern Glacier de Miage. The host of the Pierre Pointue was prepared with "*encore un gigot,*"

JAKOB.

as he always was, because experience taught him that the enduring Englishman would be persuaded to buy it. While waiting for this, we amused ourselves by examining the wonderful assortment of garments which were then considered necessary to a successful ascent of Mont Blanc. The most remarkable of these was a kind of knitted helmet of mediaeval shape and ferocious appearance. I have the best reason to remember it, for once, when I was very green, I wore one on a high expedition. I was fresh from England and my complexion was delicate. The woollen covering preserved it in perfection, all except my unfortunate nose, which was cooked into a resemblance to a well-browned cutlet.

Soon after we took to the ice, it became clear that our work was cut out for us, owing to the depth of fresh snow. It soon reached halfway to our knees, and, at the Grands Mulets, a halt for breakfast was an acceptable relief. We stood outside, for the rocks were covered with fresh snow, and no appetite could stand the stale concentrated smell of the *cabane*, caused by the surplus scraps left behind by several Mont Blanc parties, which means no small pickings, as anybody can tell, who has had to pay a provision bill at Chamouni.

Leaving the Grands Mulets we crossed the glacier, and got on to the lower slopes of the Dôme by some steep rocks, forming the commencement of the cliff which, higher up, overhangs the Petit Plateau. We chose this way because, being the most direct, we thought it would be the shortest, and also because we hoped that the snow would not have rested in such quantities, on the exposed ridge, as in the valley. But this very circumstance proved a hindrance, as the hot weather of July had consolidated the *névé*, and where it had been blown clear of snow, steps had to be cut in hard ice. Opposite the Petit Plateau the ridge we were on begins to expand into great swelling fields and hills of snow, and over these it was not particularly easy to steer a correct course through the haze which now closed in upon us. It was on these wide white hills that Mr. Nettleship so gallantly fought for his life this summer, and lost. This ridge and the adjacent ice-laden valley, an area scarcely larger than Hyde Park, might be described as the *Gehenna* of the Alps, so fatal has it been to travellers.

We were puzzled by one of those semi-transparent mists which admit a good deal of diffused light, but are a decided relief from the full blistering glare of the sun. It is altogether rather a cheerful atmospheric condition than otherwise, but it effectually obscures your vision of distant objects. Once we were brought to a standstill by finding ourselves on a round hill, which might or might not be the top of the Dôme. The slope fell away in front of us, and we could not see enough to pronounce whether the next rise was the Dôme or the Bosse. We rightly decided that our hill was a spurious imitation, and started again up the next slope. In another half-hour a break in the cloud showed us our position. We were a few hundred yards from the top of the Dôme, and had worked round to the west side of it, so that we were opposite to, and on a level with the Aiguille de Biomnassay.

We were also now able to survey the connecting ridge for which we had felt such a repugnance, when on the Aiguille at its other extremity. It certainly seemed to us that we had been well advised not to cultivate a closer acquaintance on that occasion. By the map it must be nearly three thousand yards in length. It was important to us to find its junction point with the buttress which comes down from the Dôme to meet it, because we knew that this spot had been reached from the south, by a branch of the southern Miage Glacier, which offers a perfectly easy means of descent on that side. But the momentary interval of clear weather was succeeded by more mist, which closed in upon us thicker than before. The bellying curves of the Dôme were confusing when half seen through such a veil, but we kept on in what we believed to be the right direction. A very slight error might send us to left or right of the junction point which we sought. In the latter case we should without knowing it return to the northern side of the chain, down the Bionnassay Glacier. In the former—but as that was the error which we *did* make, I will describe in due course what we found. It was now one o'clock, but owing to the soft snow and hard ice, we had taken five and a half hours from the Grands Mulets, and including halts, thirteen from Chamouni. We had a descent before us of quite six thousand feet, before we could reach the main ice-stream of the Miage Glacier. The haze again thinned out a little, and when we came to the edge of a precipitous slope we mistook it for the head of the affluent Glacier which we wished to descend, and which lay, in reality, more than a mile farther westwards. We could see some hundreds of yards down the slope which, although steep, was covered with a great accumulation of fresh, but not powdery, snow and seemed easy. At any rate this *facilis descensus* looked so inviting after our long grind, that we yielded to the temptation.

We descended, I should think, fifteen hundred or two thousand feet, ploughing comfortably up to our knees, and were beginning to see the flatter surface of the glacier below, while there was still enough haze to diminish the apparent distance, and make all look smooth and pleasant in front, when Grove's hat blew off, and trundled downwards. We were carefully watching where it would go, with a view to recovering it at the bottom, when it suddenly disappeared, and we then noticed what seemed to be a faint line drawn across the *névé* at that place, and that beyond it, what appeared to be the continuation of the slope was of a yellower colour than the snow close at hand. In a few minutes more we were near enough to see that the line was the edge of a cliff of some sort, and that the yellow *névé* beyond was, in fact, many hundred feet below it.

The whole glacier seemed to have slipped away from its source, causing a fault, to use a geological term,—a cliff of ice, stretching in a curved line, without a break, completely across the stream. For the greater part of its height it was not perfectly precipitous, and was so much broken that it seemed just possible to cut a way down it, but its upper portion was a sheer glassy wall. The rocks on both sides had our first attention, but they were almost as steep as the ice, and there was no footing on them. We unfastened ourselves from the rope and ran up and down the edge, each on his own account, looking for some means of escape, and finding none; and then we followed Jakob or Cachat about, in hopes of hearing some word of consolation from their oracular lips. At one place the cliff was vertical for only thirty feet, or thereabouts, and it would have been possible to drive in an axe, and let ourselves down, but the landing below, in that place, was hardly less precarious than the wall itself. There was another place nearer the side of the glacier which to my eyes seemed so hopeless that I scarcely looked twice at it—a great three-cornered *sérac*, which had parted from the edge, and was tottering to its fall, causing a rift in the face of the cliff which might or might not extend to the foot of the wall. Twice Jakob lay down on his stomach and peered over the edge at this place, but each time he had come away with a shrug and a grunt, and gone back to the place where the cliff was lowest and in which Cachat seemed to place most reliance. An old general of Persia once said: "If you oppose everything that is proposed and do not advance something certain, you must fail in your plans." Jakob, if he had never read Herodotus, had imbibed the maxim. Once more he returned, drew back a few steps for a short run, and boldly leapt from the edge on to the *sérac*. From thence he was better able to judge of the possibility of turning the cleft into a subway. After a long inspection he called on us to follow. I confess that I didn't like this leap into the unknown. My artist has perhaps somewhat exaggerated it, for in itself the chasm was easy to spring across, but the great hunk of ice had sunk as well as separated, and it was several feet lower than that from which it had parted. To spring back was obviously impossible. However, our confidence in Jakob was boundless, and swallowing our scruples, one by one we leapt the chasm. Immediately below us the cleft was blocked with snow to within a few yards of the surface, and we were lowered on to this one by one, the last man coming down with a run, while those below stood firm to catch him, a system of tactics that we had recourse to many times during the afternoon. The snow we had alighted on gave us good footing, and we descended some distance farther into the bowels of the glacier by its means. When this

JAKOB INVITES US TO LEAP.

came to an end, Jakob proceeded to cut diagonally downwards, planting his steps on each side alternately. This was slow work, and the smooth blue walls drew largely on our stock of vital heat.

There is no foundation for the popular definition of *névé*, namely unconsolidated snow. These same walls were composed of ice as hard and transparent as any to be found in the artificial caves at Grindelwald. And yet we were at a height of twelve thousand feet, and many thousands of feet above the limits of what is generally called *névé*. I question whether the layer of powdery or granulated snow is ever more than a few feet thick on the top of the denser material. The effect of the weather is so quickly to granulate the surfaces and cause a superficial resemblance to snow that none but a fresh breakage exhibits the clear ice.

All this time that we worked downwards, or rather that Jakob worked and we supported ourselves with outstretched legs, the interest was too absorbing for us to think much of the cold, as we were never able to see for many yards what was before us. But at last light began to be reflected on the walls in front of us as well as from above, and, on turning a corner in the *crevasse*, we saw out through the split that it made in the face of the cliff. At the bottom of the split, which we could easily have reached, the cliff outside was too sheer for a footing, so Jakob cut upwards again towards a higher point where it looked more promising. As the *crevasse* here became too broad for a pair of legs to stretch across, this was a grand difficulty. The manner in which Jakob solved it was a masterpiece of mountaineering skill, quite the *chef-d'œuvre* of the many really scientific dodges to which he had recourse that day. I cannot tell how he defied the laws of gravitation while he cut the necessary supports for us, and while we were waiting round the corner, but as each of us came to pass the difficulty, he found, first a series of big pigeon-holes for his feet in the perpendicular wall, then a corresponding series of little ones above the level of his head for his left hand, and finally, a third series of small deep holes in the opposite wall, which was distant six or seven feet. The use of these last was to bring out the capabilities of the axe as a third leg. This was held at arm's length against the opposite wall, the holes being intended to prevent the point slipping. We were then able by its means to jam ourselves against the ice, and move along, tripod fashion, till, on reaching the edge, a big red hand was thrust round the corner, and seizing ours, drew us round into broad daylight, on to a small platform of limited character on the outside, and one by one we emerged like rabbits, a hundred feet lower than where we had entered.

We had only got about a third of the way down the cliff, but what remained, although it was hardly less sheer, and gave ample opportunity for the display of Jakob's ingenuity and sticking powers, offered some slight shelves and points of support, and after our late triumph we hardly believed in anything which could stop him. There was obviously only one possible way, and that Cachat strenuously maintained was impossible. He detached himself and went to look for a better, but came back in ten minutes and in silence resumed the rope.

After three hours of ingenious manœuvres and cramping positions, and masterly combinations of finger-holds, always so arranged that our weight should be distributed over many points of support, and our safety never allowed to depend on the stability of one (which is the secret of safety in a bad place), we reached the foot of the ice cliff, and pausing a moment under the sheltering cave formed by a large fragment, to stretch ourselves, and to recover Grove's hat, which lay on the snow close at hand, we started and ran as fast as we could over the remains of avalanches which covered some acres of the glacier, till we were out of their range. We kept down the middle of the Glacier whose fortunes we had unwittingly followed, instead of those of the Miage Glacier, into whose deep straight trough it pours. Soon we came to the top of an icefall. This was not apparently of any great difficulty, and the Chamouniard of course proposed that we should make our way down it, but the German, as was his nature to, chose the rocks on the left bank.

I cannot say for certain that we should have done better on the glacier, but it soon became evident that, as it was, we had no longer any chance of getting clear of the ice before night. The rocks proved more obstinate than we anticipated, and, though we encountered no great difficulty, it was repeatedly necessary to detach the party and use the whole rope to let them down one by one, like sacks, over some steep face of rock or awkward ledge, to surer footing below. Time passed quickly, and our progress was slow. Another night bivouac seemed now inevitable, and we began to look about anxiously for a favourable place to spend it in. The rocks we were on would not do at all, as they were far too steep to allow of stamping about in the night, a most important, if not essential condition. The only place in sight was a *moraine* some way down the glacier, on its opposite bank, if we could get there in time.

After three more hours on the rocks, we got down to the level ice-stream, with a short half hour of daylight left to make the best we could of, and we *did* make the best of it. We started off at a round trot, and kept it up as long as the nature of the glacier permitted; and even when it didn't, the pace was not slackened, for we made up our minds at all hazards not to improve on our night on the rocks of the Bionnassay, by spending this one on the open glacier. Once, we were nearly floored by a long big split at right angles to our course. It seemed rather broad for a jump, but time pressed, and no other means of escape except a long detour presenting itself, there was no help for it. There was barely rope enough between us, but as each man jumped, the next on the line followed as near as he dared to the edge, to allow as much tether as possible, while he himself was held up by those behind. The rope was severely strained at each successive leap, and one or two of us were nearly jerked off our legs into the abyss. Only poor Cachat, who was last, had no one to restrain him from behind, and was obliged to spread himself flat on the ice and anchor his arm in a hole to avoid this catastrophe. This was the last obstacle, and throwing off the rope, we strolled across a level slope of ice which separated us from the *moraine*, congratulating ourselves on the superior nature of our accommodation. One big rock had attracted our attention when yet a great way off, and to our delight we found it partly hollow underneath. Here we established ourselves, after pulling out the most knubbly stones, and made favourable comparison between this and our night quarters on the Bionnassay. There was but one drawback; we had no water, and our wine was all gone. Cachat went in search of a stream as soon as we arrived, but it was so dark that he was unable to find any.

After two hours of restless and intermittent dozing, the sky grew light behind the jagged edge of Mont Broglie, and the full moon rose. The light was so brilliant that things were almost as plainly seen as by day. We were so comfortable, that if it had not been for want of water, I think we should have stayed where we were. But we could hear a rivulet gurgling under the ice in a tantalising manner a few yards off, and this aggravated our thirst to such a degree, that, in the hope of finding some lower down, we started again, and before long came upon a spring, which was, however, too stinging cold to drink from, except sparingly.

We now got on to the lowest spur of the buttress which divides the Glacier du Dôme from that of the Northern Miage. The last few hundred feet were steep enough to be a bore in the deceptive light of the moon and in our tired condition, so telling the men to find out the best way and then call us, we curled ourselves up in a hollow and dozed again. In a quarter of an hour a voice below told us to come on, and at twelve o'clock we got down on to the Miage Glacier, whose comparatively level stream we ought to have begun to follow ten or eleven hours before. From that time I remember nothing but many an unsatisfying drink and many a sleepy stumble, till we reached the broad level path of the Allée Blanche. There all fear of glacier pools and loose stones being at an end, I believe I went soundly asleep as I walked, and dreamt comfortable dreams of trout, and cutlets, and champagne. Once or twice I faintly suggested spending the rest of the night where we were, but the idea was treated with scorn by my more persistent companions, and I trudged on, a hungry somnambulist, until at last broad daylight and pleasant anticipation quickened the sleepy blood and lifted the heavy eyelids. At half-past five we entered Bertolini's, and then—may his shadow never grow less—my dreams were more than realised.

After this the weather forbade any more high expeditions, and I returned home over the pass of Mont Cenis in the diligence, enjoying by the way an experience which, I venture to think, is rather uncommon. At Susa I secured my place in the *coupé*, the other corner being occupied by a neat little French damsel. Two is company but three is none. At the last moment a German bagman got in and wedged himself between us. His diameter was large, and his odour of garlic offended me. Indeed his presence there at all was superfluous. I hoped to console myself with sleep, but this was impossible, for these two talked incessantly the whole night through. She was a dressmaker, and he "travelled" in ribbons and buttons, so they had a bond of union to start with. More and more voluble waxed their talk as we toiled up the zigzags; and as we rattled down on the French side their mutual confidences became quite embarrassing to a shy man like myself. Finally, about six o'clock in the morning, totally disregarding my presence, he offered her his hand and his fortune. If he did not throw himself into the conventional attitude it was solely because to turn round was impossible. At this point I was almost inclined to intervene and implore her to refuse the brute, but it was unnecessary. After an anxious minute of suspense, she curtly dismissed him, if that be a correct expression when her lover remained necessarily glued to her side for another two hours. Happily his disconsolate position reduced him to silence for a time, so that I slept, and was only roused by a fresh discussion about *ces bourgeois d'Anglais*, and especially

THE AUTHOR.

INDEX

Abdullah, 138
Accident, 65, 66, 67, 86
  ,,   On Salt Mountain, 116
Achmet, 284, 298, 310, 312
  ,,   Ben Saâd, 153
Afioum Kara-Hissar, 319
Ahmar Khadou Range, 149
Aidin Railway, 197
Alfa grass, 132
Alfred's mount, 311
Ali, 138
Allée Blanche, 397
Anderegg, Jakob, 385
  ,,   Melchior, 385
Andreas, 68, 132
Antelope rupicapra, 36 et seq.
Antonio, 237, 253
Aoudad, 123
Arab dinner, 118
Arabas, 315
Arabs hawking, 144
  ,,   Method of warming themselves, 138
  ,,   Wear sandals of *alfa* grass, 137
Arwi, 123
Asia Minor, 193 et seq.
Athens, 197
Atlas Mountains, 123 et seq.
  ,,   ,,   Waterless, 130
Aurès Mountains, 128, 149
Autumn colours, Alps, 40
  ,,   Sport, 361

Bara Singha deer, 279
Barbary sheep, 123 et seq.
  ,,   ,,   Power of concealment, 134
"Barfod," 321
Basques, 236

Bears, 47, 166, 257 et seq., 333
  ,,   As guardians of herds, 261
  ,,   Attacking horses, 261
  ,,   Boy's successful encounter, 263
  ,,   Driving, 333
  ,,   Encounters with hunters, 260
  ,,   Fondness of berries, 261
  ,,   In Asia Minor, 289
  ,,   Scarcity of, 116
  ,,   Tale about, 260
  ,,   The author spies one, 266
  ,,   Turberville's account of, 262
  ,,   Will dive when wounded, 262
  ,,   Winter habits of, 260
Beavers, 103
  ,,   Manner of trapping, 103
Bed-bugs, 174
"Ben a Chouf," 154
Berbers, 119
Bergschrund, fall over, 67
Bergwagen, accident with, 56
Bernardo, 50, 72
Big-horn sheep, 114
  ,,   Rams, Gerald's successful stalk of, 117
Bionnassay, Aiguille de, 372 et seq.
  ,,   Glacier de, 389
Birds of Scandinavia forest, 161
Biskra, 125, 149
Bleeding, Arab custom of, 149
Boar, 24, 150, 301
Bonifacio, Straits of, 1
Bosse du Dromadaire, 378
Bou Arif, 154
Boulai, 204, 285
Bouchero, 353
Box bushes, 229, 252
Brèche de Roland, 353

2 D

Brigandage, 10, 203, 318
Brooke, Sir Victor, kills a bear, 253
Brugière heath, 21
Buffalo Fork, 90
Bustard, the Great, 316

Caccia grossa, 8, 26
Cachat, 372
Cagliari, 6
Camels, 223, 314
Camp in the Pyrenees, 233
　,,　A dry, 320
Campoggiolo, 72
Cantonière, 11
Capercailzie, 161
Capra œgagrus, 193 *et seq.*
　,,　　,,　　Driving, 210
　,,　　,,　　Habits of, 208
Carabinieri, 10
Cartridge hangs fire, 71
Cartridges, passage of, through France, 368
Caves used for shelter, 230
Celestin, 3, 199, 284, 290
Chamois, 36 *et seq.*
Chamouni guides; preference of ice over rocks, 375, 395
Chardak, 197
Chawia, 149
Cheese, Norwegian, 339
Chot, or salt marsh, 130
Christiansund, 272
Circassians, 219
Circular hollows in limestone, 360
Clarke's ranch, 85
Cliffs, 230
Colani, 41
Col de Voza, 372
Colour of clothes deceives the izzards, 356
Constantinople, 197
Cook, a faint-hearted, 60
Corniches, 233
Corsican pine, the, 283
Cotton-wood, 83
Cow, in unexpected place, 256
Cris, 77, 106
Croz, Jean Baptiste, 385
Cyprian mouflon, 21

DATES, 149
Desert sparrows, 152
Diavel, Pitz, 63
Dog-harness, 169
Dogs, Norwegian, 324

Dogs, distance at which they wind deer, 328
　,,　For reindeer hunting, 327
Dôme du Gouter, 372 *et seq.*
Double snipe, 162
Douglas pine, 83
Driving reins in Norway, 186
Dust columns, 152
　,,　Spout, 316

EAGLES, 198, 294
Edmi, 144, 154
Eikisdal, 342
Electricity, stream of, audible, 378
El Gattar, 152
Elk, the, 159 *et seq.*
　,,　Dogs, 163
　,,　Driving, 184
　,,　Food of, 171
　,,　Ground, description of, 161
　,,　Habits of, 170
　,,　Hearing of, 170
　,,　Intelligence of, 183
　,,　Numbers of, 164
　,,　"Rights," 167
　,,　　,,　　Cost to hire, 174
　,,　Sign, 169
　,,　Swimming, 188, 191
Emir Dagh, 314
Enricetto, 12

FALLEN timber, 87, 115
Fat herrings, 274
Feshtal, 126
Fires, accidental, in America, 116
Fjeld, 343
Fladbröd, 337
Flea-powder, 299
Fleas, 12
François, 285

GAVARNIE, 350
Gazella dorcas, 144
　,,　　*Kevella*, 144
Geese, wild, 198
Geitauns, 134
Gentleman's Recreation, the, 162
Geof, 273
Geyser Basin, 80, 94
Gigi, 12
Glissade, 66
Goat-skin, Yuruk shod with, 310
Grands Mulets, 387
Graubunden, jealousy of people of, 40
Gros Ventre, 95

Guest-house, 218, 317

HADJI, 200
Hammâm, 150
Hazel-Grouse, 162
Heifer, accident to, 256
Herodotus, 133, 143
  ,,   Description of Salt Mountain, 111
Hevne Fjord, the, 165
Hitteren, 165, 257
Hjerpe, 162
Hoass, 323
Holbne, 335
Hunting, Sard method of, 14
  ,,   On horseback, 82
Hyena, 217

IBEX, Pyrenean, 229 et seq.
  ,,   Dogs used to hunt, 235
  ,,   Driving, 237
  ,,   Falling over cliff, 246
  ,,   Form of horns of, 230
  ,,   Habits of, 234
  ,,   Skill in concealment, 235
Ilex, 23
India-rubber soles to boots, 137
Indian, the North American, 75
Iron pegs to scale cliffs, 234
Izzards, 349 et seq.
  ,,   A good day at, 359, 360
  ,,   Distinction between chamois and, 349
  ,,   Falling over cliff, 356
  ,,   Ground frequented by, 352

JACKSON'S Hole, 95
Jani, 285
Jays, 238
  ,,   Indicate presence of deer, 305
Jebel Metlili, 126 et seq.
Jemtland, 187
John Wallan, 177

Kapek, 220
Khan, 319
Kirkesæter, 166
Klonglevik, 166, 262
Klonglevik's rifle, 263
Konia, 314
Kous-Kousou, 118
Kroksen, the, 259
Krokstad, 274

LÄMMERGEIER, 17, 239

Leg-johren, 18, 17, 54
Leghorn, 4
Lemmings, 326
Leopard, 217
Levanger, 166, 187
Livigno, 46
Long shots, 357, 359
Löschund, 161
Lourdes, 350
Lovöen, 173
Lynx, 217

Macquia, 7, 16
Madden, 79
Maimun Dagh, 197
Main Divide, 80, 81, 105
Malaria, 197
Malciccati, 6
Marmot, 46
Mermen and Mermaids, 260
Miage, Col de, 382
  ,,   Glacier, 383
Miss-fires, 246
Mont Broglic, 397
  ,,   Cenis, 398
Moose, 103
Moritzburg, Castle of, 225
Mouflon à manchette, 123
  ,,   Best season for stalking, 35
  ,,   Colour of, 147
  ,,   Dimensions of horns of, 20
  ,,   Driving, 35
  ,,   Saddle-mark, 20
  ,,   Sardinian, 2
  ,,   ,,   craftiness of, 21
Mountain Gazelle, 154
Mud-waggon, 7, 71
Municipal Institutions, 236
Mushrooms, 301

Narcissus Moschatus, 250
Native weapons, 321
Night in the open, 64
Norway, cost of labour in, 332
  ,,   License to shoot on public lands, 318
  ,,   Scenery in, 343
Nuraghe, 5

OASES, 125
"Odas," 317
Ofener Pass, 54
Ogliastra wine, 9
Olaus Magnus, quotation from, 326
Old silver, 333

"Old Soldier," the, 365
Oristano, 6
Othman, 320
Ovis montana, 114 *et seq.*
„ *Musimon*, 21 *et seq.*
„ *Tragelaphus*, 123 *et seq.*
Oxendal, 331

PACK HORSES, 79, 88
Palm culture, 149
„ Trees, noise made by leaves of, 125
Partridges, 199
Pastorale, 29
Payot, 372
Photography, amateur, 96
Pierre Pointue, 386
Pilaff, 285
Pine marten, 95, 239
Pinus mughus, 47, 54
Pisidia, 281
Pliny, quotations from, 134, 217, 296
Pole-cat, the marbled, 294
Pontoppidan, Bishop, 161, 259
Porpoises chasing herrings, 274
Priest of Livigno, 62
Proposal, a, 398
Pyrenean streams, 233
„ Sheep-dogs, 251

RACIAL Characteristics, 9
Rats, 109
Rawlins, 74
Red deer, 222, 279 *et seq.*
„ Ancient records of, 295
„ Beds made by, a good indication of numbers, 294
„ Behaviour when started, 291
„ Difficulty of finding horns, 284
„ Difficulty of hunting, 292
„ On Hitteren, 257
„ Roaring, 299
„ Sardinian, 27
„ Search for wounded, 309
„ Smell of, 296
„ The big head, 280
„ Travelling stags, 300
Reindeer, 323 *et seq.*
„ Skins, used as mattresses, 174
„ Tame, 173, 188
Rocks, resonance of, in Atlas Mountains, 137
Rocky Mountains, 73 *et seq.*

Romsdal, 345
Roosevelt, Mr. Theodore, 107
„ Capture of thieves by, 107

SADDLES, Mexican, 80
Sæters, 335
Sage brush, 83
„ Hens, 75
Sahara, Desert of, 122 *et seq.*
„ Climate of, 122
Salt Lake, 197
„ Lick, 52
„ Mountain, 143, 144
Sard language, 11
Sardinia, 1 *et seq.*
Sardinian bread, 8
„ Game, 27
„ Guns, 26
„ Railway, 5
Sebbo, 166
Shed horns, 101
Sheepfolds, 173
Shoshone Dick, 76
Sledges, 182
"Smoke," 287
Smyrna, 197
Snake River, 91, 101
Snowstorm, 28
Solitaire chamois, a, 71
„ Lives in woods, 72
„ Restlessness in October, 361
Southerly wind, effect of, 374
Spanish mountaineers, 236
„ Valleys, description of, 230
Spinas, 49
Spöl Ravine, 53
Spying, 15, 36
Stagni, 6
Steam-launch, 165
Step-cutting, 376
Stillness of the air, 293
Stone pines, 206
Strike of guides, 384
Striker of rifle, loss of, 68
Sundal, 324
Susa, 398
Suut Dagh, 198

Tasso, 272
Taugwald, 384
Taurus, 195
Terranova, 4
Teton Peaks, 87, 96
The *Alcalde*, 237
Thunder-shower, 282

Thunderstorm, 378
Timber, destruction of, in Turkey, 283
Tinned meats, American, 81
To-gwo-tee Pass, 81
Topography in Norway, 176
Tortoises, 198, 217
Tostin, 324
Tower on Jebel Metlili, 139
Tramontana, 4
Trout, 105
  ,, For luncheon, 170
"Tump," 167
Turkomans, 218
Turks, hospitality of, 218, 317
  ,, Manners of, 200
  ,, Marriage customs, 219
  ,, Procrastination of, 314

Union Peak, 109

Val del Aqua, 71
  ,, Fain, 58
Vendetta, 10
Vermin, 317
Village priest, 62
Vinge Fjord, 272
Von Tchudi, 41

Vulture, 198

Wall Creeper, 239
Wapiti deer, 83, 90
  ,, Attacked by scab, 102
  ,, Bull, craftiness of, 100
  ,, Gerald's first, 83
  ,, Head, best attitude to mount, 102
  ,, Lured with a penny whistle, 110
  ,, Reckless destruction of, 114
  ,, Toughness of horns, 101
  ,, "Whistling," 98, 109
  ,, With palmated antlers, 114
Washakie Fort, 75
Water, difficulty with, 131
  ,, Scarcity of, 197
Westerners' partiality for fresh meat, 105
White Mountain, the, 281
Wild raspberries, 255
Wind River, 80
  ,, ,, Mountains, 86
Wolf, gray, 101
Wolverine, 100
Wood grouse, 161
Wyoming, 79

Yruck, 200, 219

THE END

www.ingramcontent.com/pod-product-compliance
Lightning Source LLC
Chambersburg PA
CBHW030556300426
44111CB00009B/1002